One Hundred

Nature Walks

in the Missouri Ozarks

One Hundred Nature Walks in the Missouri Ozarks

by Alan McPherson

Cache
River
Press

Vienna, Illinois

©Cache River Press, 1997

Library of Congress Catalogue Card Number 97-66301
ISBN 1-889899-00-3

1st edition

Author:
Alan McPherson

Publisher:
Cache River Press
2850 Oak Grove Road
Vienna, IL 62995
USA

(888) 862-2243

Printed in the United States of America

Dedicated to

Richard J. McPherson, my brother,

who showed me the Missouri Ozarks

*"I wonder that others have not discovered
the real beauty of the Ozarks."*

Harold Bell Wright, *Shepherd of the Hills*, pg. 249

Table of Contents

100 Nature Walks in the Missouri Ozarks

Foreword

Missouri is blessed with millions of acres of public lands, much of which are national forest, plus the Missouri Department of Natural Resources, state forests, Department of Conservation and state park lands total thousands more acres. The Nature Conservancy also holds thousands of acres that are open for public use.

The terrain available to hikers varies from marshy bottomland along our major rivers to the rugged hills and hollows of the Ozarks and glades and prairies in between. Most of this land has some sort of trail system. The most ambitious project is the Ozark trail which, when completed, will run from St. Louis to the Arkansas border where it will join the Ozark Highland Trail in Arkansas for a total of 700 miles. The Blair Creek section in Missouri is maintained by the Sierra Club.

Another major project undertaken by the Sierra Club along with The Nature Conservancy and other conservation organizations is the restoration of Missouri's glades to pre-settlement condition by clearing non-native flora species by cutting and controlled burning.

Alan McPherson is to be commended for completing this ambitious project. I'm sure every ornithologist, botanist and just plain nature walker who enjoys the great Missouri outdoors will find this book a valuable addition to their library.

Robert J. Gestel
Ozark Chapter Sierra Club

Acknowledgements

A special thanks with deep gratitude to all individuals who generously contributed to the making of this book. The author and publisher are deeply grateful for the help of personnel of the Mark Twain National Forest Service in the Missouri Ozarks, especially Darsan Wang who took a deep interest in the book. They also thank Marjorie Russell for editing and design work and especially Karen Fiorino for map composition.

*F*inally, most of all, we thank the numerous individuals who encouraged us to describe the natural wealth and beauty of the Missouri Ozarks.

Author and Publisher

Preface

*B*etween the East and the West, the Ozark Plateau contains more wild areas and higher elevations than any other region in the Central United States. The 55,000 square miles of ancient, deeply eroded plateau, also referred to as the Ozark Mountains, is roughly bounded by the Mississippi River to the east, the Missouri River to the north, the Osage and Neosho Rivers to the west, and the Arkansas River to the south. The State of Missouri claims the lion's share of the Ozarks, followed by Arkansas, Oklahoma and Illinois. The Missouri Ozarks encompass nearly 33,000 square miles of rock-bound hills and mountains, level tablelands and deep valleys. Hundreds of springs, sinkholes and caverns dot the Ozark region. To fully appreciate the special spirit of the Missouri Ozarks, you must explore on foot.

*R*esidents and visitors alike are fortunate in having an abundance of publicly accessible natural areas to explore along foot trails for all seasons. Being outside and freely hiking is a memorable experience. The main focus of *One Hundred Nature Walks in the Missouri Ozarks* is to guide families, weekend naturalists, intrepid travelers and all lovers of the outdoors to over 100 places where walking trails have been established, ranging from short and easy to long and rugged. The majority of nature walks in this guide may be traversed in one day but there are also plenty of overnight backpacking experiences. Nearly all of the 100 nature walks are located south of Interstate 44. Within a day's drive, many Midwesterners and Southerners can experience one of the best wild regions near the center of our vast country.

*N*early all nature walks in this book were hiked, photographed and described by the author during 1995 and 1996. The brief trail write ups include a capsule heading that lists the location of the nearest community, the county or counties the trail covers, the name or names of the U.S. Geological Survey 1:24,000 (one inch equals 2,000 feet) topographical map or maps, the trail mileage, parkland acreage, recreational activities and facilities available and any fees charged. The main focus of the material body is to inform about the outstanding site features, trailhead locations, trail surface, and how to arrive by highway. All write-ups have been checked for accuracy by the administering property agencies. Maps and black and white photographs accompany the written material for further directional understanding and aesthetic appreciation. More than a trail guide, the natural and cultural history of the Missouri Ozarks is also included to further enhance the enjoyment of the many splendors of these interior highlands.

Alan McPherson

Discovering the Missouri Ozarks

Boardwalk at Devils Well, Ozark Riverways

"The Ozarks have other places that equal it,
though none exceed it in beauty."

Richard Rhodes, *The Ozarks*, pg. 31.

*T*he Ozarks are a major region of the country that most Americans recognize and often picture as a land of forested hills and hollows. However the Ozarks (French, aux arcs or aux arks, "with bows") are also low mountains shaped by spring-fed rivers, caves and other geological formations such as natural bridges and arches, waterfalls and shut-in gorges, pockets of prairie within desert-like glades that often appear as hilltop "balds" and a myriad of other natural surprises.

*C*asual walkers and serious hikers will find enjoyment and satisfaction in the Missouri Ozarks, the area covered by this guidebook. Hiking provides nearly everyone with a unique opportunity for appreciating the great outdoors. Despite more than a century of taming the Missouri

Ozarks by mining, forestry, farming and industry, the land is still wild. There are eight wilderness areas and thousands of acres of public lands to explore on foot along hundreds of miles of trails. Knowing where the trails are located, what to expect, and how to get to them by highway are the three basic questions this guidebook addresses.

*D*esigned for ease of access, the 100 nature walks are arranged into nine sections: seven forest service areas or districts, the National Park Service's Ozark Riverways and the Ozark Trail, which is administered by several governmental agencies and private organizations. For convenience sake, the forest service district arrangement was used. However it often overlaps and includes public properties that are not National Forest lands such as state parks and conservation areas. The Ozarks comprise 40 percent of the lands of Missouri. The Missouri Ozarks are divided into seven natural divisions: the Ozark Border, St. Francois Mountains, Upper Ozark, Lower Ozark, Springfield Plateau, White River and Elk River.

*T*he 100 nature walks are numbered and correspond to a regional map for general site location. Trail and highway maps pinpoint the site for ease of access. The information includes a general capsule heading and specific details of what to expect and road directions.

*A*ll levels of government administer public accessible parklands for recreational and other multi-use purposes. So do private organizations such as The Nature Conservancy, an international conservation organization, whose objective is the preservation and protection of environmentally significant lands.

*W*alking is instinctive. No special skills are necessary to be a lifetime walker, except to have legs and a desire to "stretch them." To further enhance your enjoyment and safety in the outdoors, there are tips worthy of mention. Exercise different styles of walking but most of all, walk for pleasure. Walking is personal and you don't have to join a hiking club even though walking for enjoyment may eventually lead you to it. A backpacker is a hiker who is prepared for overnight stays. Plan and study ahead your special needs for either a short walk, a day hike or several overnights. There is no doubt that extending your time in nature will bring you closer to nature. Walking is half the fun of getting there.

*C*onsider your physical comfort in the humid continental climate of the Missouri Ozarks. Spring and fall are especially ideal times to set out on foot. Today's hikers have a broad choice of comfortable rugged footwear since most manufacturers have some type of hiking shoe or boot. The best choice for Ozark terrain is a lug sole cross between a tennis shoe and a hiking boot. The average walking speed is about 2 miles per hour or 20 minutes per mile. The best safeguard against blisters is properly fitting shoes. If your feet feel good, you feel good.

Protect yourself from the elements with outerwear so you can walk in rain, wind, or even snow and still feel at ease. Wearing appropriate clothing makes you feel good about the experience. Good fitting and roomy clothing is essential. Cotton is good for summer and wool and other synthetics for winter. Keep warm in the coldest weather by layering dark clothing of natural wool, cotton and high-tech synthetics. Be extra cautious of frost bite, hypothermia and dehydration in winter and heat exhaustion and sunstroke in summer. Several outdoor and sporting stores have everything for hiking and backpacking needs, plus the malls and army surplus stores are also worth shopping.

*S*uggested day pack essentials or options may include rain gear, map(s), compass, flashlight, pocket knife, hand lens, pedometer, water, butane lighter, plastic bags, first aid kit, insect protection, toilet paper, emergency food, fresh food and a guidebook to your favorite nature study like birds or geology. A hat, sunglasses, sunscreen, and gear plus a camera or binoculars should fit into one or two day packs or fanny packs.

*B*ackpacking overnight will, of course, require additional gear, especially in winter. Well broken in boots, several pairs of socks, gaiters, long underwear, wool shirt, sweater and trousers will help to keep the cold at bay. Sleeping gear such as sleeping bag, ground pad, and cloth, plus a tent shelter adds more pounds. Kitchen cooking gear, food, personal gear and miscellaneous items will also add to the load of your external pack frame. It is easy to say, the lighter your pack, the easier the trail, but cutting back on necessities is not so easy. Additional overnight items that may be included are candles, repair kits and camp shoes or sneakers. Large plastic bags may serve as makeshift emergency raincoats for backpacks and hikers. If matches are preferred, buy or make waterproof matches. Overall, gear should be compact, simple, light and necessary. When it comes to backpacking gear, think of Thoreau's saying, "more is less." All in all, you can explore the Ozarks without expensive gear. Some day hikes require only a quart of water and a map and compass. Before leaving, always tell your family and friends your hiking plans. Make sure your vehicle is road worthy to take you and others to a destination and back. Arrive alive.

*T*rail quality and their conditions will vary. Ancient vulcanism, uplifts and earthquakes have made the Ozarks a rocky experience. Pieces of chert stone seem to be underfoot at every step and are particularly noticeable in burnt over areas. The oldest rock in the Ozarks is found in the St. Francois Mountains. Prairie glades or "balds" are rocky habitats that are composed of either limestone, sandstone, dolomite or granite. The stream-dissected land has been cut down through the plateau. Erosion has taken a heavy toll along many of the trails especially on the steep ascents and descents. Expect to keep your eyes on the trail during many outings. Trails are rated easy, moderate, more difficult, most difficult and rugged. Due to the lack of maintenance, expect trails to have poor surface conditions, possibly be overgrown and have little signage.

Excessive horseback riding has resulted in heavily eroded and compacted trails. Hikers should always yield to horses and their riders and watch for all-terrain bicycles. Few trails are paved and accessible to all. Some trails are well blazed and consistent in trail marker style and spacing while other trails are unmarked, such as the wilderness trails where maps and a compass are necessary.

*W*hen planning a hike, consider the length of daylight hours, especially during the shorter days of late fall, winter and early spring. Steep hikes will cut your hiking time in half. Expect wet feet from springtime seeps and numerous stream crossings. Trail rules may vary, but basically all expect fire control, trash and sanitary containment and proper disposal. Please respect private property and people. Hikers should be aware of the potential dangers of hunting, especially during the fall deer season. Accidents do happen.

*N*early all 100 hiking trails have property maps available, some at the trailhead. Off-road exploration is secure if compass and map plus the knowledge of how to read them, are available. Topographic quadrangle maps feature natural detail with symbols. A map in the scale of 1:24,000 shows 2,000 feet as one inch. A square mile is two inches square. A "topo" covers 7.5 minutes of latitude and longitude. Color used is real to life – green for woodlands, brown lines for earth contours, blue for water and black for human works. "Topos" and other maps may be purchased from the following addresses:

Missouri Department of Natural Resources
Maps and Publications
P. O. Box 250
Rolla, MO 65401
(573) 368-2125

Mark Twain National Forest
401 Fairgrounds Road
Rolla, MO 65401
(573) 364-4621 or (573) 341-7455 (TTY)

Over the Counter Sales –
Division Headquarters
Buehler Building
111 Fairgrounds Road
Rolla, MO 65401
Monday through Friday
8 a.m. - noon; 1 p.m. - 5 p.m.

*F*ederal land maps are available at local ranger districts in Fredericktown, Poplar Bluff, Potosi, Salem, Doniphan, Van Buren, Winona, Houston, Willow Springs, Ava and Cassville.

*M*aps for the Ozark Riverways, National Park Service are available at the headquarters on Business U.S. 60, Van Buren, MO or by writing; Superintendent, P.O. Box 490, Van Buren, MO 63965 (573) 323-4236 (voice), or (573) 323-4270 (TDD).

*S*everal backpacking and outdoor stores in the larger cities carry topographical maps. Prices vary. Expect to pay $2.25 to $5 each on average. Check libraries for maps.

*I*nsect pests are also part of being outside and the Missouri Ozarks has its share of noxious creatures, including bloodsucking chiggers, ticks and mosquitoes. Chiggers (harvest mites or red bugs) and ticks are common in thick brush or grass from summer to frost. Avoiding their habitat, using a miticide such as powdered sulphur, and wearing long pants is advised. Since the 1950s, deet is the major ingredient used in most insect repellents. Insecticides containing 30 percent deet or less is recommended by foresters. Avoid sitting in herbaceous and grassy openings; pick a rock instead. Any overgrown trail could be potential chigger and tick habitat, especially from mid to late summer. Ticks can transmit several major diseases such as Rocky Mountain spotted fever, tularemia, ehrlichiosis and Lyme disease. Always do a tick check anytime after being outside during their season. Promptly and carefully remove all ticks by grasping them between your nails near their jointed heads and pulling them straight out. Do not crush the tick with your fingers which could inject infectious fluids through your skin into your body. Clean the bite area. Light colored clothing should be worn to make ticks readily visible. The Missouri Ozarks has three spring and summer "waves" of ticks. The early dog tick is usually large enough and slow enough to be seen and felt moving on the skin. It usually moves from the ankles up, and is not considered the vector tick of Lyme disease but does carry the rarely transmitted Rocky Mountain spotted fever. Later, in June and July, the smaller, forest-dwelling deer and aggressive Lone Star ticks become active. The third wave of ticks are young nymph larvae that are nearly invisible and therefore considered a greater threat. Nearly 80 percent of Lyme disease cases are transmitted by the bite of young nymphs of the deer tick.

*M*osquitoes appear to be the hungriest at dawn and dusk but may appear at anytime in warm weather, especially when there is ample rainfall. They can hatch in the smallest of pools such as in the crotch of a tree branch, or even in dew. The dryness of late summer and early fall eliminates most mosquitoes in the Ozarks.

*T*he female deer fly, like the female mosquito, needs blood for protein to produce young. Deer flies breed in wet areas and are especially noticeable along reservoirs or wet woodlands or swamps. A hat, long sleeved shirt and pants help keep them from biting, as do certain insecticides. They are strong fliers and will pursue their victims for miles. Usually they are not a problem after mid-August, but may persist until frost. The wood gnat can be a pest of the eye as well as the ear, nose and mouth in late summer.

*M*issouri has inventoried more than 300 species of spiders. The largest spider is the hairy and harmless Missouri tarantula which has a sharp bite and is most often encountered crossing trails and roads, wandering in the dry open glade country of south and central Missouri. Hikers in late summer often encounter the webs of the triangulate and spiny-bellied orb weavers, strewn across the path like cotton candy. The jumping gray tree trunk spider is often found on shagbark hickory tree trunks. Wolf spiders are usually found in moist habitats along streams. The chances are greater of encountering a brown recluse than a black widow. Both can inflict non-fatal bites that can cause severe pain and infection. Both spiders are often found under rocks and around old, undisturbed buildings. Ozark ants do not inflict painful stings (fire ants are farther south) but Missouri is home to several species of stinging social wasps and bees, particularly paper wasps, yellow jackets, bumblebees and honeybees. There are also scorpions in the drier western areas. Know if you are severely allergic to stings and if so, purchase a sting kit by prescription at most pharmacies. Bees can be provoked by scented cosmetics and shiny objects. Keep an eye out for gypsy moths and report their whereabouts to the forest service.

*T*here are 52 species and subspecies of snakes in Missouri and about 35 are found in the Ozarks. Most are harmless but will bite if provoked. There are five pit vipers or poisonous snakes found in Missouri and four are found in the Ozarks: the Osage copperhead, western cottonmouth, western pygmy rattlesnake and the timber rattlesnake. The Osage copperhead and its southern subspecie is by far the most common of the four poisonous serpents, often seen from April to November (they are usually nocturnal during the hot summer months). Copperheads prefer rocky hillsides, forest edges, brushy streamsides, and abandoned farm buildings and even occupied homesites. Medical treatment is necessary but the bite is rarely fatal. The semi-aquatic cottonmouth, or true water moccasin, has a spotty distribution in the Missouri Ozarks, but usually is found around spring-fed rocky creeks, from April to early October. The cottonmouth can inflict a fatal bite. There are two entirely different types of rattlesnakes. The western pygmy is one of the smallest species of rattlesnakes in North America. It lives under rocks on cedar glades or south-facing rocky open hillsides. Its bite is serious but not fatal. The timber rattlesnake is the Ozark's largest venomous snake, ranging in length from 36 to 54 inches. It inhabits densely wooded rocky hillsides and ledges and it is active from April through October, being nocturnal in summer.

*S*nakes are often encountered basking on the trail in early spring during the day, but with the hot weather of summer, they become more active at night. Consider the worst possible scenario – you are hiking alone,

10 miles from your car and you get a snake bite. Try to stay as calm as possible and use a snake bite kit, if possible. Some general snake rules are: stay away from habitats where they may congregate such as swamp, marshes and bluffs, wear protective footwear and clothing, do not place your hands or feet in unseen places, keep your eye out and step lively when hiking. Several state park nature centers have excellent specimens displayed and the Springfield Dickerson Park Zoo has an outstanding reptile collection. It is unlikely you will ever encounter a black bear or bobcat in the Missouri Ozarks, but while at the Dickerson Park Zoo, visit the latest Missouri Habitats section to see what they look like up close.

*L*earn to identify poison ivy and avoid it. If you encounter the vine, use rubbing alcohol to remove the oils, then bathe as soon as possible to neutralize the urushiol. Woodland stinging nettle can be painful as can be greenbriar, and briars from roses, raspberry and blackberry canes. It is remotely possible that an encounter with a skunk may result in being sprayed. Even more remote is a bite from a rabid raccoon or other animal. The safety rule for lightning is to seek out dense woods, ravines, ditches and groves of immature trees. Do not shelter underneath large solitary trees, hilltops, high ground or rock ledge outcrops. The spring months, especially March through May, are tornado months.

*S*ome native Ozarkers believe there is a five month spring, four month summer, two month fall and one month winter. Of course that is stretching it, but usually the ideal times in the Missouri Ozarks are from mid March to mid May and late September to deer hunting season in mid November. However, there are many good days in between for nature outings.

*A*fter a long hike, treat your feet to a warm water soak, a cool rinse, easy drying, a massage and maybe some foot powder. If handy, put on a fresh pair of socks. Be flexible, leisurely, and prepared for all your trips in the outdoors. Whether hiking with a friend or alone, always inform others of your plans. When lost, do not panic and try to stay level headed.

*T*rail routes are always changing. New trails are being added, old trails are neglected, re-routed, improved or abandoned. All trails listed here have been read and checked for accuracy by the administering agencies, however, errors may exist. Errors and corrections should be brought to the attention of the author and the publisher. Be aware that Cache River Press and the author are not responsible for any accident or injury that may occur while using this guide.

*E*xplore the land, with its many moods and wonders, and make it a time also of self discovery.

Abbreviations Used

ATB . . . . all terrain bicycle
ATV . . . . all terrain vehicle

CA . . . . Conservation Area
CCC . . . . Civilian Conservation Corps
CR . . . . County Road

DNR . . . . Department of Natural Resources

Elev . . . . elevation above sea level

FH . . . . fish hatchery
FS . . . . Forest Service road

Hwy . . . . Highway

I . . . . Interstate

MDC . . . . Missouri Department of Conservation

NA . . . . Natural Area
NHS . . . . National Historic Site
NPS . . . . National Park Service
NWR . . . . National Wildlife Refuge

ORV . . . . off-road vehicle
OT . . . . Ozark Trail

RA . . . . Recreation Area

SHS . . . . State Historic Site
SPK . . . . State Park
SR . . . . State Road

TNC . . . . The Nature Conservancy

US . . . . United States
USGS . . . . United States Geological Survey
USFS . . . . United States Forest Service

WA . . . . Wild Area

YCC . . . . Youth Conservation Corps

100 Nature Walks in

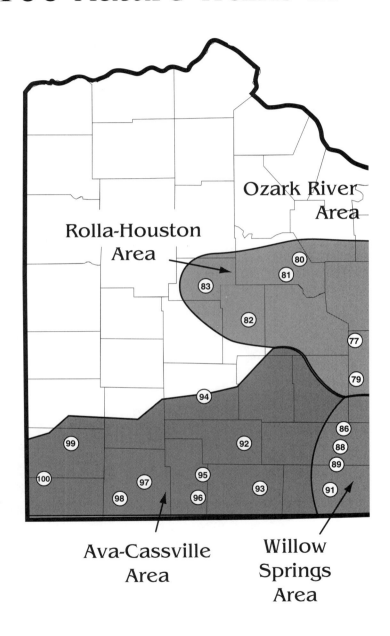

Ozark River Area

Rolla-Houston Area

Ava-Cassville Area

Willow Springs Area

the Missouri Ozarks

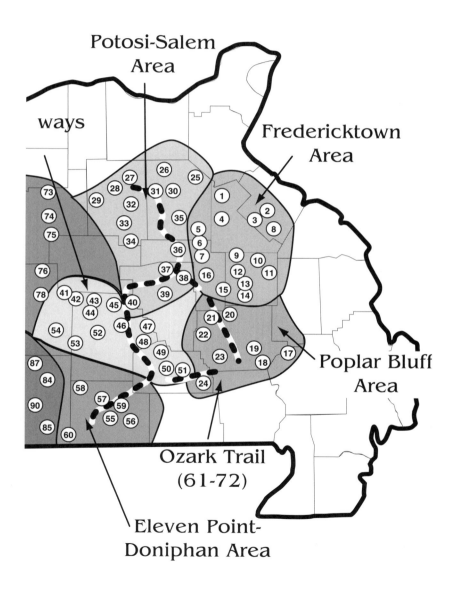

Potosi-Salem
Area

ways

Fredericktown
Area

Poplar Bluff
Area

Ozark Trail
(61-72)

Eleven Point-
Doniphan Area

One Hundred

Nature Walks

in the

Missouri Ozarks

TRAIL 1: **St. Francois State Park**

*W*ildness is the essence of St. Francois State Park. The lush Pike Run Hills and hollows are coated with an aging oak and hickory forest, prairie-like glades, boggy wet meadow fens, limestone bluffs of the Big River and clear, free-flowing Ozark streams. Nearly 80 percent of the park lands are designated a Missouri Wild Area. This Ozark border park is in the transition zone where the Ozarks blend with the open country to the north and east. The main bulk of the acreage was first purchased over 30 years ago by the generous citizens of St. Francois County. The Missouri Department of Natural Resources (DNR) is the administering agency.

*S*t. Francois State Park is located off I-55 on U.S. 67, 50 miles south of St. Louis.

*T*he scenic naturalness and varying distance trails attract even the most casual walker. There are four maintained and color-coded trails with varying conditions. Three trails are for hikers only, however the Pike Run Trail is open to equestrian use in addition to hiking and backpacking. Three trails loop through the Coonville Creek Wild Area. All trails are easily accessed and range from easy to moderately difficult.

*T*he 2.7-mile Mooner's Hollow Trail is a loop path. It begins and ends at the north picnic area parking lot next to Coonville Creek, downhill from the park office and highway entrance. A trail guide booklet is available at the trailhead registration box. Enroute along Coonville Creek and adjoining uplands there are 14 interpretive stops, numbered to correspond to entries in the trail booklet. Succession, erosion, stream life, watershed, bedrock, seeps and glades are described. Blue arrows blaze the footpath in both directions along the stream and ridge slopes.

*B*e leisurely and allow two hours for the hike (elev. 700-800 ft.). The spring-fed, cold waters of the cascading creek once supplied illegal moonshiners with a valued ingredient in making whiskey. Several stills were located along the perennially flowing 3-mile-long stream, thus giving rise to the name, Mooner's Hollow.

*T*wo miles of Mooner's Hollow and Coonville Creek, or about 50 acres, are dedicated as a natural area. Several species of fish inhabit the stream, including uncommon darters. Spring is a fine time to see returning migratory warblers, tanagers, vireos, thrushes and flycatchers. The wet meadow fens grow rare wildflowers such as queen of the prairie, bog coneflower, mountain mint and cowbane. The semi-arid glades support a host of herbaceous prairie plants.

*D*own the road from Mooner's Hollow picnic area and just north of the campground, is the trailhead and parking area for the 11-mile-long Pike

NATURE WALK
1

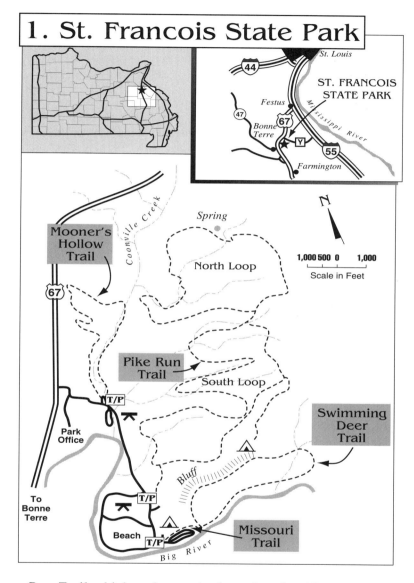

1. St. Francois State Park

Run Trail which makes an invigorating day hike or overnight backpacking trip. Historically, the Pike Hills were a refuge for Confederate outlaws during the Civil War, but now the hills offer refuge to modern day walkers. The old logging trail roads serve equestrians as well as hikers so expect rough, eroding ascents and descents (elev. 700-900 ft.). The rugged ridge and ravine trail is divided into a yellow-blazed South Loop (6.7 miles) and a North Loop (4.3 miles) interconnected by a short trail marked with green arrows. To reach

NATURE WALK
1

the North Loop you must hike a section of the South Loop. A quarter-mile-long spur trail from the South Loop leads to an overnight backpack camp at the base of a hollow. Expect limestone glade overlooks as well as small creeks and waterfalls, especially in springtime. Backpackers should pack in their own water. A small spring is located trailside near the mid-point of the North Loop.

*T*wo trails exclusively for hiking are located in the camping area. Non-camping visitors should park their vehicles in the visitors parking lot next to the showerhouse and walk to the trails. The half mile, orange arrowed Missouri Trail begins near the first restroom adjacent to the amphitheater and follows a woodland path, skirting the north edge of the campground. The short point-to-point forest trail leads to the Swimming Deer trailhead.

*T*he 2.7-mile-long Swimming Deer Trail loops along the forested floodplain and bluffs of Big River at the east end of the campground. Green arrows mark the path. Warblers and other spring migrants are plentiful amidst the sycamore, ash, Ohio buckeye, silver maple and black walnut trees. Canoeists ply the waters of Big River and 24 mile floats downstream to Washington State Park are popular. Allow two hours to hike this scenic trail. Join the park naturalist on scheduled warm season hikes along the park trails.

*T*he park entrance is located 5 miles north of the community of Bonne Terre east of U.S. 67. From I-55 take Crystal City exit 174 onto U.S. 67 south. Continue south on U.S. 67 about 21 miles to the park entrance on the east side of the highway.

Area/Location/County:
Fredericktown/Bonne Terre/St. Francois County

U.S.G.S. Map(s):
1:24,000 Bonne Terre

Trail(s) Distance:
four trails total approximately 17 miles

Acreage:
2,735 acres

Activities:
hiking, backpacking, natural and wild areas, naturalist, nature programs, amphitheater, picnicking, shelters, swimming, fishing, canoeing, launch ramp, equestrian trail, basic and electric camping

Fee(s):
picnic shelter rental, camping

NATURE WALK
1

TRAIL 2: *Hawn State Park*

Pickle Creek Trail sunny path

*H*awn State Park is named in honor of Mrs. Helen Hawn, who generously donated the initial acreage to the State of Missouri and the Department of Natural Resources in 1952. It is a perennial favorite among hikers. Trails lead to an outstanding old growth shortleaf pine and oak forest that thrives on the 800-foot-high sandstone knobs, far above the stream-carved canyon of Pickle Creek. Those interested in geology will discover one of the few places in Missouri where sedimentary sandstone and igneous granite are found together in the same streambed.

*S*hortleaf pine is abundant and attracts numerous small birds year around. Pink flowering azalea is common in spring along the ridge slopes. Nearly 700 species of plants are found here, including several rare northern-ranging plants such as rattlesnake orchid, hay scented fern and partridge berry. There is a restored pine savanna between the campground and picnic area. The two hiking-only trails traverse the 58 acre Pickle Creek Natural Area and the 2,080 acre Whispering Pine Wild Area.

*T*he 1-mile-long Pickle Creek Trail (elev. 600-800 ft.) follows the riparian north bank of the stream valley. Shut-ins and sandstone bluffs are

NATURE WALK
2

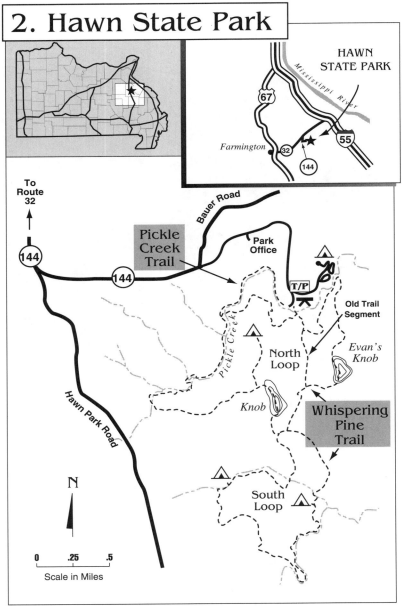

2. Hawn State Park

scenic natural area features. The clear Ozark border streambed has rocks and boulders of volcanic granite rock, crystalline gneiss rock and sandstone that greatly contribute to the natural beauty in this narrow forest valley. The rocks, pines and rushing waters combine to give a western United States or northern Canada atmosphere, especially on a sunny spring day.

NATURE WALK
2

*T*he trailhead begins at the picnic area and heads west, blazed by green arrows. Although a point-to-point trail, a loop hike is possible by returning on a mile long, red blazed section of the Whispering Pines Trail which ascends the south bluff on the opposite (south) side of Pickle Creek, returning to the picnic area and parking lot.

*T*he 10 mile Whispering Pine Trail is considered one of Missouri's best hikes. Two loops wind through the 2,080 acre Whispering Pine Wild Area, covering nearly half of the park's acreage. Established in the late 1970s, the scenic trail was constructed with the help of the Ozark Chapter of the Sierra Club. The North Loop is about 6 miles in distance and the South Loop is 4 miles. The trailhead begins south of the picnic area and parking lot where the trail crosses a footbridge over Pickle Creek. The forest trail is signed in a counterclockwise direction. Red arrows identify the North Loop and blue arrows mark the South Loop. White arrows are used to identify spur trails leading to the three primitive backpack campsites (one in North Loop, two in South Loop). The 36 acre Botkins Pine Woods Natural Area is some distance off the trail, protected, as is the 120 acre Orchid Valley Natural Area nearby. The River Aux Vases is east of the South Loop. There is a point of confusion on Whispering Pine Trail at the base of Evans Knob where an old forest road bypasses Evans Knob, returning near the trailhead bridge over Pickle Creek. There are great vistas from the knobs. Both loops can be comfortably hiked in one day but the well-spaced backpacking camps allow for overnighters.

*T*o reach Hawn State Park from I-55 exit Mo. 32 and drive west to Mo. 144, east of Farmington turning left (south). Proceed about 4 miles to the park entrance. St. Louis is about 70 miles to the north.

Area/Location/County:
Fredericktown/Coffman/St. Genevieve County

U.S.G.S. Map(s):
1:24,000 Coffman, Weingarten

Trail(s) Distance:
two trails total 11 miles

Acreage:
3,271 acres

Activities:
hiking, backpacking, natural and wild areas, seasonal naturalist, nature programs, picnicking, shelters, playground, Scout Area, basic and electric camping

Fee(s):
camping, shelter rental, group rental special area

NATURE WALK
2

TRAIL 3: *Pickle Springs Natural Area*

Pickle Spring

Double Window Arch

NATURE WALK
3

*I*f you could hike only one trail in the Missouri Ozarks, this should be that one choice. It is the 500 million-year-old geological features that make the 180 acre natural area uniquely special. Father Time has carved unusual sandstone formations and canyons. The 2 mile gravel Trail Through Time loop is lined with rock shelters, waterfalls, arches, bluffs, caves, "hoodoos" or rock pillars, a box canyon and spring named after an early pioneer, William Pickles. The rugged landscape supports a remnant of northern plant life that survived the area's change to a warmer climate inside the cool, damp canyon. Pickle Springs Natural Area is owned and maintained by the Missouri Department of Conservation (MDC) and is recognized as a National Natural Landmark by the National Park Service.

*H*ikers should slow down and take their time on the Trail Through Time, allowing two hours for exploring. A 16 page trail guide with fine pen and ink illustrations is available at the trailhead registration box. From the trailhead, walk in a clockwise direction going left (east) to The Slot, a narrow passageway or "gateway" to other natural features: Cauliflower Rocks, Terrapin Rock, Double Window Arch, The Keyhole, Bone Creek, Mossy Falls, Spirit Canyon, Owl's Den Bluff, Dome Rock, Hoodoo Cave (halfway point), Pickle Spring, Rockpile Canyon, Headwall Falls and Piney Glade.

*P*ickle Springs Natural Area is located 4 miles west and southwest from Hawn State Park. From I-55 at Ste. Genevieve, exit Mo. 32 west and drive approximately 15 miles to the junction of Hwy. AA and turn left (south). Continue on AA 1.7 miles south to Dorlac Road and turn left (north). Proceed four-tenths of a mile to the parking area and trailhead on the south side of Dorlac Road. The natural area is closed from 10 p.m. to 4 a.m. daily.

Area/Location/County:
Fredericktown/Farmington/St. Genevieve County

U.S.G.S. Map(s):
1:24,000 Sprott, Coffman

Trail(s) Distance:
2 mile loop

Acreage:
180 acres

Activities:
nature walk, nature study

Fee(s):
none

NATURE WALK
3

3. Pickle Springs Natural Area

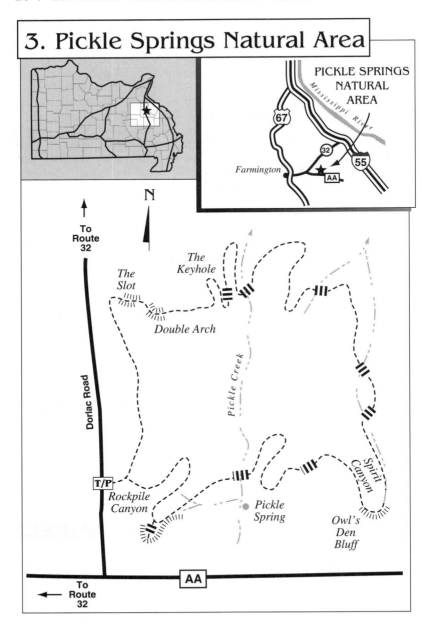

NATURE WALK
3

TRAIL 4: **Missouri Mines State Historic Site and St. Joe State Park**

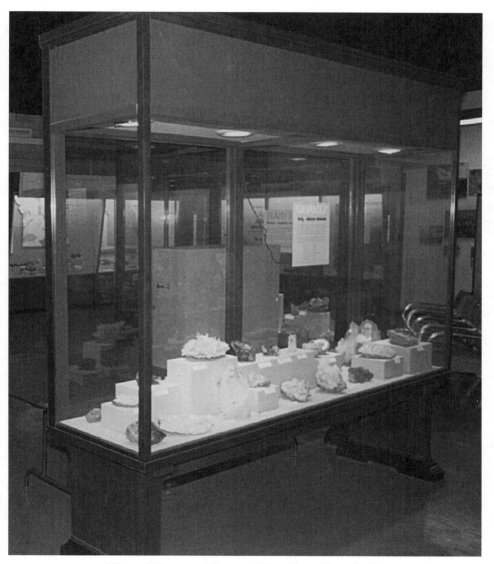

Mineral Museum, Missouri Mines State Historic Site

NATURE WALK
4

*T*he Ozark Plateau cannot be discussed without mentioning the role of geology. A wealth of different geological materials are found at the earth's surface and below. The most important mineral mined in the Missouri Ozarks is lead ore or galena. For more than 100 years, mining was the major industry in the "Old Lead Belt," centered around Flat River (now renamed Park Hills). Total production was more than 8.5 million tons of lead ore. From 1907 to 1963 the area was the major lead ore producing district in the United States, in many years accounting for 80 percent or more of the United States' total.

*I*n recognition of the significance of the state's mining history, the Missouri Mines State Historic Site features a premier museum of Ozark geology and mining. The adjoining 8,561 acre St. Joe State Park is comprised of exhausted lead mines that are now utilized for recreational purposes. Since 1864, the St. Joe Minerals Corporation has operated a lead mine in the area and in the process has carved nearly a thousand miles of underground mine tunnels where mine trains run.

*T*he powerhouse of Federal Mill No. 3 has been transformed into a museum of Missouri mining, history and technology. The first of three museum galleries contains underground mining equipment used in the "Old Lead Belt." The second gallery features exhibits on lead, geology and mineral resources and an outstanding mineral collection. Displayed minerals and fossils of Missouri are on loan from members of the Mineral Area Gem and Mineral Society. One prominent display is a scale model of the powerhouse complex as it appeared when built in 1906. There is also a small theater where a 1950s film about lead mining and milling is viewed. The third gallery is the partially-renovated power room, containing giant air compressors that supplied air power to the mine and mill complex.

*M*issouri Mines State Historic Site is located at the south edge of Park Hills, just north of St. Joe State Park. Entrance to the historic site is off the south end of the Mo. 32 overpass at Flat River Drive. Follow the directional signs to Federal Mill entrance road.

*A*djacent south of the historic mines site is St. Joe State Park, Missouri's second largest park. St. Joe State Park is not a "hiking park," however, an 11 mile-long paved bicycle and hiking trail circles the ORV riding area and 23 miles of horse trails are open to hikers and all-terrain bicycles. The ORV riding area covers about 800 acres of mined sand flats which are a visual oddity. The four manmade lakes on the sandflats – Monsanto, Pim, Jo Lee and Apollo – are open to swimming, fishing and non-motorized boating. In addition there are ORV, horse and public campgrounds as well as picnic areas.

NATURE WALK
4

St. Joe State Park is reached from Mo. 32 at Park Hills by going south on the Pimville Road at the junction of the Pimville Road and Hwy. B.

Area/Location/County:
Fredericktown/Park Hills/St. Francois County

U.S.G.S. Map(s):
1:24,000 Flat River

Trail(s) Distance:
museum and historic site tour, 11 miles of paved bicycle and general hiking trails in adjacent St. Joe State Park

Acreage:
25 acres

Activities:
nature walk, nature study, historic site, guided tours

Fee(s):
museum entrance, guided tours, group rates available, camping at St. Joe State Park

NATURE WALK
4

4. Missouri Mines State Historic Site & St. Joe State Park

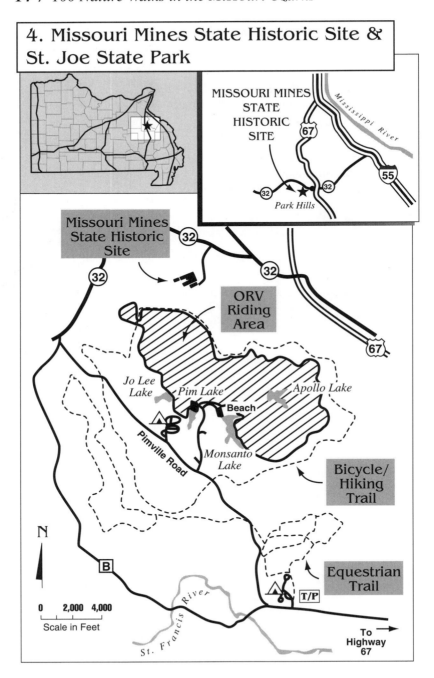

MISSOURI MINES STATE HISTORIC SITE

Mississippi River

67

55

32

32

Park Hills

Missouri Mines State Historic Site

32

32

67

ORV Riding Area

Jo Lee Lake

Pim Lake

Apollo Lake

Beach

Pimville Road

Monsanto Lake

Bicycle/ Hiking Trail

N

B

Equestrian Trail

T/P

0   2,000   4,000

Scale in Feet

River

St. Francis

To → Highway 67

NATURE WALK
4

TRAIL 5: *Hughes Mountain Natural Area*

Crest at Hughes Mountain

*T*he half mile climb to the summit of Hughes Mountain not only has great views of the surrounding St. Francois Mountains, but yields up-close views of an unusual geological formation known locally as the Devil's Honeycomb. The rare formation is a prime example of igneous rock that, when cooled, formed four- to six-sided, joint columns of Precambrian rhyolite, or volcanic rock that is the lava form of granite. The rhyolite columns are 8 to 10 inches in diameter and 3 to 4 feet in height. Pieces of the fractured rock are strewn about the igneous glades that comprise about half of the 333 acre natural area. The rest is forest land and includes portions of Lost Creek and Cedar Creek. The day use natural area is maintained and administered by the Missouri Department of Conservation.

*T*he linear, point-to-point trail begins at a mini parking area (about six cars) at the west base of Hughes Mountain and heads nearly straight uphill through young oak and hickory forest along an eroded former trail. The trail breaks into open rocky glades near the summit. The path becomes lost somewhat in the treeless glades but hikers should follow the stone cairns and somewhat obvious worn foot path curving south

NATURE WALK
5

and east to the pinnacle. At the top are found the best examples of honeycomb-shaped, jointed rhyolite. A classic Old World example of this type of rock pattern is found in Ireland, where it is known as the Giant's Causeway. The return trip down the mountain may be more confusing than ascending, so keep your eye on landmarks enroute.

*H*ughes Mountain Natural Area is located about 3 miles southwest of Irondale and about 7 miles north and east of Caledonia. From the junction of Mo. 8 and Mo. 21 at Potosi, drive south 10 miles on Mo. 21 to the junction with Hwy. M and turn left (east). Continue on Hwy. M 4 miles and turn right (south) on Cedar Creek Road/CR 541. Drive on two-tenths of a mile to the parking area at the left (east) side of the county road at the hillcrest. Be careful of oncoming vehicles.

*W*hile in the vicinity, consider walking the 1 mile loop trail at Bootleg Access on Big River, 4.2 miles west and 1 mile north of Hughes Mountain. Local Scouts worked with the Missouri Department of Conservation (MDC) to establish the wood chipped and grassy trail. Several large trees are signed, and include black walnut, red cedar, white oak, chinquapin oak, burr oak and shellbark hickory.

*T*he foot trail leads to a blufftop with an observation overlook deck above Big River. The second half of the hike is riparian through floodplain forest, along bluffs and open herbaceous fields. There are benches, foot bridges and there are three primitive camp sites near the trailhead. The boat ramp is a "carry down" access.

*B*ootleg Access is located 10 miles south of Potosi on Hwy. 21. Turn at the entrance on the east side of Hwy. 21, just north of the Big River bridge. From Hughes Mountain, the 303 acre access is located 1 mile north of the junction of Hwy. M and Mo. 21.

Area/Location/County:
Fredericktown/Irondale/Washington County

U.S.G.S. Map(s):
1:24,000 Irondale

Trail(s) Distance:
1 mile one way (2 miles round trip)

Acreage:
330 acres

Activities:
nature walk, nature study

Fee(s):
none

NATURE WALK
5

5. Hughes Mountain Natural Area

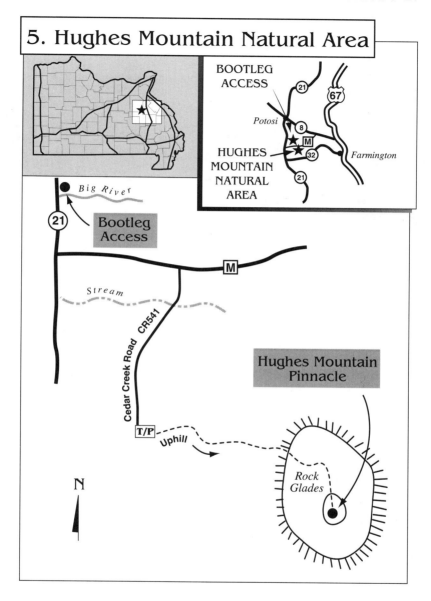

TRAIL 6: *Buford Mountain Conversation Area*

Northern Fence Lizard

Scenic 1,740-foot Buford Mountain overlooks the Belleville Valley. Atop its magnificence are open rhyolite glades that appear on the cluster of knobs that comprise Buford Mountain. Bald Knob (elev. 1,674 ft.) is the largest and most scenic glade on the mountain with heavenly vistas of the valley below. This is a great spot to rock hop and investigate the wildlife.

At one time this part of the St. Francois Mountains was inhabited by prehistoric woodland mounds builders. In 1812, William Buford acquired the land through a Spanish land grant. The mountains were logged and charcoal was produced during the late 1800s. Old charcoal kilns still existence around Buford Mountain. The Nature Conservancy was very active in acquiring Buford Mountain which is now administered by the Missouri Department of Conservation.

A 10 mile loop begins and ends at the locked metal gate at the Hwy. U parking lot. Follow the service road on foot north and east one-quarter mile to a second parking area and the actual trailhead on the north end. At this time, the trail blaze is a "Bubble" man hiker symbol. Follow the eroded path up the mountain about 700 feet to the first of five knobs and the connecting ridge saddles. Continue west along the ridge crest trail about 2 miles to the trail fork at the top of the third knob. The loop trail is signed in a counterclockwise direction, however if you prefer to visit the glades at Bald Knob, walk clockwise or left from the trail fork three-quarters of a mile to the 10 acre open glade.

NATURE WALK
6

6. Buford Mtn. Conservation Area

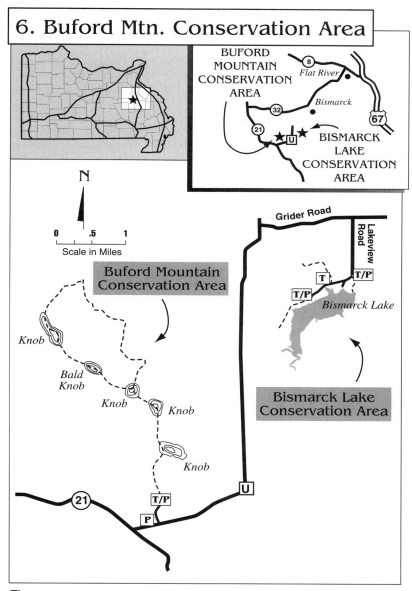

*G*oing counterclockwise as signed, the trail descends 600 feet into a hollow, past a pond, crossing a small stream, then continues north and west uphill to a saddle and turns due west uphill to Buford Mountain (ATVs have made the trail confusing in places). Arriving at the mountain crest, the loop trail continues south and follows the most scenic knob section of the trail to Bald Knob and back to the trail junction and trailhead.

NATURE WALK
6

*B*uford Mountain Conservation Area is accessible from the Hwy. U parking lot which is located 8 miles north of Ironton on Mo. 21 to Hwy. U. Turn right (east) on Hwy. U and drive four-tenths of a mile to the signed parking lot on the north side of the highway. Located a few miles south of Hughes Mountain Natural Area, Buford Mountain is just over 2 miles from Belleview and 3 miles from Graniteville and Elephant Rocks State Park.

*N*earby 210-acre Bismarck Lake Conservation Area also has some Ozark scenery worth seeing. Unfortunately there are no trails completed around the lake or connecting to Buford Mountain but there are three old forest roads on the north lakeside of the 1,188-acre area. Formed by the headwaters of the St. Francis River, the lake is over 50 years old. It was purchased by the Missouri Department of Conservation (MDC) in 1951 from the Hanna Mining Company and was then called Ozark Ore Company Lake. It makes a fine canoeing lake with its good size and scenery.

*T*o reach Bismarck Lake Conservation Area from the Hwy. U parking lot at Buford Mountain Conservation Area, drive east and north on U.S highway about 5.5 miles to Grider Road and turn right (east). Continue on Grider Road 1.5 miles to Lakeview or Lake Bismarck Road and turn right (south). Continue 1 mile to the lakeshore parking area.

*A*lso from the junction of Mo. 32 and Hwy. N in Bismarck, drive south on Hwy. N, 1.8 miles to Grider Road and turn right (west). Continue on Grider Road 1.1 miles to Lakeview/Lake Bismarck Road and turn left (south). Continue 1 mile to the lakeshore.

Area/Location/County:
Fredericktown/Belleview/Iron, Washington, St. Francois counties

U.S.G.S. Map(s):
1:24,000 Graniteville

Trail(s) Distance:
10 miles

Acreage:
3,743 acres

Activities:
hiking, backpacking, nature study, seasonal hunting

Fee(s):
none

NATURE WALK
6

TRAIL 7: *Elephant Rocks State Park*

Unusual Rock Formations

Unique Trail Loop

NATURE WALK
7

*L*ike elephants standing end to end, trunk and tail, in a circus, Elephant Rocks are indeed a curious geological "herd." "Dumbo," the largest rock, weighs 680 tons, and is 27 feet tall, 35 feet long, and 17 feet wide. Sculptured by time, the huge, round granite boulders are ancient, about 1.2 billion years old, dating back to the Precambrian Era. In short, over the eons the volcanic magma cooled to form granite, and weathering reduced the mountaintop to separate massive boulders. Dr. John S. Brown, a retired geologist, purchased and gave the property to the State of Missouri and the Department of Natural Resources (DNR).

*A*lthough user paths are conspicuous, there is a maintained 1 mile paved interpretive trail loop that has 22 interpretive stations with braille signage, a first in Missouri. The "Elephant Walk" Trail was also the first National Recreation Trail in Missouri. There is a designated seven acre natural area at the Elephant Rocks, within the 129 acre park. The area has a major quarry history, active from 1845 to 1869, but fortunately Elephant Rocks were spared. Allow an hour for this easy geological wonder walk. This St. Francois Mountain spot has plenty of shaded woodland picnic sites and quarry fishing.

*E*lephant Rocks State Park is located seven-tenths of a mile northwest of Mo. 21 and Graniteville, 5 miles south of Belleview, and about 5 miles north of Pilot Knob and Ironton.

*A*nother nearby location to discover is Ft. Davidson State Historic Site, also administered by the Missouri DNR. Although no maintained trails are established, the spacious open grounds of the 31 acre site in the Arcadia Valley at the base of 1,608-foot Shepherd Mountain and 1,400-foot Pilot Knob, is a fine place to stretch your legs.

*O*n September 27, 1864, the Civil War battle of Pilot Knob took place at Ft. Davidson and the Confederates won a costly, hollow victory with many casualties, no prisoners or captured munitions. The Confederate campaign failed to relieve the eastern front from Union victory. Only earthwork remnants remain of Ft. Davidson located just northwest of the visitors center.

*T*he Federal-style visitors center contains exhibits that interpret the battle and books and gifts about Missouri's social and natural history are for sale. The center is open year around from 10 a.m. to 4 p.m. Monday through Saturday and from noon to 5 p.m. on Sunday. The fort and the surrounding grounds are open dawn to dusk. A picnic area and playground are situated south of the visitors center.

*F*t. Davidson State Historic Site is south of Elephant Rocks State Park in the community of Pilot Knob, north of Ironton. From Mo. 21 turn east on Hwy. V. Drive to the four-way stop and turn right to the entrance, parking lot and visitors center.

*H*ikers be aware that the Historic Taum Sauk Trail, an 8 mile, Boy Scout maintained, point-to-point trail, extends from Ft. Davidson to Taum Sauk Mountain State Park.

*I*n summary, the white blazed trail crosses Mo. 21 and proceeds west on West Maple Road to Shepherd Mountain Road for about a mile. The trail leaves Shepherd Mountain Road and ascends Shepherd Mountain (trail rocky, vista after leaf fall), descending south along a ridge to Shepherd Lake, the municipal water supply for Ironton.

*T*he historic trail crosses Hwy. M from Shepherd Lake and follows a gravel road west, crossing over Stouts Creek and heads southwest through the forest toward 1,726-foot Russell Mountain, crossing Hwy. CC on its way to Taum Sauk Mountain State Park. (See also Ozark Trail, Taum Sauk Section and Taum Sauk Mountain State Park.)

Area/Location/County:
Fredericktown/Graniteville/Iron County

U.S.G.S. Map(s):
1:24,000 Graniteville

Trail(s) Distance:
1 mile paved loop

Acreage:
129 acres

Activities:
nature walk, nature study, picnicking, shelter, playground, quarry fishing, naturalist hikes and programs

Fee(s):
none

NATURE WALK
7

7. Elephant Rocks State Park

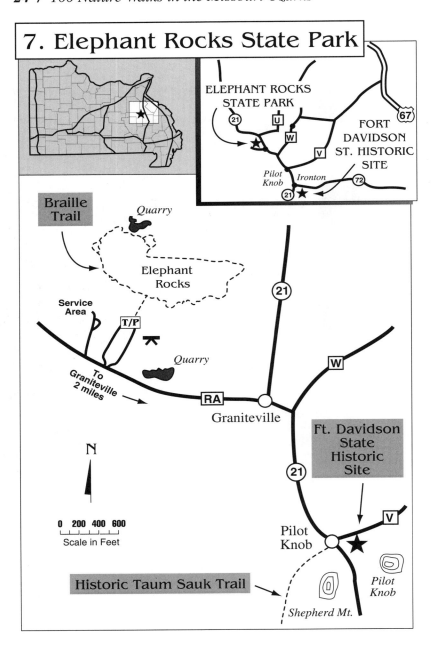

TRAIL 8: **John James Audubon Trail**

Bidwell Creek

*T*he easy to rugged 13 mile, double loop trail follows mostly single track through forest and along stream, old forest roads and sections of FS 2199. The non-motorized trail is maintained by the St. Louis Council of the Boys Scouts, Troop 657, in cooperation with the U.S. Forest Service. The pathway is named in honor of naturalist-painter, John James Audubon (1785-1851), who lived, painted and was a merchant in nearby Ste. Genevieve in the early 1800s. The Forest Service land is located in southwest Ste. Genevieve County about 3 air miles southeast of Hawn State Park.

*T*he trailhead is at the Bidwell Creek ford on FS 2199 about 5 miles north of Womack and Hwy. T. There is ample parking for five or six vehicles in the pullouts and there are primitive camping sites adjacent to the

NATURE WALK
8

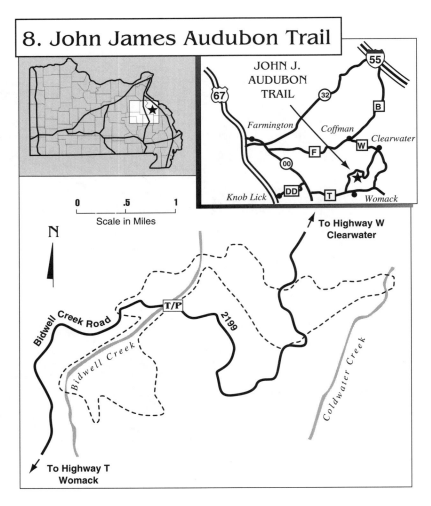

8. John James Audubon Trail

JOHN J.
AUDUBON
TRAIL

55

67   32   B

Farmington   Coffman   Clearwater

F   W

00

Knob Lick   DD   T   Womack

0   .5   1
Scale in Miles

N

To Highway W
Clearwater

Bidwell Creek Road

T/P   2199

Bidwell Creek

Coldwater Creek

To Highway T
Womack

forest road and creek. The Bidwell Creek trailhead is near the middle of two loops: the Bidwell Creek, West Loop and the Coldwater Creek, East Loop (8 miles and 5 miles long). The well-worn trail is blazed in both directions with 2- by 6-inch, white painted vertical rectangles, identical to those on the Appalachian Trail. The suggested direction is clockwise.

*T*he trail follows the hills and hollows of the Ozark Border with an elevation change of 300 feet (elev. 700-1,000 ft.). The uphills and downhills can be steep, with muddy and rocky segments. There are stream crossings over Bidwell Creek and Coldwater Creek and road crossings and travel on FS 2199. Three primitive campsites are situated on Coldwater and Bidwell Creeks. The trail splits into two loops about a mile downstream from the Bidwell Creek trailhead where a short

NATURE WALK
8

connector spur enables you to cut the hiking distance to 8 miles. Experienced hikers or ambitious beginners may hike the entire 13 miles in a long day. Backpackers can make it in a leisurely two day trek.

*I*n brief, the Bidwell Creek, West Loop Section is 8 miles long and follows and crosses Bidwell Creek and its tributaries. The Coldwater Creek, East Loop Section is 5 miles long and follows the ridges and hollows of Coldwater Creek. Salamander Hollow is a candidate to become a natural area. Hiking is good year around but is especially nice during sunny April days with free-flowing creeks and the promise of flowers everywhere.

*F*rom I-55 exit Mo. 51 east at Perryville and drive to Hwy. T and turn left (west). Follow T west to Womack and Bidwell Creek Road/FS 2199. Turn right (north) and drive 4.6 miles to the Bidwell Creek trailhead at the stream ford.

*F*rom Fredericktown, go north on Hwy. 00 about 9 miles to the junction with Hwy. T and turn right (east). Follow T 5 miles east to Bidwell Creek Road/FS 2199 at Womack and turn north (left). Go north 4.6 miles on Bidwell Creek Road/FS 2199 to the trailhead at the Bidwell Creek Ford.

Area/Location/County:
Fredericktown/Womack/Ste. Genevieve County

U.S.G.S. Map(s):
1:24,000 Womack

Trail(s) Distance:
13 mile loop (two loops, 8 and 5 miles)

Activities:
hiking, backpacking, nature study, mountain biking, seasonal hunting

Fee(s):
none

NATURE WALK
8

TRAIL 9: *Knob Lick Mountain Lookout Tower*

Shadblow Bloom in April

*E*asily accessed via U.S. Hwy. 67, this Missouri Department of Conservation day use property sits atop and around Knob Lick Mountain, the highest point for miles (elev. 1,333 ft.). Situated at the eastern edge of the St. Francois Mountains, the tower site provides fine views but little in the way of walking. However, there are two short jaunts: one along the glade area at mountain crest and another down ridge from the tower to the base of the mountain. Both trails are short and easy to negotiate.

*F*rom the parking area adjacent to the lookout tower, walk south, west and east to form a loop through the five acre glade of boulders and flowers. The 400 yard wide open space provides fine views of the St. Francis River valley. Take time to look close up at life on the glade, the so-called "Missouri Desert."

A second, longer grassy trail begins "backside" of the lookout tower at the grass-forest edge. The easy, wide path goes downhill about one-third of a mile and dead ends at a gate on private property. Retrace your steps up the mountain back to the tower site and parking area. Vistas are better when the leaves are down.

*K*nob Lick Mountain Lookout Tower provides great views, short walks, and excellent picnicking. From U.S. 67 near Knob Lick, located

NATURE WALK
9

9. Knob Lick Mt. Lookout Tower

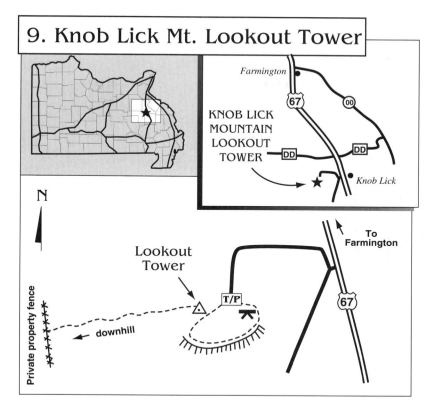

between Farmington and Fredericktown, turn west on Canterberry Road and make an immediate turn right (north) onto a gravel road. Follow the gravel road 1 mile to the parking area. Watch for the road signs.

Area/Location/County:
Fredericktown/Knob Lick/St. Francois County

U.S.G.S. Map(s):
1:24,000 Knob Lick, Wachita Mountain

Trail(s) Distance:
approximately 1 mile total

Acreage:
80 acres

Activities:
nature walk, nature study, picnicking

Fee(s):
none

NATURE WALK
9

TRAIL 10: *Silas Dees Azalea and Wildflower Preserve*

*T*he Nature Conservancy owns and manages this donated five acre roadside preserve, a small haven of spring wildflowers. There are no established walking paths but user and deer paths weave about the fenced preserve. April to mid-May is the best time to visit, when the level bottom and hillside are littered with colorful flowers.

*T*he sweetly-scented, pink to white tubular flowers of the azalea illuminate the rocky, open wooded hillside and are considered by many to be the Ozark's most beautiful native shrub. Azalea (*Rhododendron prinophyllum*) is often called rose azalea or wild honeysuckle. The shrub goes unnoticed most of the year except when flowering in late April and early May. The knee high, perennial shrub has dark, weak stems and thrives in the dry, acidic, cherty soils of open ridge slopes. The delicate 1- to 1.5-inch-long flowers appear in showy clusters at the tips of the twigs. Additional spring flowering plants found in the preserve include flowering dogwood, paw paw, bedstraw, goats rue, several ferns, wild ginger, cohosh, and low bush blueberry.

*T*o reach Silas Dees Azalea and Wildflower Preserve from Fredericktown, drive north from the junction of Hwy. OO and Mo. 72, 7.1 miles (1.75 miles north of the Madison and St. Francois county line) on Hwy. OO and park in the roadside pullout (room for two cars max and this can be a busy highway). To enter the preserve, look for the yellow and green Nature Conservancy property signs and the open fence gap. The community of Fredericktown hosts an annual Azalea Festival the first weekend in May.

*A*nother nearby roadside azalea preserve is located 14.3 miles from the Silas Dees Preserve. Drive east from the Fredericktown junction of Hwy. OO and Mo. 72, on Mo. 72 just west of the Madison and Bollinger county line. The Spiva Azalea Roadside Park is on the north side of Mo. 72 and is signed. The small preserve needs to be replenished with new azalea plantings. The Missouri Department of Highways maintains the roadside park but a garden club needs to adopt it.

*A*long the back roads of the St. Francois Mountains, wild azalea can be prolific. The forest service properties of Silver Mines and Cathedral Canyon are scenic areas where rock, pine, water and azaleas blend together in mid spring. A remote area in the Eleven Point District is noted for azalea blooms. From Thomasville in Oregon County, drive north on Mo. 99 for 2.7 miles and turn right (east) on FS 3173/Spring

NATURE WALK
10

10. Silas Dees Azalea & Wildflower Preserve

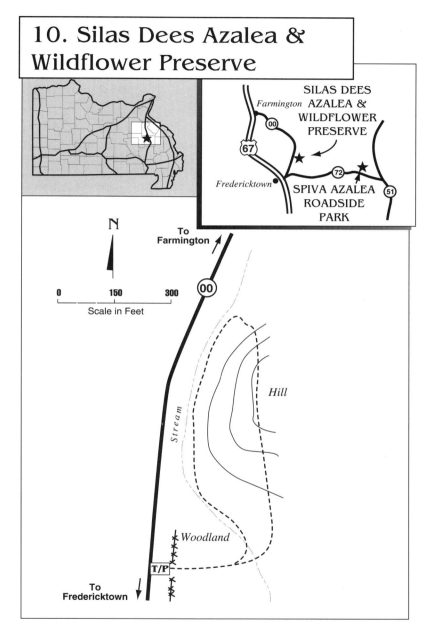

Creek Road. Drive 1.7 miles east to FS 4155 and turn left (north). Proceed north on FS 4155 eight-tenths of a mile to a road fork. This is a good area to park and walk the forest road. Most of the azaleas can be found in the first quarter mile beyond the fork (U.S.G.S. Map 1:24,000 Birch Tree).

NATURE WALK
10

*F*arther west in the Ava/Cassville District is the 2.6 acre Alma Peterson Azalea Memorial, a Nature Conservancy preserve in Douglas County. The roadside gate may be closed most of the year (but never locked) except late April to mid-May when the azaleas flower. There is an old woods lane that leads north from the gate and stone memorial. The preserve is located 14 miles southeast of Ava and 1.2 miles southeast of Sweden just off Mo. 14.

*F*rom the junction of Hwy. P and Mo. 14, drive east on Mo. 14, 1.3 miles to a gravel road with a roadside sign with directions to the preserve. Turn right (south) and follow the gravel road six-tenths of a mile to the road bend and jog east three-tenths of a mile to a roadside pullout, the gate, and the Alma Peterson stone memorial (U.S.G.S. Map 1:24,000 Ava).

Area/Location/County:
Fredericktown/Farmington/St. Francois County

U.S.G.S. Map(s):
1:24,000 Knob Lick

Trail(s) Distance:
short user and deer paths

Acreage:
5 acres

Activities:
nature walk, nature study

Fee(s):
none

NATURE WALK
10

TRAIL 11: *Amidon Memorial Conservation Area*

Hahns Shut-Ins on the Castor River

*W*ithin Amidon Conservation Area is the Castor River or Hahn's Mill Shut-ins Natural Area, the only shut-ins (narrow gorge) found in the Castor River valley. It is considered to be one of the Ozark's most beautiful and it appeared on the cover of the 1995 Missouri Conservation Atlas. The smooth, water-carved, granite boulders are locally called "pink rocks," alluding to their dazzling coloration. The 209 acre designated natural area is located along the upper 2.5 miles of the river. Amidon Memorial Conservation Area was acquired in 1984; a portion of the property was donated by the Amidon family.

*T*he 1 mile Cedar Glade Trail loop is considered easy with some upland walking. The mixed cedar, pine and deciduous forest amid the rocky shut-ins makes it a year around nature walk. During the warm months, wading and sunbathing are popular pursuits. In the 1870s, a gristmill owned by the Hahn family operated at the downstream junction of Madison County roads 253 and 208. An old trail, no longer maintained, follows the west bank of the Castor River from the Cedar Glade Trail and the Hahn's Mill shut-ins, downstream to the historic old Hahn's mill site. Walk leisurely.

*A*midon Conservation Area is due east of Fredericktown about 12 miles. Take Mo. 72 east about 3 miles to Hwy. J and turn left (east). Continue 4.6 miles to the junction with Hwy. W and turn south (right). Go 2.4 miles on Hwy. W to the end of the pavement and Madison CR 208. Turn left (east) on CR 208 and drive 1.1 miles to the junction with CR 253. Turn left (north) on CR 253 and proceed nine-tenths of a mile to the parking area and trailhead on the right (east) side of the gravel road.

NATURE WALK
11

11. Amidon Memorial Conservation Area

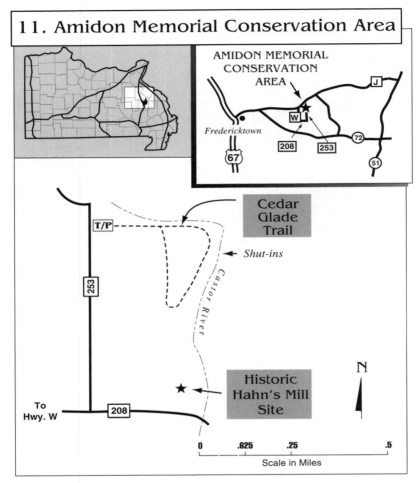

Area/Location/County:
Fredericktown/Fredericktown/Madison and Bollinger counties

U.S.G.S. Map(s):
1:24,000 Fredericktown, Higdon

Trail(s) Distance:
1 mile loop

Acreage:
1,632 acres

Activities:
nature walk, nature study, natural area, picnicking, fishing,
primitive camping, seasonal hunting

Fee(s):
none

NATURE WALK
11

TRAIL 12: *Silver Mines Recreation Area and Millstream Gardens Conservation Area*

Missouri Whitewater Championships

*F*or the nature walker, these two adjoining public properties seem like one. Developed in a cooperative effort between the U.S. Forest Service and the Missouri Department of Conservation, the 3-mile-long Turkey Creek Trail (point-to-point) extends from the USFS Silver Mines Recreation Area, Riverside picnic and boat ramp at the Hwy. D bridge to the MDC Millstream Gardens Conservation Area parking lot, about half a mile south of Mo. 72. Highlights along this whitewater section of the St. Francis River include the old Silver Mine Dam and Shut-In, Mud Creek Shut-In, Bluff Hole, Tiemann Shut-In and Big Drop, Double Drop and Cat's Paw.

*T*urkey Creek Trail follows the rocky, 200-foot-high, riverside bluff above Silver Mines Shut-In, along the east bank of the St. Francis River, north from the Riverside picnic area at the Hwy. D bridge to the Turkey Creek picnic area. The trail becomes floodplain level after crossing the footbridge over Turkey Creek (about a mile walk).

NATURE WALK
12

12. Silver Mines Recreation Area & Millstream Gardens Conservation Area

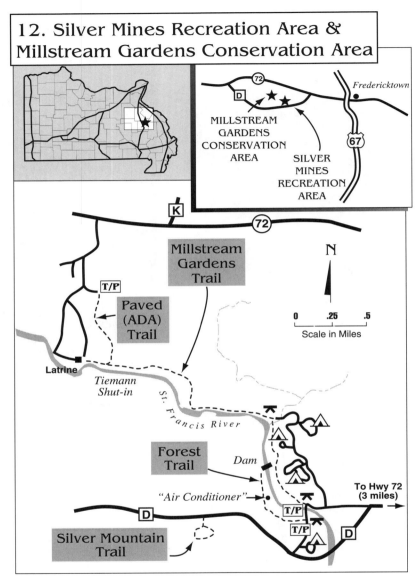

MILLSTREAM GARDENS CONSERVATION AREA

SILVER MINES RECREATION AREA

Fredericktown

Millstream Gardens Trail

Paved (ADA) Trail

T/P

N

0 .25 .5
Scale in Miles

Latrine

Tiemann Shut-in

St. Francis River

Forest Trail

Dam

"Air Conditioner"

To Hwy 72 (3 miles)

Silver Mountain Trail

*H*ere the trail continues north another 1.5 miles, upstream along a riparian path to the Tiemann Shut-In and the 20 acre St. Francis River Natural Area. The trail becomes paved at the wooden overlook and heads uphill to the upper parking lot. Car shuttle or retrace your steps the 2.5 miles back to Silver Mines and the Hwy. D bridge trailhead at riverside. Campground trail spurs feed into Turkey Creek Trail at Silver Mines Recreation Area. This portion of the St. Francis River is popular with kayakers and canoeists. The annual Missouri Whitewater

NATURE WALK
12

Championship races are held here in late March and are easily viewed from Turkey Creek Trail.

A second nature trail originates and ends in the USFS riverside camp loop near Hwy. D, across the St. Francis River from Turkey Creek trailhead, south terminus. At the north side of the parking area is the trailhead for the Silver Mines Trail. The half-mile-long rugged path follows the west bluffs of the St. Francis River upstream to the old 1936 dam and Einstein Silver Mine. The trail returns the same way for a mile-long hike round trip. Experience the coolness of the old mine shaft called the "Air Conditioner."

*T*he third trail is located half a mile west of Riverside camp loop on Hwy. D, uphill and on the left side of the highway. The quarter-mile-long Silver Mountain Historic Trail loops about the foundations, streets and sidewalks of the ghost mining town of Silver Mountain. From 1877 through 1938 the busy village housed the workers of the Einstein Silver Mining Company. The USFS purchased the former mining land from the Silver Dam Realty and Mining Company.

*T*o reach Silver Mines Recreation Area from Fredericktown, take Mo. 72 west about 6 miles and turn left (south) on Hwy. D. Follow D about 4 miles to the recreation area at the St. Francis River bridge.

*T*o reach Millstream Gardens Conservation Area from Mo. 72 at Fredericktown, go west 8.5 miles to the property entrance on the left (south) side of the highway. Continue half a mile south to the parking area and trailhead for Turkey Creek Trail.

Area/Location/County:
Fredericktown/Fredericktown/Madison County

U.S.G.S. Map(s):
1:24,000 Rhodes Mountain

Trail(s) Distance:
three trails total about 4 miles

Acreage:
600 acre Silver Mines RA/684 acre Millstream Gardens CA

Activities:
Silver Mines RA: hiking, nature study, historic sites, picnicking, swimming, fishing, canoeing, kayaking, launch ramp, camping, group camping
Millstream Gardens CA: hiking, nature study, picnicking, shelter, swimming, fishing, canoeing, kayaking, paved trail, special event, seasonal hunting, archery range

Fee(s):
camping at Silver Mines Recreation Area

NATURE WALK
12

TRAIL 13: *Cathedral Canyon*

*T*he outdoor experience at Cathedral Canyon is as uplifting as its place name. However the site is also known as Dark Hollow of Lower Rock Creek, a more "down-to-earth" title. Most visitors would agree the deep canyon is the most picturesque in the St. Francois Mountains. The 400-foot-high, vertical rock bluffs tower over the rushing boulder-filled stream. Glade-dotted Black Mountain (elev. 1,502 ft.) and Trackler Mountain (elev. 1,400 ft.) flank Cathedral Canyon to the south and north. Lower Rock Creek drops 100 feet in gradient per mile in the last 4 miles before joining the St. Francis River. The canyon is easily accessed on foot but hiking becomes challenging in Dark Hollow. You cannot get lost following Lower Rock Creek upstream or downstream in Cathedral Canyon. Private property borders the U.S. Forest Service property at both ends of the canyon.

*T*o reach Cathedral Canyon from Fredericktown, go west on Hwy. E from the junction with U.S. 67, about 10.4 miles, just beyond the St. Francis River bridge crossing. Turn right on Madison CR 511 and follow the gravel north three-tenths of a mile to a forest road on the left just beyond the stream ford. Turn left on the forest road and park in the available pullouts or continue on to the USFS metal gate and park. This trailhead location is known as Wolf Hollow.

*W*alk past the locked gate, cross the stream, and take the first immediate trail junction left (south) to Cathedral Canyon instead of following the forest road uphill to Trackler Mountain. The unmarked trail spur to Cathedral Canyon is an easy mile-long forest trek. The worn path passes between two ridges, sliding over a low saddle and dropping down into Lower Rock Creek.

*A*rriving at Lower Rock Creek, stop and mark in your mind this return-to-trailhead spur. Lower Rock Creek may be explored downstream or upstream to a point where forest service land borders private property. The Cathedral Canyon portion of Dark Hollow of Lower Rock Creek is upstream about three bends or 1 mile from entering the canyon. A user path cuts through the overgrown terrace and sometimes crosses the stream. Hiking the canyon will be slow, so take a friend and be leisurely. If you go in springtime, the strong mountain feeling comes through with dashing water, blooming flowers such as ninebark and azalea, and boulder rock all around.

*C*athedral Canyon is 7 road miles east of the U.S.F.S. Marble Creek Recreation Area on Hwy. E.

NATURE WALK
13

13. Cathedral Canyon

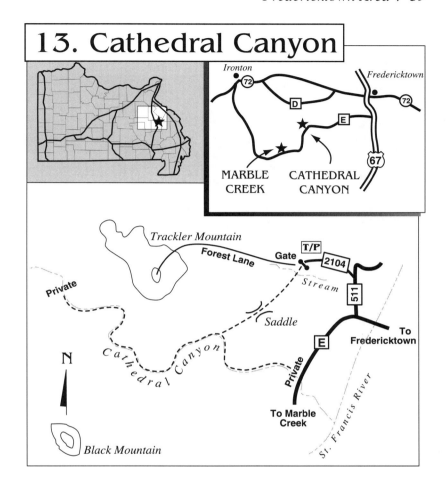

Area/Location/County:
Fredericktown/Fredericktown/Madison County

U.S.G.S. Map(s):
1:24,000 Lake Killarney, Des Arc NE, Rhodes Mountain, Rock Pile Mountain

Trail(s) Distance:
approximately 4 miles round trip

Activities:
hiking, backpacking, nature study, fishing, seasonal hunting

Fee(s):
none

NATURE WALK
13

TRAIL 14: *Rock Pile Mountain Wilderness*

Trailhead Marker, Little Grass Mountain

*O*f the eight wilderness areas in the Missouri Ozarks, Rock Pile Mountain is the smallest in acreage but holds one of the biggest archaeological mysteries. To date, archaeologists are uncertain as to who or what prehistoric culture piled the ancient circle of granite rock at the crest of Rock Pile Mountain (elev. 1,270 ft.). The suggested trail route of old forest roads may be hiked in a day but allow a backpacking overnight to explore the bluffs, Turkey Hollow and the St. Francis River. Overall the trail is open and not overgrown, has little erosion (except for the ups and downs at Rock Pile Mountain and Cave Branch), and has little horse impact due to difficult access. Maps and compass are a necessity in unmarked wilderness areas.

*T*he trailhead begins and ends at Little Grass Mountain (elev. 1,306 ft.), the highest point on the trail. The trailhead and registration box are located at the west end of the parking lot near a granite boulder on which are carved the words, "Rock Pile Mtn. Wilderness." The forest mountainside path switchbacks down the southwest slope of Little Grass Mountain quickly to descend 300 feet to a lower ridge. For the next 2 miles or so the unmarked but obvious path heads south along the ridges (bear right at an old road junction) to connect at the "T" trail junction with the wilderness loop (approximately 7.5 miles) which leads to Rock Pile Mountain and Cave Branch and back to the trail junction at Little Grass Mountain trailhead parking.

*A*t the "T" trail junction beginning and ending the loop, walk left or clockwise up the old ridge forest road to Rock Pile Mountain (about 2 miles). Stay right at all old road trail junctions. The old road trail ascends Rock Pile Mountain (elev. 1,270 ft.). At the mountain crest is a cedar glade where the trail follows the igneous knob ridge. The ancient

NATURE WALK
14

14. Rock Pile Mt. Wilderness

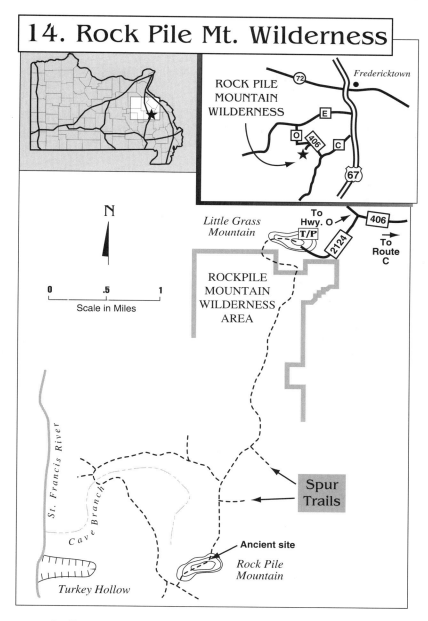

rock pile will be at the right of the trail a short distance from the middle of the crest.

*F*rom Rock Pile Mountain the trail descends the southwest slope, bearing right at the the junction of two old forest roads, and gradually follows the ridges to Cave Branch (elev. 500 ft.; about 2 miles).

NATURE WALK
14

*F*rom Cave Branch, the next half mile of the loop trail crosses the branch and ascends a ridge and bears right (east) past the two old road spurs that lead to the St. Francis River, Turkey Pen Hollow, and the river bluffs. (Backpackers or canoeists have more time to explore these special wilderness areas).

*C*ontinue on the loop 2 more miles by walking east along the ridges above Cave Branch to the junction with the original access trail spur that leads back north to Little Grass Mountain trailhead.

*T*o reach Rock Pile Mountain Wilderness Area trailhead at Little Grass Mountain, go south 3 miles from Fredericktown on U.S. 67 to the intersection with Hwy. C at Cherokee Pass. Drive west on Hwy. C about 5.5 miles to the junction with Madison CR 406/Tower Road and turn right (west). Continue on CR 406/Tower Road 2.5 miles to FS 2124 and turn left (south). Proceed 1.1 mile on FS 2124 to the trailhead.

A second scenic route from Fredericktown would be to go west on Hwy. E at the junction with U.S. 67. Follow Hwy. E 6 miles to Hwy. O and turn left (south). Continue on Hwy. O 2.1 miles to Madison CR 406/Tower Road and turn left (east). Proceed on CR 406/Tower Road 1.4 mile to FS 2124 and turn right (south). Continue 1.1 mile to the Little Grass Mountain trailhead parking.

*F*or hikers who desire solitude and beautiful surroundings, try Rock Pile Mountain Wilderness.

Area/Location/County:
Fredericktown/Fredericktown/Madison County

U.S.G.S. Map(s):
1:24,000 Rock Pile Mountain

Trail(s) Distance:
loop of approximately 10 miles

Acreage:
4,131 acres

Activities:
hiking, backpacking, nature study, seasonal hunting

Fee(s):
none

NATURE WALK
14

TRAIL 15: *Crane Lake Recreation Area*

Crane Pond Creek Shut-Ins

*O*ne-hundred acre Crane Lake was formed in 1973 with the creation of a dam on Crane Pond Creek and a day use U.S. Forest Service recreation area was established. The main outdoor activities are picnicking along the lakeshore, fishing from the gentle banks, canoeing the waters, birding the bays and hiking the coves. Never crowded and always peaceful, hikers will appreciate the Crane Lake (North) and Crane Pond Creek (South) loops plus the 8 mile, point-to-point Ozark Trail section from Crane Lake to Marble Creek Recreation Areas.

*C*rane Lake Trail, a designated National Recreation Trail, was constructed by the Youth Conservation Corps (YCC) in 1975. The maintained trail is marked with forest service white diamonds and some cairns on the rocky glades on South Loop near the dam. The two trail loops total 5 miles.

*T*he 3 mile North Loop (and Ozark Trail) trailhead begins and ends at the parking lot adjacent to the picnic area in the northeast shore of Crane Lake. The path is easy and level as it circles the open wooded shore, but near the dam the trail descends and crosses Crane Pond Creek Shut-Ins and ascends back to lake level. There are several finger cove bays and the northwest shore is nearly solid white oak due to TSI (Timber Stand Improvement) by the Forest Service.

NATURE WALK
15

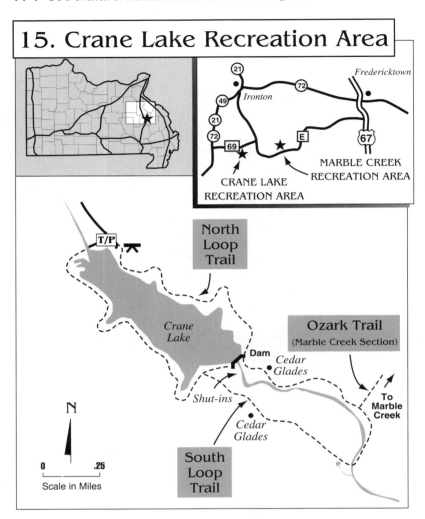

15. Crane Lake Recreation Area

The 2 mile South Loop begins and ends at either side of the dam. From the southeast side of the dam (hiking clockwise) follow the South Loop through the rocky glades where the trail may become obscure. Look for cairns and arrow-painted rocks. The trail leaves the glade for the forest and meadow, following an old farm lane. As the trail curves back to cross Crane Pond Creek, the Ozark Trail departs from South Loop and heads east 8 miles to Marble Creek Recreation Area, crossing Crane Pond Creek, The South Loop moves along level bottomland to forest and the rocky glades on the opposite bluff of the shut-ins, emerging above the dam and North Loop.

The Ozark Trail, Marble Creek Section of the Eastern Loop begins and ends at the Crane Lake picnic area and shares the east shore of the North

NATURE WALK
15

Loop and the cedar glade, forest and field of the east section of the South Loop. Leaving the South Loop, the Ozark trail heads east 8 miles to Marble Creek Recreation Area. (See Ozark Trail: Marble Creek Section.)

*T*o reach Crane Lake Recreation Area from Ironton, go south on Mo. 21/49, 12.2 miles to Chloride and turn left (east) on Iron CR 120/FH 69. Cross the railroad tracks and follow the gravel road nearly 5 miles to the four-way junction (Black Stallion Trade Store on southwest corner) and turn right (south) on Crane Pond Road. Continue 1.9 miles to the Crane Lake parking area and trailhead.

*Y*ou may also turn on Hwy. E, 2 miles south of Ironton or half a mile south of Arcadia, at the junction of Mo. 21/49 and Hwy. E. Travel about 8 miles east to FH-69 and turn right (west). Proceed 2.8 miles to the four-way junction and turn left (south) on Crane Pond Road. Go 1.9 miles to Crane Lake Recreation Area.

*F*rom Fredericktown, drive about 21 miles west on Hwy. E, (past Marble Creek Recreation Area, 18 miles) to FH-69 and turn left (west). Go 2.8 miles to the four-way junction and turn left (south) on Crane Pond Road and proceed to the recreation area.

*M*arble Creek Recreation Area (seasonal camping, picnicking, wading, swimming, fishing, Ozark Trailhead) is located on Hwy. E, 14 miles east of Ironton and 18 miles west of Fredericktown on the north side of the highway. Watch for signs. Walk the user paths along Marble Creek and enjoy the pink marbled shut-ins.

Area/Location/County:
Fredericktown/Chloride/Iron County

U.S.G.S. Map(s):
1:24,000 Des Arc NE, Glover

Trail(s) Distance:
5 mile double loop
8 mile Marble Creek Section, Ozark Trail

Acreage:
100 acre Crane Lake

Activities:
hiking, backpacking, nature study, picnicking, fishing, non-motorized boating, seasonal hunting, (seasonal campgrounds at Marble Creek RA)

Fee(s):
seasonal camping at Marble Creek RA

NATURE WALK
15

TRAIL 16: **Taum Sauk Mountain State Park**

*T*aum Sauk Mountain (elev. 1,772 ft.) has the distinction of being the highest natural point in the state of Missouri and also having the highest waterfall in the "Show-Me State," as well as some of the best scenery that is accessible only by foot. The billion-year-old dome-shaped mountain, "the geologic core of the St. Francois Mountains," is covered with a groundmass of igneous purple or dark red porphyry rock that keeps your eyes to the trail while hiking. A rugged 3 mile Mina Sauk Falls Trail loop leads hikers from the park's trailhead parking area to Missouri's High Point, Mina Sauk Falls and back to the start. The south segment of Mina Sauk Falls Trail is shared with the Eastern Loop of the Ozark Trail, Taum Sauk Section. It is a 33 mile point-to-point hiking-only trail that stretches from Bell Mountain Wilderness east through Johnson Shut-Ins State Park and Taum Sauk Mountain State Park to terminate at Mo. Hwy. 21, Claybaugh Creek trailhead parking in Ketcherside Mountain Conservation Area. In addition, the Boy Scouts of the St. Louis Council maintains the Historic Taum Sauk Trail that leads from Taum Sauk Mountain State Park to Russell Mountain, on to Shepherd Mountain to end or begin at Ft. Davidson State Historic Site in Pilot Knob, a distance of 8 miles. (See also Ft. Davidson State Historic Site.) Offers great spring or autumn hikes!

*T*railhead parking for Mina Sauk Falls Trail and the Ozark Trail at Taum Sauk Mountain State Park begins and ends at the far end of the park road, west of the campgrounds and picnic areas, adjacent to the restroom, brochure and trailhead registration box. The spur trail to the loop and Missouri's High Point is paved. At High Point, a sign-in book reveals the names and home towns of many visitors who have or plan to visit the high points of the 50 states and the world.

*T*he red-blazed, counterclockwise, Mina Sauk Trail Loop is as rocky as walking in a dry (and sometimes wet) streambed. Arriving at the waterfalls, the forest breaks into open vistas to the west of Wildcat, Church, and Proffit mountains. Historic Sauk and Piankashaw Indian legends say the Great Spirit created the cascading volcanic ledges and the waterfall with lightning. The place name, Mina, may possibly mean "waterfalls" and Sauk is a French corruption of Osakiwuk or Asakiwaki, "people of the yellow earth," an Indian tribe driven south by war. Various legends say Mina Sauk, the daughter of Chief Taum Sauk, committed suicide at the waterfall when her people killed her lover from an enemy tribe. The word Taum, may be derived from the Sauk word, Tongo, meaning "big."

*F*rom the waterfall, the Mina Sauk Trail curves back to the trailhead along the seasonal cascades. The westbound Ozark Trail passes through the

NATURE WALK
16

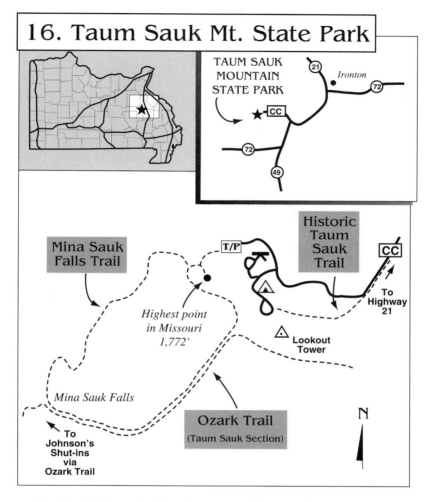

16. Taum Sauk Mt. State Park

TAUM SAUK
MOUNTAIN
STATE PARK

Ironton

Mina Sauk
Falls Trail

T/P

Historic
Taum
Sauk
Trail

CC

To
Highway
21

*Highest point
in Missouri
1,772'*

Lookout
Tower

Mina Sauk Falls

To
Johnson's
Shut-ins
via
Ozark Trail

Ozark Trail
(Taum Sauk Section)

N

Devil's Toll Gate, Proffit Mountain and Johnson Shut-Ins State Park, a 12 mile hike. Consider walking a mile one way to the Devil's Toll Gate, a keyhole through two giant boulders. The eastbound Ozark trail heads down and up to Russell Mountain and the Claybaugh Creek trailhead at Mo. 21/49, north of Royal Gorge Natural Area in Ketcherside Mountain Conservation Area. There is also Ozark Trail access on Hwy. CC at the Russell Mountain pullout enroute to Taum Sauk Mountain State Park (see also Ozark Trail: Taum Sauk Section).

*T*he 8 mile, point-to-point, historic Taum Sauk Trail that is maintained by the Boy Scouts begins and ends at the Taum Sauk Mountain State Park (go left at the state park entrance on Hwy. CC). The historic trail heads east down Hwy. CC from the lookout tower to connect with the trail that leads through the woods and recrosses Hwy. CC just west of

NATURE WALK
16

Russell Mountain Ozark Trailhead. The Taum Sauk continues northwest to Stouts Creek, Hwy. M, Shepherd Lake and Shepherd Mountain, crossing Mo. 21 to conclude at the Ft. Davidson State Historic Site. The trail is heavily eroded in places, especially on Shepherd Mountain.

*T*o reach Taum Sauk Mountain State Park from Ironton, drive south on Mo. 21/49 to Hwy. CC, just past Tip Top Hill picnic area, and turn right (west). Travel about 3 miles on Hwy. CC to the park entrance and another mile to the trailhead parking. Look for Russell Mountain trailhead (signed) and white blazes of the Historic Taum Sauk Trail enroute along Hwy. CC.

Area/Location/County:
Fredericktown/Ironton/Iron County

U.S.G.S. Map(s):
1:24,000 Ironton

Trail(s) Distance:
3 mile Mina Sauk Falls trail loop trailhead to Ozark Trail
Taum Sauk Section (33 miles)
trailhead to BSA Historic Taum Sauk Trail (8 miles)

Acreage:
6,508 acres

Activities:
hiking, backpacking, nature study, picnicking, basic camping

Fee(s):
camping

TRAIL 17: *Mingo National Wildlife Refuge*

*E*stablished in 1944, the vast Mingo National Wildlife Refuge marks the eastern edge of the Missouri Ozarks, where rugged, rocky hills meet swampy flat bottomlands; floristically, where shortleaf pine meets bald cypress. The national wildlife refuge is 20 miles long and 3 to 5 miles wide. Mingo Wilderness is one of eight wilderness areas in the Missouri Ozarks and the only one outside the boundaries of the Mark Twain National Forest.

*D*espite a century of economic reaping before preservation during the New Deal, Mingo remains the largest hardwoods swamp in Missouri, an important link in the Mississippi River bird flyway. Peak waterfowl populations of 125,000 mallards and 75,000 Canada geese have been recorded. The refuge contains about 15,000 acres of hardwood bottomlands, 1,275 acres of cropland, 700 acres of grasslands and 5,000 acres of marsh and water. The 3,000 acre Monopoly Lake, one of Missouri's largest natural lakes, is a remnant of an ancient Mississippi River channel that remained after the river shifted east 18,000 years ago.

*T*he canoeist is more at home at Mingo than the hiker, however there are three short foot trail loops, one a boardwalk, that begins and ends by the visitor and nature center near the entrance. Overlooking Rockhouse Marsh, the visitor center is also an outstanding nature center that features displays about the natural and cultural history of Mingo Swamp, now administered by the U.S. Department of Interior's Fish and Wildlife Service. The visitors center is open from 8 a.m. to 4 p.m. Monday through Friday year around and 9 a.m. to 4 p.m. Saturday and Sunday, March 15 through June 15 and September 15 through November 15. The refuge is open for day use from March 15 through September 30. The remainder of the year visitors should contact the visitors center for specific hours.

*T*here are also self-conducted auto tours (25 miles, two hour drive) during Sunday afternoons in April and Sunday afternoons in October and November. Available brochures and signs point out 16 points of interest along the auto route, some requiring getting out the car (short walk stretches). Along the route visitors will experience swamp, marsh, bottomland and upland forests, river bluffs, rocky wooded hills, pasture, croplands and old, abandoned fields. The croplands are wildlife food plots. A checklist is available listing the 246 birds sighted on the refuge, which is also home to 10 state and national champion trees.

Trail Summary:

*T*he 1 mile Boardwalk Nature Trail allows visitors to experience the bottomland hardwood swamp up close. The trailhead begins and ends

NATURE WALK
17

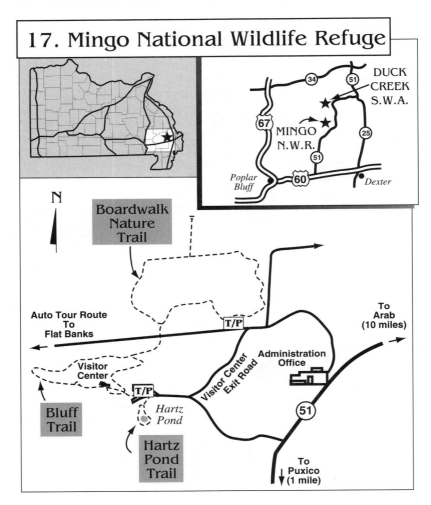

17. Mingo National Wildlife Refuge

DUCK
CREEK
S.W.A.

MINGO
N.W.R.

Poplar
Bluff

Dexter

N

Boardwalk
Nature
Trail

Auto Tour Route
To
Flat Banks

To
Arab
(10 miles)

T/P

Visitor Center Exit Road

Administration
Office

Visitor
Center

T/P

Bluff
Trail

*Hartz
Pond*

Hartz
Pond
Trail

To
Puxico
(1 mile)

at a small, signed parking area at the base road below the visitors center. Hikers may also access via the Bluff Trail connector spur near the visitors center. There are 15 numbered stations enroute that include bald cypress and tupelo. A two-tenths mile-long boardwalk spur leads out to an observation deck tower from the main boardwalk loop, providing views of Rockhouse Marsh. A spotting scope on the deck tower enhances wildlife viewing.

*T*he four-tenths of a mile Bluff Trail loop begins and ends at the visitors center, interconnecting with the Boardwalk Nature Trail. Forested, spring wildflowers and vistas of Rockhouse Marsh are trail highlights.

*H*artz Pond Trail, two-tenths of a mile long, circles a small wildlife pond directly south of the visitors center. Descend steps and walk the rim of

NATURE WALK
17

the pond. The short path is popular with students of aquatic biology students.

*T*he vehicle entrance fee station is located 1.75 miles north of Puxico on the west side of Mo. 51, about 30 miles northeast of Poplar Bluff.

*I*mmediately north of the boundary of Mingo National Wildlife Refuge is the 6,234 acre Duck Creek Conservation Area which has a fine auto tour of 5 miles but no maintained walking trails. The auto tour circles the 1,800 acre Pool One where bald eagles and waterfowl may be viewed. The property hours are from 4 a.m. to 10 p.m. daily. Primitive camping is offered at Duck Creek along with fishing, boating and hunting.

*T*he conservation area is 5.25 miles north of Mingo National Wildlife Refuge on Mo. 51, 7 miles north of Puxico on the west side of the road. Property map, bird checklist and auto tour guide is available at the property headquarters adjacent to the Mo. 51 entrance.

Area/Location/County:
Poplar Bluff/Puxico/Stoddard, Wayne and Bollinger counties

U.S.G.S. Map(s):
1:24,000 Puxico, McGee, Wappapello, Acorn Ridge, Sturdivant

Trail(s) Distance:
1 mile boardwalk trail loop
two short loops total six-tenths of a mile
25 mile seasonal auto tour

Acreage:
21,676 acres

Activities:
nature walks, nature study, visitor nature center, picnicking, shelter, observation towers, canoeing, bicycling, fishing

Fee(s):
entrance

NATURE WALK
17

TRAIL 18: *Wappapello Lake*

*T*he 8,400 water acres of Wappapello Lake are derived from the dammed waters of the St. Francis River and its tributaries. Constructed by the U.S. Army Corps of Engineers and completed in 1941, the dam's primary roles are flood control and recreation. Despite the focus on water based outdoor recreation, there are three hiking trails that border the lake reservoir, an old historic walking trail to former Greenville, plus the Ozark Trail's Wappapello Lake Section. The 20 mile Ozark Trail section follows the west bank of the St. Francis River from Sam A. Baker State Park south to near Hendrickson and Hwy. O. The lake's place name is derived from the nearby village that was named after an early nineteenth century Shawnee Chief, Wapepilse, who was friendly to the pioneers and hunted the local area.

*T*rail brochures are available for the three hiking trail loops which are considered easy to mildly difficult. All three trails are also classified as national recreation trails by the National Park Service.

Trail Summary:

*T*he well marked trailhead of Pine Ridge is located below the dam at the Spillway Recreation Area (picnicking, shelter, play courts playgrounds, amphitheater). The trail forms a double, short and long, loop of about half a mile and one mile. There are plenty of shortleaf pine (*Pinus echinata*) and other scientifically identified Ozark trees (described in a brochure listing 18 stops to view trees) growing on this hillside, sandwiched between the tailwater and a ridgetop picnic area.

*T*he 1 mile woodchipped Lost Creek Trail loops counterclockwise on a forested ridgetop that overlooks Wappapello Lake's waterfowl refuge on the northeast shore. A brochure interprets the 10 numbered stations. The hike includes lake vistas and good birding. The signed trailhead is located 5 miles north of the dam off Hwy. D, 3 rough road miles on Piso Point Road to the dead end of Wayne CR 523.

*J*ohnson Tract Natural Area Trail is a hiking and backpacking path that circles the 1,136 acre natural area clockwise along forest road trails (elev. 400-710 ft.). Highlights include the St. Francis River, cedar bluff top glades and open abandoned fields. There are two primitive backpacking camps. Be advised that seasonal walk-in hunting is permitted. The trailhead is located 8 miles north of the dam.

*N*ear U.S. Hwy. 67, 1.5 miles south of present-day Greenville lies Old Historic Greenville. Surrounded by the Greenville Recreation Area, Old Historic Greenville awaits visitors along the mile-long Memory Lane Historic Walk. Established in the early 1800s along the banks of

NATURE WALK
18

18. Wappapello Lake

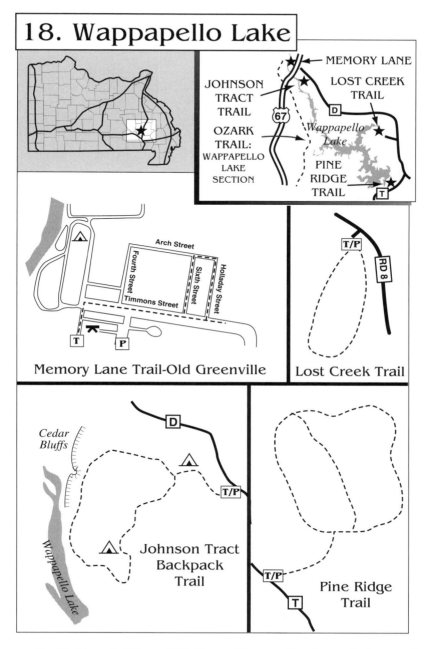

MEMORY LANE

JOHNSON TRACT TRAIL

LOST CREEK TRAIL

67

OZARK TRAIL: WAPPAPELLO LAKE SECTION

Wappapello Lake

PINE RIDGE TRAIL

Arch Street

Fourth Street

Sixth Street

Holliday Street

Timmons Street

Memory Lane Trail-Old Greenville

Lost Creek Trail

RD 8

Cedar Bluffs

D

Johnson Tract Backpack Trail

Wappapello Lake

Pine Ridge Trail

the St. Francis River, Old Greenville saw its share of glory and flooding. Finally the county seat was moved to its present, high and dry site during the 1930s and early 1940s. Aging sidewalks, foundations and historical landmarks and markers all testify to a living past, and are

NATURE WALK
18

the "grave markers" of a ghost town. Listed in the National Register of Historic Places, the Greenville Recreation Site is located 21.2 miles from the dam and also offers picnicking, shelter, fishing, boat ramp and dock and campgrounds.

*N*ature walkers may also explore the secluded finger cove lakeshore during the winter when the pool level is lower from mid December to March. In addition, the beaches at Peoples Creek, Redman Creek and Rockwood Point Recreation Points are great year around. There are naturalist programs during warm weather.

*T*he Ozark Trail: Wappapello Lake Section is a 20 mile trek that begins and ends at the Mo. 143, south entrance of Sam A. Baker State Park and ends and begins near Hendrickson and Hwy. O. There are about 10 trailhead access parking sites. There are numerous road and stream crossings. The Ozark Trail covers mostly U.S. Army Corps land but also some U.S. Forest Service lands. The closest trailhead access from the lake dam is along the north side of Mo. 172, east of U.S. 67.

*W*appapello Dam's management office and visitor center is located 16 miles north and east of Poplar Bluff. From Poplar Bluff, at the intersection of U.S. 60 and U.S. 67, drive east on U.S. 60, 5.5 miles to Hwy. T and turn left (north). Drive 11.5 miles on Hwy. T to the area by the dam.

Area/Location/County:
Poplar Bluff/Wappapello/Wayne and Butler counties

U.S.G.S. Map(s):
1:24,000 Wappapello, Shook, Hendrickson

Trail(s) Distance:
three trails total 7 miles
1 mile historic walk loop
20 mile Ozark Trail:Wappapello Lake Section

Acreage:
8,400 Wappapello Lake

Activities:
hiking, backpacking, visitors center, naturalist programs, historic sites, amphitheater, picnicking, shelters, playground, beaches, swimming, fishing, pier, playcourts, playfields, boating, boat launches, marinas, lodging, restaurant, camping, group camping, walk-in-tent, special events

Fee(s):
camping, shelter rental, boat rentals

TRAIL 19: **Lake Wappapello State Park**

Lake View Trail, Lake Wappapello State Park

*A*mid all the Wappapello Lake acreage managed by the U.S. Army Corps of Engineers, there exists on the southwestern shore of the lake's Allison Peninsula, Lake Wappapello State Park. There are three short, lakeside loop trails that explore the Allison Peninsula and make fine half day hikes. The 15 mile Lake Wappapello Trail loop is rugged and is also shared with mountain bicyclists and horse riders.

Trail Summary:

*T*he Lake View Trail is a half mile long loop that gets close to the lake and is signed clockwise with blue arrows. The trail begins and ends in the day use area near the picnic shelter, descending the ridge to the east and switching back along the lakeshore slope to the starting point. It accesses Allison Cemetery Trail.

*A*llison Cemetery Trail is a 3.5 mile loop trail may also be accessed from the day use area parking near the picnic shelter and the Lake View Trail. A second trailhead is on the north side of the park road leading to the cabin area. Shorter hikes are possible (1 mile and 2.5 mile loops) by using the two white arrow-blazed connector trails. The trail moves clockwise and is signed by green arrows. The easy, wide path follows the ridge to the Allison Cemetery and along the lakeshore, connecting with Lake View Trail.

*A*sher Creek Trail is about 2 miles long and has two connector white-blazed trails that allow shorter optional walks: a two-tenths of a mile trail loops about the bluff and lakeshore and a half mile loop traverses the lakeshore, cove and an upland forest ridge. The 2 mile loop offers more of the same. The red-blazed trail begins and ends on the west side

NATURE WALK
19

of the campground and follows a clockwise direction along the cove bay, a designated waterfowl refuge, and back up along the ridges. Day users should park at the visitors parking lot near the campground gate.

*T*he Lake Wappapello Trail (elev. 360-550 ft.), the longest trail in the park, also crosses Corps land, MDC University Forest Conservation Area and some private property. The 15 mile hiking and backpacking trail loop is signed in a counterclockwise direction blazed with yellow arrows. The rugged single track is also utilized by bicyclists and equestrians.

*T*he segment of trail alongside Wappapello Lake is scenic but the trail surface is compacted, trashy and has lots of poison ivy, probably related to the high and low water pools of the lake. There are three road crossings and the most confusing is the Mo. 172 crossing in a residential area (MDC University Forest CA) west of the state park. There is also a point-to-point trail spur that leaves the loop and heads northeast to Chaonia Landing Point, U.S. Army Corps, accessible from Hwy. W via Mo. 172 (boat ramp, picnicking, camping). The trailhead and parking area is adjacent to Mo. 172 at the park's west boundary.

*L*ake Wappapello State Park is located about 25 miles north and east of Poplar Bluff. Drive north on U.S. 67 from Poplar Bluff and turn right (east) on Mo. 172. Continue east to the park entrance, 9 miles on Mo. 172.

Area/Location/County:
Poplar Bluff/Williamsville/Wayne County

U.S.G.S. Map(s):
1:24,000 Wappapello

Trail(s) Distance:
three short trails total 6 miles
15 mile trail loop

Acreage:
1,854 land acres
8,600 Lake Wappapello

Activities:
hiking, backpacking, picnicking, shelters, bicycling, beach, swimming, fishing, boating, launch ramps, water skiing, cabins, camping

Fee(s):
camping, lodging, shelter rental

NATURE WALK
19

19. Lake Wappapello State Park

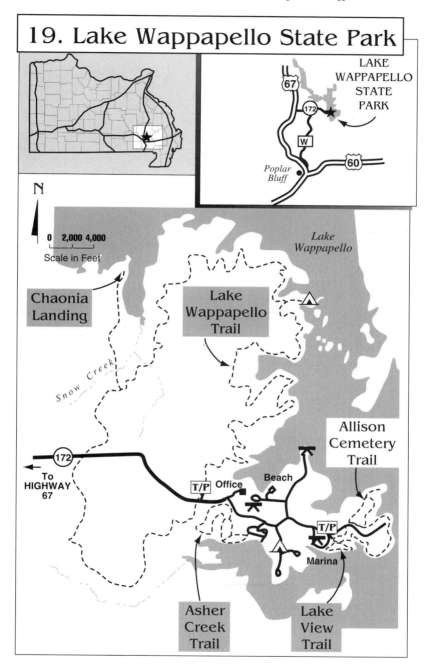

N

0 2,000 4,000
Scale in Feet

Chaonia Landing

Lake Wappapello Trail

Lake Wappapello

Snow Creek

Allison Cemetery Trail

172

To HIGHWAY 67

T/P Office

Beach

T/P

Marina

Asher Creek Trail

Lake View Trail

NATURE WALK 19

TRAIL 20: *Sam A. Baker State Park*

Speckled King Snake

*S*am A. Baker State Park is situated along the southeastern edge of the scenic St. Francois Mountains. Administered by the Missouri Department of Natural Resources, Division of State Parks, the public land was first acquired in 1926, thereby making it one of the earliest state parks in the "Show Me" State. The state park is named in honor of former Missouri governor and educator, Samuel Aaron Baker.

*H*ikers and backpackers will appreciate the unspoiled wilderness area of the 4,180 acre Mudlick Mountain Wild Area and the 1,370 acre Mudlick Mountain Natural Area that comprise most of the park's acreage. Trails are moderately rugged to extremely rugged. Rocks and uphill climbs should be expected. Natural features of these wild landscapes include old growth oak and hickory forest, canyon-like Big Creek Shut-Ins, deep hollows, desert-like glades, rocky talus slopes and bluffs where the rare yellowood tree thrives. At 1,313 feet high, Mudlick Mountain is the highest point in the park and one of the highest dome-shaped Precambrian knobs in the Missouri Ozarks. Green Mountain, which is also over 1,000 feet elevation, forms the park's western boundary. The St. Francis River and Big Creek shape the eastern boundary of the park.

NATURE WALK
20

*T*wo connecting trails provide access to the wild natural areas of the park. The 1.5 mile Shut-Ins Trail begins and ends at the north end of the park adjacent to the dining lodge along Mo. Hwy. 143. A parking lot across the highway will accommodate several vehicles. The Shut-Ins Trail is marked in blue and follows the base of Mudlick Mountain approximately 1.3 miles along Big Creek to a scenic shut-in. The last two-tenths of a mile scales the bluff to an Appalachian-style hiking shelter. Hikers can retrace their steps back to the dining lodge trailhead or make a loop by utilizing a segment of the Mudlick Trail. The 300 foot climb overlooking Big Creek valley is worth the effort.

*T*he 12 mile Mudlick Trail loop, a designated National Recreation Trail, circles the perimeter of Mudlick Mountain and the park's boundaries. A shorter loop may be formed by following connecting trails directly to Mudlick Mountain. The rugged trail is marked by yellow blazes and moves in a counterclockwise direction but may be hiked both ways. The main hiking trailhead begins at the same location as the Shut-Ins Trail, across from the dining lodge near the north park entrance. Two additional trailheads are available in other developed sections of the park along the park road, Mo. 143. Two backpacking camps are located along Big Creek and Logan Creek and the three Appalachian-style stone hiking shelters along the bluffs overlooking Big Creek are open for overnight use from October 1 to May 15.

*M*udlick Trail gradually climbs out of the Big Creek valley and follows the bluffs northwest to descend into Mudlick Hollow. Enroute a spur trail connects with the loop and leads to the top of Mudlick Mountain. The three-quarters of a mile segment along Mudlick Hollow Creek is considered to be the most scenic portion of the trail with its waterfalls and shut-ins. From Mudlick Hollow the trail begins a gradual climb up Green Mountain.

*W*hen leaves are down, the Green Mountain segment provides fine vistas of Mudlick Mountain and other high points to the west. At the south end of Green Mountain the trail descends along switchbacks into the Logan Creek valley. Hikers may find the final segment of the trail the most difficult as it crosses a talus slope of Mudlick Mountain's east face back to the trailhead. Hikers may choose to follow the connecting equestrian trail spur on Miller's Ridge to the fire tower atop Mudlick Mountain. The 2 mile-long service road that connects Mudlick Mountain fire tower with the camping area along Big Creek may also serve hikers as an alternative route. Take plenty of water. Stream water from Mudlick, Big and Logan creeks may be treated in your preferred manner for drinking.

*B*e sure to stop by the nature visitors center to enjoy the exhibits that interpret the natural features of the park. Park naturalists provide educational nature walks, programs and other activities.

NATURE WALK
20

*S*am A. Baker State Park, south entrance, is located 4 miles north of Patterson on Mo. 143 in Wayne County. From Des Arc at the junction of Mo. 143 and Mo. 49, follow Mo. 143 11 miles to the park's north entrance.

*T*he north terminus of the 20 mile Wappapello Lake Section of the Ozark Trail begins and ends at the roadside trailhead parking area near the south entrance to the state park along Mo. 143. The riparian corridor trail heads south to Hendrickson near Hwy. 0, the south terminus. The U.S. Army Corps of Engineers maintains most of this section along with the U.S. Forest Service and the Missouri Department of Conservation. Sample the trail from the state park south to Mo. 32 and back, about 6 miles round trip. (See also Ozark Trail: Wappapello Lake Section.)

Area/Location/County:
Poplar Bluff/Patterson/Wayne County

U.S.G.S. Map(s):
1:24,000 Brunot, Patterson

Trail(s) Distance:
nearly 20 miles of trails
north terminus of Ozark Trail: Wappapello Lake Section

Acreage:
5,168 acres

Activities:
hiking, backpacking, bridle trail, picnicking, shelters, nature center, naturalist, canoeing, launch ramp, river fishing, swimming, volleyball, playground, seasonal camp store, laundry, dining lodge, seasonal cabins, campground (electric), campground (water), trailer dump station, equestrian campground, July Mountain Bluegrass Festival

Fee(s):
camping, canoe rental, seasonal cabin rental from March 25 through October 31

NATURE WALK
20

20. Sam A. Baker State Park

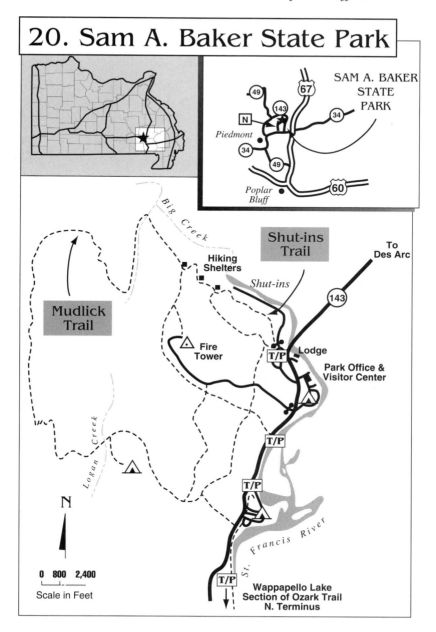

NATURE WALK
20

TRAIL 21: *Lon Sanders Canyon Conservation Area*

As local legend has it, Lon Sanders Canyon was the hideout for the James and Younger brothers after they robbed the nearby Gads Hill train on January 31, 1874. Today's visitor can see how the wild area served to hide train robbers, especially along the recesses of the McKenzie Creek

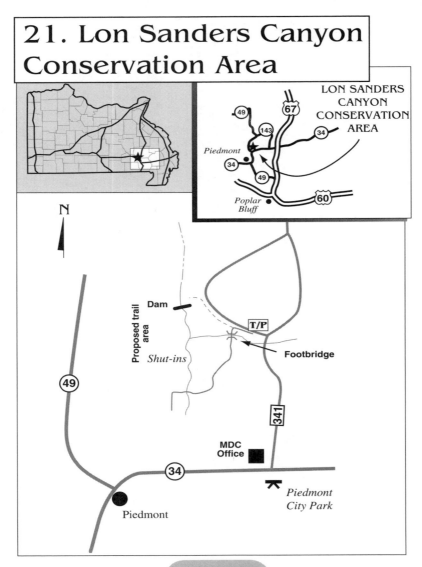

21. Lon Sanders Canyon Conservation Area

LON SANDERS
CANYON
CONSERVATION
AREA

Piedmont

Poplar
Bluff

N

Dam

Proposed trail area

Shut-ins

T/P

Footbridge

49

341

MDC
Office

34

Piedmont
City Park

Piedmont

NATURE WALK
21

Shut-Ins. The place is named after an engraver who was in love with the canyon. Part of the land was donated as a wildlife study, hiking and nature area by Nan Gardner Weber, who devoted most of her life to Missouri conservation.

*T*he trailhead begins and ends at the stone pillar gates and mini parking lot adjacent to Wayne CR 341, 1 mile north of Mo. 32 and the MDC Clearwater Forest District Office. The 1 mile trail follows an old service lane and single track, forking at the wooden footbridge over a tributary to McKenzie Creek. Across the bridge, the stone-worked trail goes bluffside along the shut-ins. The purple granite rock was quarried in the late 1800s for cobblestones in the streets of St. Louis. The trail crosses the creek and dead ends downstream about 100 yards, so retrace your steps. (A loop trail has been marked out with red ribbon but has not been cleared). There are two small dams on the stream located on the old forest lane west from the footbridge fork. The old lane becomes a thicket on the other side of the stream. Retrace your steps.

*T*his 130 acre historic and attractive conservation area is located 1.5 miles north and east of Piedmont. From the junction of Mo. 34 and Mo. 49, go east on Mo. 34, four-tenths of a mile to Canyon Road/Wayne CR 341 and turn left (north). The MDC District office is on the corner across from the park. Proceed north on Canyon Road/Wayne CR 341 one mile to the parking area on the left (west) side of the road. The seemingly remote area is a gem of a nature spot.

Area/Location/County:
Poplar Bluff/Piedmont/Wayne County

U.S.G.S. Map(s):
1:24,000 Piedmont

Trail(s) Distance:
1 mile hiking trail

Acreage:
130 acres

Activities:
nature walk, nature study

Fee(s):
none

NATURE WALK
21

TRAIL 22: *Clearwater Lake*

Canada Geese

*T*he south flowing Black River and its numerous tributaries fill Clearwater
Lake, a flood control and recreation project constructed between 1940
and 1948, the first Missouri lake to be constructed by the U.S. Army
Corps of Engineers. Hiking trails are few along the 27 miles of steep
shoreline bluffs and bays, but there are two easy, short loops of about
1 mile total at River Road and Bluff View Recreation Areas.
Clearwater Lake is often billed as a "wilderness lake" and in some
ways it is with its backcountry camping (permit required). Consider
visiting the recreation areas at Webb Creek and Old Highway K and
walking the lakeside and riverside.

*T*he Black River Nature Trail is a four-tenths of a mile loop that begins
and ends on the southwest side of the dam, east of the visitor

NATURE WALK
22

information center off Hwy. HH at the River Road Recreation Area on the south or right bank. The easily accessed trail walks counterclockwise from the trailhead, a pine studded blufftop overlooking Black River tailwater. It leads to a wooden staircase leading down to the Black River, looping back along the developed streamside where there are fishing platforms, picnicking tables and parking. The trail goes back uphill to the blufftop trailhead via a second "1,000" step wooden staircase. Clearwater dam is located 7 miles east of Piedmont and Mo. 34/49 on Hwy. HH.

*B*luff View Trail, a six-tenths mile loop, is located in the Bluff View Recreation Area campground, section C. The trailhead situation is more conducive for campers than day visitors who will need to park at the campground gate or the trailhead parking area. A Trees of the Trail brochure corresponds to numbered stops along the old forest blufftop. Identified are black walnut, black oak, white oak, northern red oak, mockernut hickory, sugar maple, hackberry, black cherry, winged elm, black gum, flowering dogwood, paw paw, sassafras and shortleaf pine.

*B*luff View Recreation Area is located northwest of Piedmont in Reynolds County. From the junction of Mo. 49 and Mo. 34, go north on Mo. 49 six-tenths of a mile and turn left (west) on Hwy. AA. Continue on Hwy. AA about 6 miles to the recreation point.

*B*oth short trails are equipped with overlook platforms which provide a relaxing place with beautiful views of Clearwater Lake.

Area/Location/County:
Piedmont/Wayne and Reynolds counties

U.S.G.S. Map(s):
1:24,000 Clearwater Dam, Piedmont, Lesterville SE, Ellington SE

Trail(s) Distance:
two short trails total 1 mile

Acreage:
18,604 land and water acres

Activities:
nature walks, nature study, amphitheater, picnicking, shelters, beach, swimming, playground, fishing, canoeing, boating, launch ramps, marinas, water skiing, camping, group camping, backcountry camping, seasonal hunting

Fee(s):
camping, shelter rental, day use fees, boat launch, swimming

NATURE WALK
22

22. Clearwater Lake

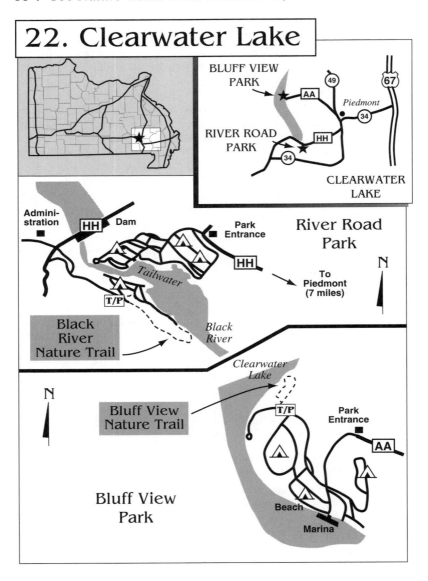

TRAIL 23: **Markham Spring Recreation Area**

*T*his beautiful spot has long been a popular gathering place. Markham Spring, one of the best flowing springs in the Black River basin, is the main attraction. The place name originates from a former owner, M. Jefferson Markham, who acquired the property in 1901 and continued operation of a gristmill there until 1907. Actually six springs flow into the three acre turquoise pond at a daily rate of 5 million gallons. The pond was built to create power to operate a gristmill as early as 1845.

*T*he present-day wheelhouse that sits at the pond's edge was built in the 1930s by Rudolph Fuchs to produce electricity for the native stone and timber home he built during the Depression. The beautiful home still stands on the opposite side of the pond from the wheelhouse. It is hoped that the U.S. Forest Service, which purchased the property in 1966, will continue to preserve the operable wheelhouse and Fuchs House for public access. (Imagine a restored electric-producing wheelhouse and a concessionaire-operated bed and breakfast at the Fuchs House.)

*T*here are three short trails, all interconnecting along the south and west bank of the Black River, about 20 miles downstream from Clearwater Lake Dam. There are rest benches and footbridges along the paths. User paths stray from the maintained trails and can make certain points confusing, but it would be difficult to become lost. The trail system begins at the parking area at the boat access near the entrance.

Trail Summary:

*F*isherman's Path or River Trail follows three-quarters of a mile along the Black River. The point-to-point path has numerous accesses leading from the day use area and campgrounds. The trail follows the top of a levee in the bottomland forest portion. The River Trail joins with the Eagle Bluff Trail at the north portion of the property near Eagle Bluff. Hikers can make a loop trail by combining the River Trail with the Eagle Bluff Trail, walking either direction starting from the boat ramp lot near the entrance.

*E*agle Bluff Trail begins across the park road from the boat ramp parking area near the Markham Spring Branch. Aging steps lead to the ridgetop where the trail curves north and follows the ridge north to Eagle Bluff overlook of Black River. A connector spur switchbacks downhill to Markham Spring and Canebrake Trail, thus making the trail a double loop. From Eagle Bluff the forest trail curves downhill to connect with the River Trail near the Sycamore and Birch loops of the campground.

*T*he Canebrake Trail circles the spring pond where the historic house and wheelhouse are located. Canebrake or hardy bamboo grows around the

NATURE WALK
23

waterfall spring outlet at the east edge of the 20-foot-deep spring pond. The tall reedgrass was utilized by Indians and pioneers alike for baskets, mats, housing material, pipestems, fishing rods, and even the young tender plant for a pot herb. Parking is nearby. The picnic area around the spring is a favorite. North and west of the spring is a planted bald cypress slough that is active with beaver.

*M*arkham Spring Recreation Area is located 26 miles northwest of Poplar Bluff, 3 miles east of Williamsville, and 9 miles west and north of Ellsinore on Mo. 49. From Poplar Bluff go north on U.S. Highway 67, 14 miles and turn left (west) on Mo. 49. Drive 9 miles on Mo. 49 to the Markham Spring entrance on the north side of the highway.

*W*hile in this part of the Lower Ozark Division, visit The Gulf, a geological sinkhole located 11 miles northwest of Markham Spring RA. An interpretive observation deck at the rim allows visitors to overlook this vertical blue hole abyss that harbors a cave and a hidden lake.

*T*o reach The Gulf from Markham Spring RA go west on Mo. 49, 3 miles to the junction of Mo. 49 and Hwy. A and turn north on Mo. 49. Continue 5.8 miles north on Mo. 49 to Wayne CR 442 (3 miles south of Mill Spring), and turn left (southwest). Drive 2.2 gravel miles on Wayne CR 442 past the Carson Hill Church and cemetery to The Gulf, parking at the second gravel road right. This is also U.S. Forest Service land.

Area/Location/County:
Poplar Bluff/Williamsville/Wayne County

U.S.G.S. Map(s):
1:24,000 Williamsville

Trail(s) Distance:
three short trails total 2.5 miles

Activities:
nature walks, nature study, historic sites, picnicking, shelters, swimming, tubing, canoeing, fishing, camping

Fee(s):
shelter rental, camping

NATURE WALK
23

23. Markham Spring Recreation Area

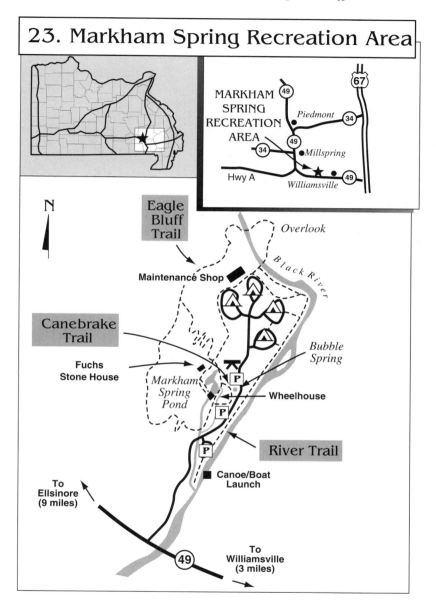

MARKHAM
SPRING
RECREATION
AREA

49

67

Piedmont

34

49

34

●Millspring

Hwy A

49

Williamsville

N

Eagle
Bluff
Trail

Overlook

Black River

Maintenance Shop

Canebrake
Trail

Bubble
Spring

Fuchs
Stone House

Markham
Spring
Pond

P

Wheelhouse

P

P

River Trail

Canoe/Boat
Launch

To
Ellsinore
(9 miles)

49

To
Williamsville
(3 miles)

NATURE WALK
23

TRAIL 24: *Pinewoods Lake Recreation Area*

Beaver Lodge at Pinewoods Lake

*D*ay tripers and overnight travellers will discover this recreation area is easily accessed by road and by foot. Not at all remote, Pinewoods Lake is about a paved half mile south of U.S. Hwy. 60, a major Ozark highway, 2 miles west of Ellsinore. There is a feeling of remoteness despite its proximity to a somewhat busy highway.

A 1.5 mile level loop circles the 31 acre lake that was created by building a dam in 1980. As the place name suggests, solid shortleaf pine stands are found along the lake pathside. Nearly half of the trail is paved and other dirt or pine needled. Beaver are active and many lakeside tree trunks are wired for protection from their sharp, gnawing teeth. There are potential wet segments at the inlet stream on the west end. The trail begins and ends in the picnic and parking area. People of all ages and condition can enjoy easily accessible Pinewoods Lake. A breezy, sunny spring afternoon with the pines "singing" and the lake "sparkling" makes for a great walk.

*T*he recreation area is located 23 miles west of Poplar Bluff. From Poplar Bluff drive north on U.S. Hwy. 67 about 7 miles and turn left (west) on U.S. Hwy 60. Proceed west on U.S. 60 16 miles to FS 3766 on the left (south) side of the highway, 2 miles west of Ellsinore. Watch for directional signs.

NATURE WALK
24

Area/Location/County:
Poplar Bluff/Ellsinore/Carter County

U.S.G.S. Map(s):
1:24,000 Hunter

Trail(s) Distance:
1.5 mile loop

Acreage:
31 acre lake

Activities:
nature walk, nature study, picnicking, shelter, fishing, canoeing, launch ramp, floating pier, seasonal camping

Fee(s):
seasonal camping, shelter rental

NATURE WALK
24

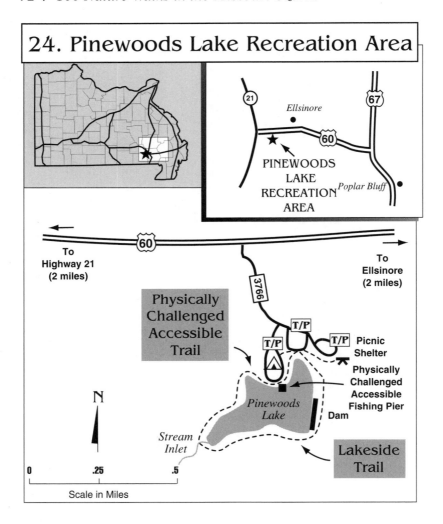

24. Pinewoods Lake Recreation Area

Ellsinore

PINEWOODS
LAKE
RECREATION *Poplar Bluff*
AREA

To
Highway 21
(2 miles)

To
Ellsinore
(2 miles)

3766

Physically
Challenged
Accessible
Trail

T/P

T/P

T/P Picnic
Shelter

Physically
Challenged
Accessible
Fishing Pier

N

*Pinewoods
Lake*

Dam

*Stream
Inlet*

Lakeside
Trail

0   .25   .5

Scale in Miles

TRAIL 25: **Washington State Park**

Rock Carving

*B*ordering Big River in the foothills that border the Ozarks, Washington State Park is a rich mix of hardwood hills, open glades, limestone bluffs and clear streams. The land was once the ceremonial grounds for prehistoric (1,000-1,600 A.D.) woodland mound builders and Middle Mississippian cultures. Petroglyphs, rock carvings of religious animal totems, are the park's main highlight. The rock carvings are easily accessed from an adjacent parking area and foot trail.

*T*rail accessible natural features of the park include overlooks of Big River from high cliffs, open valleys, prairie glades and forest cover. Big River is popular with canoeists who start from St. Francois State Park floating downstream to Washington State Park and on to the Meramec River near Eureka. Three loops of varying lengths and difficulty are maintained and open to hikers only. All three trails begin and end at the Thunderbird Lodge parking lot (the 1930 CCC-constructed lodge is reservation available for social gatherings during the warm months).

NATURE WALK
25

Trail Summary:

*T*he 1,000 Steps Trail follows the Big River floodplain to bluff top and
down again, making for a 1.5 mile loop walk that passes through the
Washington Upland Hardwoods Natural Area. The trail was built by
the Civilian Conservation Corps (CCC) during the 1930s. The "1,000"
stone steps and other structural works still survive time and vandalism,
although they are in need of repair.

*T*he trail begins and ends at the northeast edge of the Thunderbird Lodge
parking lot and moves counterclockwise, blazed by yellow arrows. The
bluff slope forest is rich in wildflowers and ferns in spring. The trail is
shared with the Rockywood Trail from the trailhead, switchbacking up
to the ridgetop restroom at the park road (elev. 550-800 ft.). The
interpretive center features displays about the natural and social history
of the park. The 1,000 Steps Trail moves down the ridge, going back to
the lodge along the floodplain. Great river vistas!

*O*possum Track Trail begins at the southwest corner of the Thunderbird
Lodge parking lot, and follows a clockwise direction, blazed with blue

25. Washington State Park

DeSoto

47

67

WASHINGTON
STATE
PARK
Potosi

47

21

0 550 1,650 2,750

N

Scale in Feet

1,000 Steps
Trail

Big River

T/P

Nature
Center

To
DeSoto

104

Rocky -
wood
Trail

21

Opossum
Track
Trail

*Petroglyph
Area*

NATURE WALK
25

arrows. The 3 mile loop crosses Mo. 104 and follows the ravine uphill, past the swimming pool, paralleling the park road, Mo. 104. The trail crosses Mo. 104, skirts the campground, and heads downhill to join with Rockywood Trail. The Opossum Track Trail turns right and follows the scenic bluffs all the way back to the Thunderbird Lodge trailhead, sharing the route with the Rockywood Loop.

*T*he Rockywood Trail Loop is a 10 mile backpacking and hiking trail that wanders about timbered hollows, high ridges, open glades and valleys. The easy to rugged trail begins at the northwest edge of the lodge parking area and is signed counterclockwise with orange arrows. In the vicinity of Thunderbird Lodge, segments of the trail are shared with the 1,000 Steps Trail and the Opossum Track Trail. The Rockywood Trail follows the perimeter of the narrow, east-to-west shaped park. Recent controlled burns have made the trail obscure in places.

*T*o reach Washington State Park from Potosi, travel 14 miles north and east on Mo. 21 to Mo. 104, the park's entry road.

Area/Location/County:
Potosi-Salem/DeSoto/Washington County

U.S.G.S. Map(s):
1:24,000 Tiff

Trail(s) Distance:
two loop trails total 4.5 miles
10 mile hiking and backpacking loop

Acreage:
1,811 acres

Activities:
hiking, backpacking, nature study, seasonal naturalist, nature programs, interpretive center, archaeological site, picnicking, shelters, river beach, swimming pool, fishing, canoeing, camp store, cabins, primitive camping, basic and electric camping, group camp

Fee(s):
swimming pool, camping, canoe rental

NATURE WALK
25

TRAIL 26: *Meramec State Park and Meramec Conservation Area*

River Trail along the Meramec River

*L*ocated across the Meramec River from each other, these two state-operated outdoor facilities have preserved an 8 mile stretch of the Meramec River valley. These publicly accessible areas will be an important link in the Ozark Trail's Meramec Section when completed. The Meramec River is one of Missouri's most scenic streams and is very popular with canoeists. Both state properties have maintained and blazed hiking trails that range in distance and difficulty. The state park's west bank is more developed and has more visitors, while the conservation area's east bank is less developed and has fewer visitors.

*M*eramec State Park, established in 1928 and CCC-developed in the 1930s, is one of the older treasures of the Missouri Department of Natural Resources. The park is biologically rich with a spring-fed river, majestic bluffs, caves, glades, forest and wet meadows, all representative of the northeastern Ozark border. The fully developed park retains a good deal of naturalness.

*T*here are six foot trails and seasonal tours of Fisher Cave. The Meramec River Section of the Ozark Trail, between Castlewood State Park and Onondaga Cave State Park, is nearly nonexistent, with the exception of the shared route with Wilderness Trail. A naturalist is on staff year around.

NATURE WALK
26

Trail Summary:

*T*he 1.3 mile Natural Wonders Trail loop begins and ends at the southeast corner of the visitor center's parking lot near the park entrance. Trail highlights include beaver ponds and meadows, old fields, glades, caves and mature upland forest. From the bottomlands to the uplands, wildlife is diverse. This is an excellent warm-up hike. Be sure to visit the outstanding visitor center to view the fine natural history exhibits and browse through the Missouri nature books available for sale.

*T*he next trail along the park road east of Mo. 185 is the 10 mile Wilderness Trail loop that travels clockwise and is marked with red arrows. The trailhead begins and ends at the north edge of the cabin, picnic and playground area. The double loop trail is comprised of a 6 mile southern loop and a 4 mile northern loop. A short cut connector trail is marked with white arrows. It is the only trail in the park designated for backpacking and eight backpack campsites are provided. Backpackers must register at the registration box 200 yards from the trailhead. The east segment is shared with the planned Ozark Trail. The single track trail covers old growth upland forest, ridge sides, wet and dry ravines, seeps and creeks, a sinkhole, and the edge of the Upland Forest Natural Area, the most remote area in the park. The trail crosses a paved park road twice. This is a great day hike!

*T*he 1.5 mile Bluff View Trail begins and ends at the dining lodge parking area. The well worn, moderately difficult path descends the ridge to overlooks and riverfront and then ascends back up the ridge to its starting point. There are two CCC trail shelter overlooks. Trail access is also found near picnic shelter No. 3 and at the trail shelter on the River Trail. The River Trail joins Bluff View Trail at the second trail shelter overlook.

*T*he dining lodge is also the trailhead of the Deer Hollow Trail, south terminus. The point-to-point 1.8 mile trail goes up and down ridges and creeks to end at Fisher Cave and amphitheater parking lot. It was one of the park's first trails constructed by the CCC's young men. Excellent forest walk with a good chance to view white-tailed deer!

*F*isher Cave is open to fee-charged seasonal tours. The 90 minute, naturalist-led tours follow a two-thirds mile-long pathway, using hand held lights. Tour size is limited. Dress for 57 degree temperatures. Cave tours are scheduled from April through October.

*W*alking Fern Trail begins and ends at the entrance of Fisher's Cave. The shortest trail in the park is a half mile loop. The trail's name is derived from a large boulder that is covered with walking ferns near the trail's midpoint. The lower segment of the trail follows the base of several bluffs, one of which contains the entrance to a prehistoric Indian rock shelter. The upper portion of the trail is dry, rock-strewn forest.

NATURE WALK
26

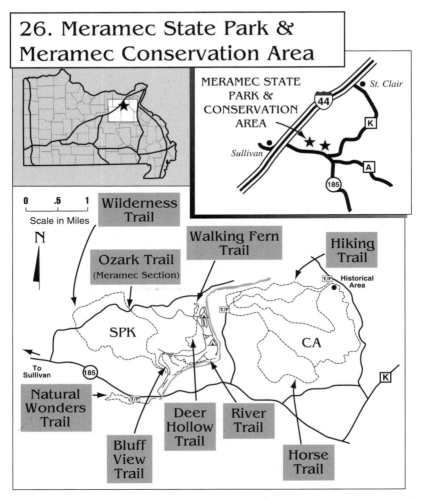

26. Meramec State Park & Meramec Conservation Area

MERAMEC STATE PARK & CONSERVATION AREA

St. Clair

Sullivan

0 .5 1
Scale in Miles

N

Wilderness Trail

Walking Fern Trail

Hiking Trail

Ozark Trail
(Meramec Section)

Historical Area

SPK

CA

To Sullivan

Natural Wonders Trail

Deer Hollow Trail

River Trail

Bluff View Trail

Horse Trail

There are several plant communities within a short distance. Good trail for children and to follow the naturalist on scheduled hikes.

*T*he River Trail is an eight-tenths of a mile loop that begins and ends at the south end of the campground near showerhouse No. 3 by the banks and bluffs of the Meramec River. A portion of the trail follows along a slough of the Meramec River where herons and kingfishers gather. At mid-point, the Bluff View Trail is accessed at the CCC trail overlook. River Trail is considered the easiest trail in the park.

*T*o reach Meramec State Park from I-44 exit 226 southeast on Mo. 185 at Sullivan. Drive 3 miles on Mo. 185 to the park entrance on the right (south) side of the road before the Meramec River bridge. The park is 25 miles northwest of Potosi on Mo. 185.

NATURE WALK
26

*A*cross the river from Meramec State Park is Meramec Conservation Area. The 8 mile hiking trail is separate from the 12 mile equestrian trail. There are two trailheads and the closest one to Meramec State Park is reached by going south on Mo. 185 from the park entrance 1.6 miles, then turning left on a gravel MDC access road. Travel 1.3 miles to a trailhead parking area at the locked gate. Horse riders share this access with hikers but soon go their own ways on separate trails, crossing each other's path twice.

*F*rom the trailhead, the trail soon enters the no-hunting wildlife refuge along the floodplain. This 2 mile segment to the historic site of Riedsville can be wet, muddy and flooded making it impassable at times. From the ghost town of Riedsville, the trail descends the forested ridge to Wet Hollow, following the hollow, then uphill to the former Lone Hill Lookout Tower. The trail finally descends Lone Hill to the river floodplain and back to the road. New trail construction has improved the trail near the trailhead's wet areas. To reach the second trailhead continue south on Mo. 185 from the first trailhead turnoff, 1 mile to the junction with Hwy. K and turn left (east). Go 1.4 mile on Hwy. K to Spanish Claim Road and turn left (north). Drive 2.3 miles to the trailhead parking on the left side of the gravel road. A trailhead spur leads south to the main hiking loop. The horse trail crossings can be confusing.

Area/Location/County:
Potosi-Salem/Sullivan/Franklin County

Map(s):
1:24,000 Meramec State Park

Trail(s) Distance:
MSPK six trails total approximately 16 miles
MCA 8 mile hiking loop

Acreage:
MSPK 6,896 acres
MCA 3,879 acres

Activities:
MSPK - hiking, cave tours, naturalist, natural area, visitor nature center, book store, picnicking, shelters, amphitheater, fishing, canoeing, launch ramp, cabins, motel, conference center, dining lodge, camp store, swimming, basic and electric camping
MCA - hiking, equestrian trail, wildlife refuge, historical sites, fishing, seasonal hunting

Fee(s):
MSPK cave tour, camping, cabin, motel, conference center rental, shelter and canoe rentals
MCA: none

NATURE WALK
26

TRAIL 27: *Onondaga Cave State Park and Huzzah Conservation Area*

Lily Pad Room, Onondaga Cave

*T*here are several miles of hiking trail between these two State of Missouri properties that are separated by the Meramec River. Within minutes visitors can change properties and activities. The Onondaga Cave tour and three hiking trails are the main attraction at the state park which is managed by the Department of Natural Resources (DNR). The primary hiking interest in Huzzah Conservation Area is the Courtois Creek Section of the Ozark Trail. Be advised that both state properties may be closed periodically due to flooding of the Meramec River, Courtois and Huzzah creeks.

*O*nondaga Cave State Park was purchased by The Nature Conservancy in 1981 and the land was transferred to the DNR. Onondaga Cave is rated by experts as one of the most spectacular caves in the United States, a National Natural Landmark. (The place name has no true connection with the Onondaga Indians of New York.) The premier cave has a nine-tenths of a mile, naturalist-guided walk through the cave, a 75 minute tour. Visitors can obtain cave tour tickets at the visitors nature center and gift shop near the park entrance. The cave is open for daily tours from March to October. On weekends only there is a separate Cathedral Cave tour that is considered rugged and which would appeal to spelunkers. For a cave tour schedule call the state park at (573) 245-6600. During the months of November, December, January and February the cave is closed to visitors except for groups that have made advance arrangements. However, those winter months are a fine time to hike the park's three trails.

NATURE WALK
27

Trail Summary:

*H*ikers often spy great blue herons along the half mile-long (one way) level Blue Heron Trail. Blue blazed arrows mark the point-to-point, wide, level earth path (some boardwalk) that begins and ends at the visitors nature center and ends and begins at the campground entrance road. Herons prefer the quiet and shallow oxbow lake that was formed when the Meramec River cut a new channel farther south a few hundred yards. The Onondaga Spring pool and waterfall are along the path. Wild flowers and ferns thrive among the rocky trailside bluffs. This is a short but sweet trail for those who want to sample a lot in a brief trek.

*O*ak Ridge Ridge Trail is a 3.25 mile loop that is a valley to ridge trail (elev. 600-9,251 feet). The red blazed trailhead begins and ends in the playground adjacent to the amphitheater and Deer Run trailhead. The trail progresses from creek, ravine, ridgeside, glades, ridgetop, ridgeslope and cove hollows. Where the trail skirts the campground there are several feeder spurs that confuse the loop's direction. This trail is a leisurely two hour hike.

*D*eer Run Trail is marked with green arrows over the 2.75 mile loop. The trailhead begins and ends at the amphitheater in the campground. The trail climbs uphill to the locked Cathedral Cave entrance. There are two road crossing, ridges, ravines and great views along the Meramec River bluffs.

*O*nondaga Cave State Park is easily accessed from I-44, 70 miles west of I-270 at St. Louis. Exit Hwy. H south at Leasburg in Crawford County. Drive 7 miles south on Hwy. H, going through Leasburg to the park and visitors parking at the entrance center.

*B*ordering Onondaga Cave State Park across the Meramec River to the south is Huzzah Conservation Area. The only maintained trail in the area is the Ozark Trail (4.5 miles completed, 8.5 miles planned). Huzzah Conservation Area is the north terminus of the Courtois Creek Section and the west terminus of the Meramec River Section (both sections are unfinished at this time).

*T*he trailhead for the Ozark Trail is at the campground turnaround on Courtois Creek, 3.5 miles south of the state park. Drive across the Meramec River from Onondaga Cave State Park and continue south on the main gravel road about 3 miles to the second crossroad and turn left on MDC 24. Proceed on MDC 24 about three-tenths of a mile to the creekside turnaround and park (room for 10 cars). The north segment of the Ozark Trail leads north along the narrow "bench" between the bluffs and creek. The first two-tenths mile of the trail is highly scenic and includes four caves, a "keyhole," pinnacle and box canyon.

*T*he trail switchbacks uphill and follows an old ridgetop road north for a mile and turns northwest passing through the Old Scotia iron furnace

NATURE WALK
27

area, and ending (at this time) on the gravel entry road. Retrace your hike back to Courtois Creek parking trailhead. An optional loop may be hiked by continuing on the gravel entry road left (south) 1 mile to the campground road MDC 24, and three-tenths of a mile back to Courtois Creek trailhead.

*T*he south segment of the Ozark Trail at Huzzah Conservation Area winds south to the Narrows and concludes. The U.S. Forest Service is working to complete a link from the southeast and the Berryman Trail and the Trace Creek Section. The southbound trailhead begins and ends at a campsite about 100 yards south of the parking turnaround at Courtois Creek campground. The trail leads through the floodplain forest and crosses Courtois Creek where hikers must wade (dangerous during high water). The path then follows downstream along the base of the bluff, curving back to hike upridge to ridgetop and on to the Narrows, concluding near the conservation property boundary. Retrace your steps.

*H*uzzah Conservation Area may also be reached from Steelville by driving east on Mo. 8 to Hwy. E and turning left (north). Drive north on Hwy. E and cross the low water bridge over Huzzah Creek. Proceed to MDC 24 and turn right and drive three-tenths of a mile to the campground turnaround trailhead parking at Courtois Creek.

Area/Location/County:
Potosi-Salem/Leasburg/Crawford County

U.S.G.S. Map(s):
1:24,000 Onondaga Cave, Huzzah

Trail(s) Distance:
OCSPK: three trails total 6.5 miles
cave walking tour
HCA: 8.5 mile Ozark Trail: Courtois Creek Section

Acreage:
OCSPK: 1,350 acres
HCA: 6,225 acres

Activities:
OCSPK: hiking, cave tours, nature study, naturalist, nature programs, picnicking, shelter, river beach, swimming, canoeing, launch ramp, gift shop, camp store, camping, Scout area
HCA: hiking, nature study, historic sites, fishing, canoeing, launch ramp, equestrian trails, primitive camping, shooting range, seasonal hunting

Fee(s):
OCSPK: camping, cave tour
HCA: none

NATURE WALK
27

27. Onondaga Cave State Park & Huzzah Conservation Area

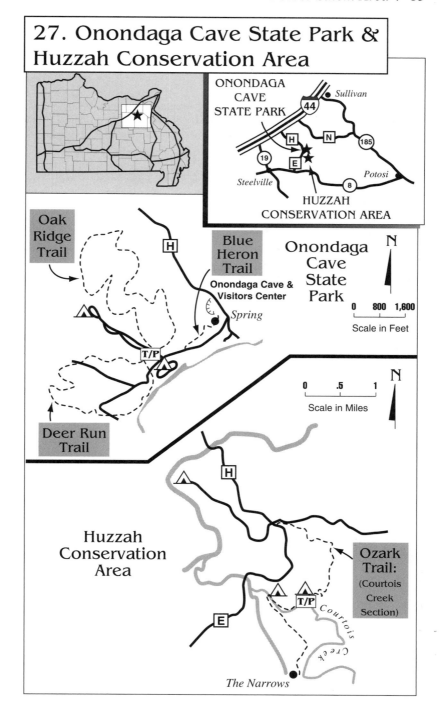

ONONDAGA CAVE STATE PARK

Sullivan

44

H

N

185

19

E

Steelville

Potosi

8

HUZZAH CONSERVATION AREA

Oak Ridge Trail

H

Blue Heron Trail

Onondaga Cave & Visitors Center

Spring

T/P

Deer Run Trail

Onondaga Cave State Park

N

0   800   1,600
Scale in Feet

0   .5   1
Scale in Miles

N

H

Huzzah Conservation Area

E

Ozark Trail: (Courtois Creek Section)

T/P

Courtois Creek

The Narrows

NATURE WALK
27

TRAIL 28: *Zahorsky Woods*

*T*his 56 acre floodplain and upland forest preserve borders the Meramec
River, 1 mile north of Steelville. In 1974, The Nature Conservancy
accepted the rich woodland as a gift in memory of a early 1900s pioneer
physician, Dr. John Zahorsky. Volunteers have constructed two
separate but adjoining self-guided loop paths that are connected by a

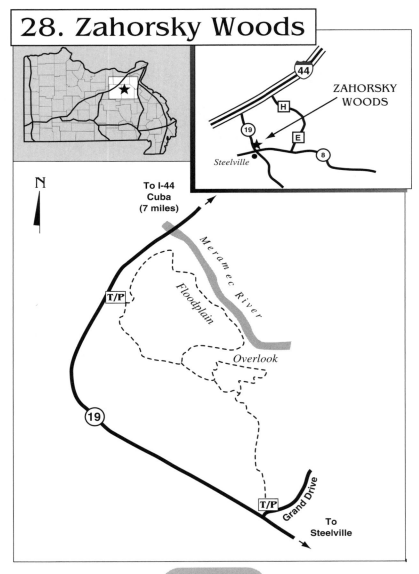

28. Zahorsky Woods

ZAHORSKY
WOODS

Steelville

N

To I-44
Cuba
(7 miles)

Meramec River

Floodplain

Overlook

19

T/P

T/P

Grand Drive

To
Steelville

linear path through the bottomlands, ravines, bluffs and ridges of the nature preserve.

*T*here are two trailheads, but the most spacious and the safest from traffic is on the southeast side of the Meramec River bridge on Mo. 19. From the north terminus, a half mile trail loops through bottomland forest which can be wet, muddy or overgrown. In addition, flooding and beaver work may obscure the trail. A steep and rugged mile-long loop climbs the bluff from the bottomland forest to a glade community and a bench that overlooks the Meramec River. There are 14 labeled trees enroute and 12 numbered trail markers that correspond to a trail map and brochure that guides visitors through the different natural communities.

*T*he main trail continues uphill into savanna woodland, crossing a powerline swath, continuing uphill along bordering private property to the south terminus at Grand Drive and Mo. 19 (half a mile north of junction of Mo. 19 and Mo. 8). There is roadside parking for two cars at the shoulder of Grand Drive. Allow two hours for a slow walk over the entire trail. Retrace your steps back 1 mile to the Meramec River Mo. 19 bridge. By the road it is seven-tenths of a mile between the two parking and trailhead entry points.

*F*rom I-44, exit Mo. 19 south at Cuba and drive 6.5 miles to the bridge crossing and the trailhead parking area on the southeast side. Zahorzky Woods begins at the south edge of the Meramec River bridge over Mo. 19, about a mile north of Steelville. Watch for the yellow and green Nature Conservancy signs.

Area/Location/County:
Potosi-Salem/Steelville/Crawford County

U.S.G.S. Map(s):
1:24,000 Steelville

Trail(s) Distance:
approximately 1.5 mile-long trail

Acreage:
56 acres

Activities:
nature walk, nature study

Fee(s):
none

NATURE WALK
28

TRAIL 29: **Maramec Spring Park**

Overflow at Maramec Spring

*M*aramec Spring Park is often listed by outdoor writers as the most beautiful place in Missouri and many visitors would agree. Maramec Spring was the first federally-registered natural landmark in Missouri. The large spring and surrounding area is privately owned by The James Foundation of Missouri and is open daily to the public, year around from dawn to dusk.

*E*arly James family ancestors from Ohio created the first successful iron works west of the Mississippi River here. Today the scenic, historical and geological park makes a great natural place to hike. Nature walkers will enjoy the Maramec Nature Center, Maramec Museum and the Ozark Agricultural Museum. There is a one loop nature walk plus a 2 mile auto tour. The naturalist offers scheduled programs and guided hikes.

Trail Summary:

*S*pring Branch Loop is an easy three-quarter mile walk along both banks of Spring Branch. It begins and ends at the furnace and forge ruins near Massey Hill picnic and parking area. Pick up the trail near the forge or

NATURE WALK
29

other streamside points and walk counterclockwise towards Maramec Spring and its rushing branch waters. The James Foundation works closely with the Missouri Department of Conservation (MDC) to maintain the trout hatchery and fishery. The amazing spring boil yields 96 million gallons daily, making it the seventh largest spring in Missouri and the largest in the Meramec River basin. The trail curves around the spring and follows the south bank of the Spring Branch past the trout-rearing pools to the Meramec River confluence. The trail crosses on a suspension cable bridge to the west bank. Downstream on the west bank of the Meramec River along the fisherman's path is the 30 acre Bottomland Forest Natural Area of the Woodson Woods Conservation Area. Continue along the spring branch upstream to the starting point at Massey Hill picnic and parking area.

*A*n auto tour travels through an area called Stringtown, named for a former mine town of houses "strung" along the road between the mine and the iron furnace. There are four large murals that depict life at four homes erected along Stringtown. This is a self-guided tour.

*T*wo new interpretative trails are currently being developed and each will be a quarter mile in length. To reach Maramec Spring Park from I-44, exit 195 south on Mo. 8 at St. James. Drive south through the city of St. James and continue on Mo. 8 about 6 miles to the park entrance, just west of the Meramec River bridge.

*O*ne and one-half miles east on Mo. 8 from Maramec Spring Park entrance is the 1834 Snelson-Brinker House that was restored by the James W. Woods Foundation.

Area/Location/County:
Potosi-Salem/St. James/Phelps County

U.S.G.S. Map(s):
1:24,000 Maramec Spring

Trail(s) Distance:
one loop trail totals three-quarters of a mile
2 mile automobile tour loop

Acreage:
1,856 acres

Activities:
nature walk, historic walks, seasonal naturalist, nature center, nature study, museums, trout hatchery, picnicking, shelters, playground, playfields, playcourts, observation tower, fishing, camping

Fee(s):
fees for entrance, shelter rental, camping

NATURE WALK
29

29. Maramec Spring Park

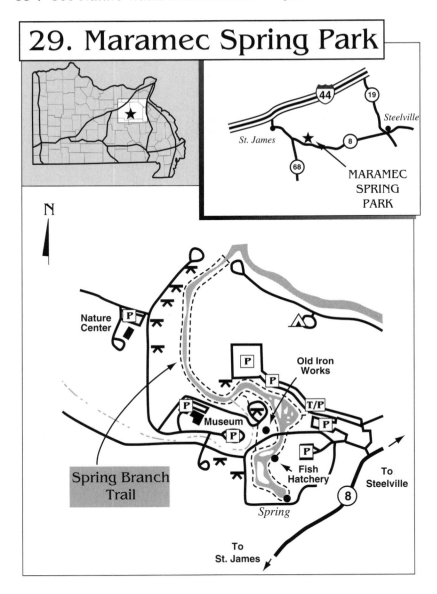

St. James

Steelville

MARAMEC
SPRING
PARK

N

Nature
Center

Old Iron
Works

Museum

Spring Branch
Trail

Fish
Hatchery

Spring

To
Steelville

To
St. James

TRAIL 30: *Moses Austin Trail*

*T*he Moses Austin Trail is developed and maintained by Troop 657 of the Boy Scouts, St. Louis Council, in cooperation with the U.S. Forest Service. The loop trail is named in honor of a famous American pioneer who came to the Potosi area in 1797 and is buried there. His son, Stephen E. Austin, the "Father of Texas," fulfilled his father's "manifest destiny" dream of a greater America. The trail is blazed by 2- by 6-inch white rectangles both ways but the suggested route is counterclockwise. The 14.5 mile trail surface is heavily eroded and can prove a challenge if "hiking through" as a day hike. Horse riders and mountain bikes also share this well-worn trail along a single track, abandoned logging roads and gravel roads (FS 2272 and FS 2438).

*R*ather than walking the entire loop, the northeast segment of the loop is the most interesting and is the suggested hiking route through this national forest land. From the Smith Road trailhead parking area, go north about 3 miles through Scott Branch Hollow to Little Pilot Knob Lookout Tower (elev. 1,412 ft.) This point-to-point walk will require retracing your steps or a car shuttle. A half mile old forest road spur heading uphill north from the Moses Austin loop to Little Pilot Knob Lookout Tower can be strenuous and is a 500-foot climb. Open meadows, low wooded hills, small creeks, springs, several crossings of Scotts Branch, ridgetop views – all are a part of the Moses Austin Trail.

*T*he trailhead of the Moses Austin Trail is located west of Potosi. Take Mo. 8 west 10 miles and turn right (north) on Hwy. AA. Drive 3.3 miles north on Hwy. AA, then west 1.5 miles on Smith Road/Washington CR 208. The trailhead parking area is located along the unmarked gravel road at an undeveloped road crossing or forest service road. Park on the north side of the road in the off-road mini parking area for three or four cars.

Area/Location/County:
Potosi-Salem/Potosi/Washington County

Map(s):
1:24,000 Shirley

Trail(s) Distance:
14.5 mile loop
suggested route of 6 miles round trip

Activities:
hiking, backpacking, mountain biking, equestrian trail, hunting

Fee(s):
none

NATURE WALK
30

30. Moses Austin Trail

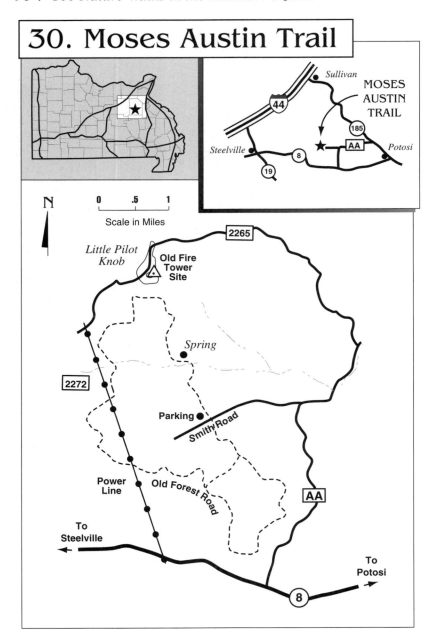

TRAIL 31: **Berryman Trail**

Edward Beecher Spring

*T*he 24 mile Berryman Trail loop has few steep climbs or descents (elev. 800-1,200 ft.) but is considered rugged due to the long segments of eroded rock and rut. Even though this National Recreation Trail was developed for horses, it has seen a lot of foot, horse, bicycle and motorized traffic over the years. Old mileage markers (some missing) are located at clockwise intervals along the loop trail that leads from creek bottoms to ridgetops, across five road crossings and as many fire trails and stream crossings. Experienced hikers can cover the 24 mile distance on a long June day, however the Berryman Trail is designed for overnight camping with four trailside camps.

*T*he best stretch of trail surface on the Berryman is from Berryman Camp northeast to Brazil Creek campground, a horse camp. From there, the trail crosses Brazil Creek and heads to Harmon Spring campground, a grassy open space. From Harmon Spring campground south past Edward Beecher Spring camp to the Berryman trailhead, the trail is a shared 10 mile trail segment with the Ozark Trail: Courtois Creek Section. The trail is blazed with white diamonds and leads through Mark Twain National Forest lands.

NATURE WALK
31

*T*here are two highway accessible trailheads. To reach Berryman trailhead and campground from Potosi, take Hwy. 8 west for 16 miles to FS 2266, 1 mile east of Berryman. Turn right (north) on FS 2266 and drive 1 mile to the marked trailhead and campground.

*B*razil Creek campground is located about 6 miles north of Berryman trailhead and campground via FS 2266 and FS 2265 and Hwy. W.

Area/Location/County:
Potosi-Salem/Berryman/Washington County

U.S.G.S. Map(s):
1:24,000 Berryman

Trail(s) Distance:
24 mile loop
10 mile Ozark Trail: Courtois Creek Section

Activities:
hiking, backpacking, nature study, equestrian use, mountain biking, camping

Fee(s):
developed camping at Berryman and Brazil Creek

NATURE WALK
31

31. Berryman Trail

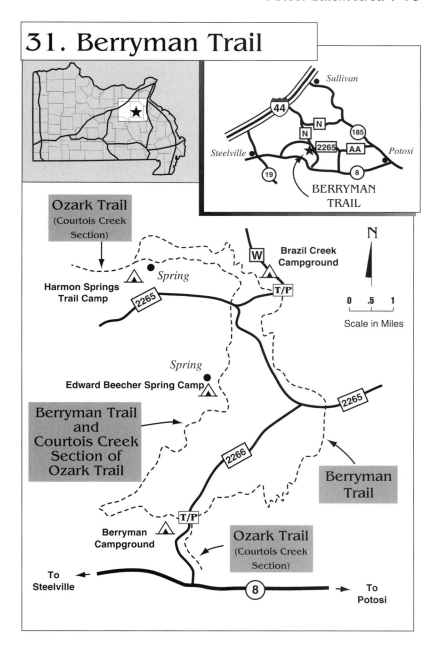

TRAIL 32: **Red Bluff Recreation Area**

Acquired by the U.S. Forest Service in 1940, the red- to brown-stained riverside bluff stands as a focal point of the recreation area. Huzzah Creek is overshadowed by this 400-foot-high colorful "painted rock," a landmark to the Osage. From the Pines campground overlook, the bluff view is spectacular. The deep valley and perennially-flowing stream attract visitors year around. There are two short maintained trails, one

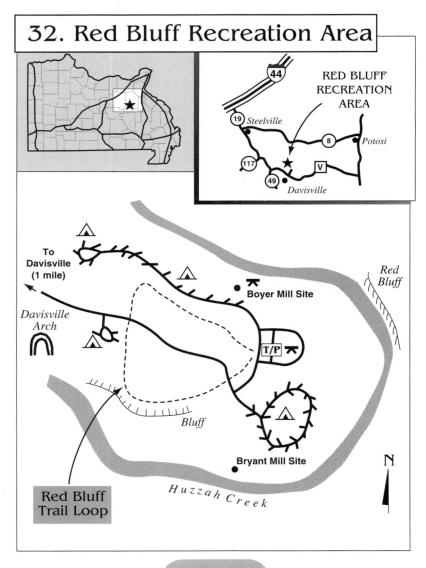

NATURE WALK
32

exploring the floodplain of Huzzah Creek and the other the upland ridges overlooking the valley.

*F*rom the parking lot trailhead at the picnic area, the Huzzah Creek Trail follows the stream edge point-to-point for about half a mile, providing a great close-up view of the iron oxide-stained Red Bluff. Near the Bryant Mill campground loop is the former gristmill site. Fishermen have extended the path upstream a few yards. This trail is a sandy and rocky floodplain walk in places but is mostly grassy path.

A second forest service path also begins and ends at the picnic parking lot. The trail starts across the park road from the red pump well and loops uphill along the property's perimeter through forest. It crosses the park road near the Pines campground and descends downhill back to the valley trailhead. There are fine views of Huzzah Creek.

*T*o reach Red Bluff Recreation Area at Davisville from I-44, exit at Steelville south on Mo. 19 and drive to Cherryville. Turn east on Mo. 49 and continue on Hwy. V to Davisville. Continue on Hwy. V one-half mile east of Davisville to the entrance on the left (north) side of the road.

*D*avisville Natural Arch is situated on the steep bluff overlooking Huzzah Creek between the entrance and Pines campground. Walk towards the bluff from the entry road about 100 yards from the entrance where the white pines are planted. The steepness of the bluff may discourage viewing the arch. This unmarked path is not maintained by the forest service and hikers in search of the natural arch, travel at their own risk.

Area/Location/County:
Potosi-Salem/Davisville/Crawford County

U.S.G.S. Map(s):
1:24,000 Davisville

Trail(s) Distance:
two short trails total 1.5 miles

Activities:
nature walks, nature study, picnicking, shelter, swimming, fishing, camping

Fee(s):
picnic shelter rental, camping

NATURE WALK
32

TRAIL 33: *Dillard Mill State Historic Site*

*D*illard Mill, like Alley Spring Mill, is one of the Ozark's best preserved and most picturesque water-powered grist mills. The restored and operational mill was built in the early 1900s and ceased commercial

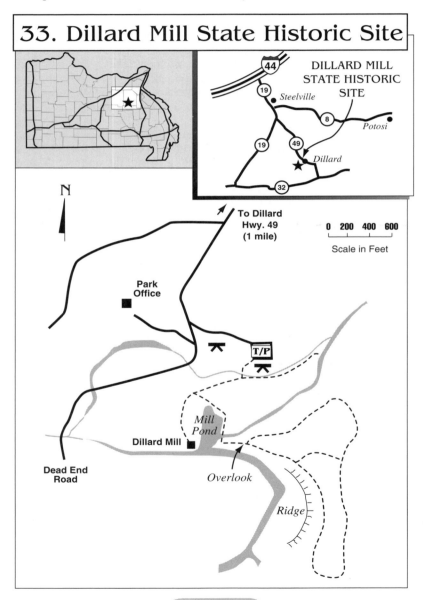

operation in the 1960s. In 1972 the property was sold to the L.A.D. Foundation of St. Louis, which leases the Dillard Mill property to the Missouri Department of Natural Resources (DNR) for management as a state historic site.

*A*t the 132 acre day use area, the two trails are short, but sweet. From the mill parking area, the Dillard Mill Trail goes down past the cemetery and picnic area to follow Huzzah Creek to the red painted mill and the confluence of Indian Creek. The mill is open daily for fee tours but is closed on the holidays of New Year's Day, Easter, Thanksgiving and Christmas.

*N*amed after the mill's first owner (Joseph Dillard Cottrell, owner from 1881 to 1889) by second owner Lester Klemme, the present day mill was built by Emil Mischke between 1904 and 1908. The 1.5 mile Upland Trail loop forks off from the Dillard Mill Trail and leads around the edge of the millpond and crosses Huzzah Creek at the outlet of the pond. Water can be high and discouraging at times. The trail heads up the bluff where there are great mill vistas that include the rock dam, waterfall and millpond below. The rocky confluence of the two small creeks at the mill site adds a unique picturesque quality. The trail continues to the ridgetop and loops along the property line down and up to return to the loop starting point at the rest bench overlook. Descend to Huzzah Creek, cross, and walk around the millpond to the Dillard Mill Trail. This is a fine place for a leisurely nature walk, picnic and tour of the beautiful old mill.

*T*he state historic site is located 1 mile south of Dillard, south of Mo. 49, west of Viburnum in Crawford County.

Area/Location/County:
Potosi-Salem/Dillard/Crawford County

U.S.G.S. Map(s):
1: 24,000 Viburnum West

Trail(s) Distance:
two trails total 2 miles

Acreage:
132 acres

Activities:
nature walks, mill tour, historic sites, picnicking

Fee(s):
mill tour

NATURE WALK
33

TRAIL 34: *Council Bluff Recreation Area*

*C*ouncil Bluff is the most developed recreation area in the Mark Twain National Forest. The 440 acre Council Bluff Lake was developed in 1985 by damming the headwaters of the Big River. The lake provides

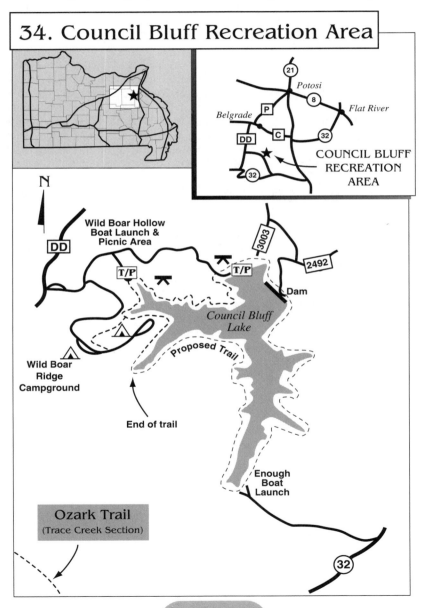

34. Council Bluff Recreation Area

NATURE WALK
34

water-oriented recreation such as canoeing, swimming, fishing, lakeside picnicking and hiking. Chapel Hill beach and picnic area opens in May and remains open daily through Labor Day. A parking fee is charged.

*T*he 3.8 mile (one way) Council Bluff Shoreline Trail begins at the southeast edge of the Chapel Hill beach parking area. The signed trailhead is at first a vehicle-wide road but quickly narrows down to a single track along the water's edge. The open wooded path follows the cedar-lined shore to the Wild Boar picnic and boat launch area (a second trailhead). Cross the parking lot and pick up the trail at the lake's edge near the boat ramp. The trail continues along the edge of the lake to a dead end point at the base of Wild Boar Ridge campground. Two campground access spur trails join the Shoreline Trail from the campground's far east end and campsite No. 40. Retrace your steps back to Chapel Hill beach and picnic parking area trailhead. Future trail development may include extending the Council Bluff Shoreline Trail completely around Council Bluff Lake and constructing a connector trail along Tellick Branch to the Trace Creek Section of the Ozark Trail.

*R*each Council Bluff Recreation Area from the junction of Mo. 32 and Mo. 21, 2 miles north of Belleview by driving west on Mo. 32 about 12 miles to the junction of Hwy. DD. Turn north on Hwy. DD and drive about 3 miles to the entrance of Council Bluff on the right (east) side of the highway.

Area/Location/County:
Potosi-Salem/Belgrade/Iron and Washington counties

U.S.G.S. Map(s):
1:24,000 Johnson Mountain

Trail(s) Distance:
4 mile (one way) shoreline trail

Acreage:
440 acre lake

Activities:
hiking, nature study, picnicking, shelters, beach swimming, pavilion, beach house, playground, seasonal concessions, fishing, canoeing, boating, launch ramps, camping, seasonal hunting

Fee(s):
beach access parking, shelter rental, camping

NATURE WALK
34

TRAIL 35: *Bell Mountain Wilderness*

Cedar glade Vista at Summit of Bell Mountain

*T*he heart of Bell Mountain Wilderness is 1,702-foot-high Bell Mountain competing with nearby 1,772-foot Taum Sauk Mountain for Missouri's highest point. Bell Mountain has been described as a long, north to south, breadloaf-shaped, igneous knob of granite glades. The trail is a climb well worth the views, so select a sunny spring day after a rain when the skies are clear to view Taum Sauk Mountain, Proffit Mountain, High Top Mountain and nearby Lindsey Mountain (a separate hike). Seven hundred vertical feet below Bell Mountain's crest is Shut-In Creek (elev. 1,000 ft.), one of the most impressive shut-ins in the St. Francois Mountains, but one that is difficult to access on foot.

*T*hree trailhead and parking areas access Bell Mountain Wilderness. The west wilderness trailhead and parking area is at Ottery Creek, Hwy. A, which is also provides trailhead parking for two sections of the Ozark Trail: Trace Creek from the north and Taum Sauk from the east (the incomplete Karkaghne Section will tie in here in the future when trail construction is completed from Sutton Bluff north). The Bell Mountain Trail loop shares the trail with the Taum Sauk Section from the Ottery Creek trailhead uphill and south for about a mile to the trail fork. This glade segment can be seepy and wet in spring.

*G*o left at the trail fork, uphill to the Bell Mountain loop (going right at the fork on the Ozark Trail leads to Johnson Shut-Ins State Park). At the unmarked but obvious loop trail junction, walk right (counterclockwise) to Bell Mountain's high point. At the mountain

NATURE WALK
35

35. Bell Mountain Wilderness

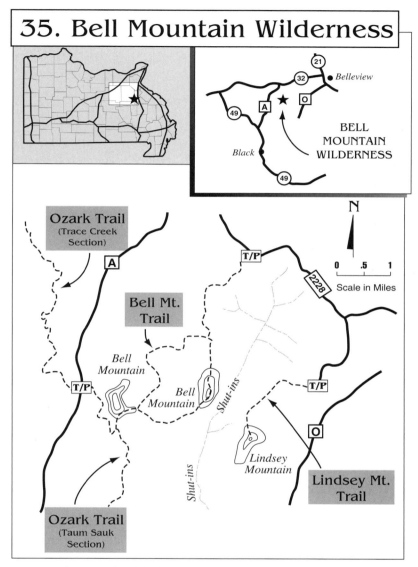

crest there are boulder-strewn, open glade overlooks to the south and east. Between Bell Mountain and Lindsey Mountain to the east lies Shut-In Creek below.

*T*he eroded trail descends Bell Mountain, curving back to junction with the second trailhead, a north wilderness access from FS 2228. Continue looping west on the main loop and descend the ridge to Joe's Creek bottoms. After a creekside mile the trail ascends lower Bell Mountain to rejoin with the original loop. Go right, downhill to the Ozark Trail

NATURE WALK
35

fork and right again, downhill, switching back to Ottery Creek trailhead at Hwy. A.

*T*he north wilderness trailhead is reached from Ottery Creek west wilderness trailhead and parking area by driving north on Hwy. A, 5.1 miles to FS 2228 (half a mile south of Mo. 32) and turning right (east). Continue 1.9 miles to the FS 2228 trailhead.

A third trailhead and a separate trail are found at the east wilderness trailhead and Lindsey Mountain. From the north wilderness trailhead parking area continue east on FS 2228, 2.8 miles (5 miles from Hwy. A) to FS 2359 and turn right (south). Follow FS 2359 south 2 miles to the dead end parking area and trailhead to Lindsey Mountain, 2 miles away on foot (one way).

*T*he trail follows an old road but turns off to a single track trail that gradually ascends Lindsey Mountain. The trail becomes overgrown and obscure the last 200 yards from the crest. If you reach the vista points along the crest of Lindsey Mountain, you earned it. Retrace your steps back to the trailhead parking. For the adventuresome, the best access to Shut-In Creek's shut-ins is probably from the Lindsey Mountain Trail but it requires traveling cross country with a map and compass and avoiding private property.

*T*o reach Bell Mountain Wilderness from Potosi, take Mo. 21 south to Mo. 32 and turn left (west). Follow Mo. 32 west 7 miles to Hwy. A and turn left. Proceed on Hwy. A south to FS 2228 and the north and east wilderness foot access or continue south on Hwy. A 5.5 miles to the Ottery Creek, west wilderness parking trailhead.

Area/Location/County:
Potosi-Salem/Black/Iron County

U.S.G.S. Map(s):
1:24,000 Banner, Johnson Mountain, Johnson Shut-Ins, Edgehill

Trail(s) Distance:
12 mile mountain loop
2 mile (one way) mountain hike
Ozark Trail junction of Trace Creek and Taum Sauk Sections

Acreage:
9,027 acres

Activities:
hiking, backpacking, nature study, seasonal hunting

Fee(s):
none

NATURE WALK
35

TRAIL 36: *Johnson's Shut-Ins State Park*

Johnson's Shut-Ins Overlook

Johnson's Shut-Ins are the best known and most photographed shut-ins in the Missouri Ozarks. The state park is one of Missouri's top natural draws and many travellers visit nearby Elephant Rocks State Park during the same excursion. The park's popularity is confirmed by the presence of seasonally staffed gates that monitor the park's attendance, allowing a maximum of 100 cars at a time into the park.

The wild rugged canyon, the park's main attraction, is easily accessible to all who seek it. Johnson's Shut-Ins is also a crossroads link in the eastern loop of the Taum Sauk Section of the Ozark Trail. The walking only scenic trails make it a hiker's paradise. There are three natural areas in the park: the 180 acre shut-ins, a nine acre fen and an 18 acre glade.

Shut-Ins Trail is a blue arrow-blazed, double loop that leads clockwise to the canyon-like gorge and back along ridgesides to the trailhead. A connector spur divides the trail into a 1 mile loop and/or a longer

NATURE WALK
36

2.5 mile loop. The Ozark Trail shares the east loop segment of the Shut-Ins Trail.

*T*he trailhead begins at the picnic area and park office where there is parking for the day use area. From the sheltered kiosk (brochures available) the quarter mile (one way) trail to the shut-ins boardwalk overlook is wide and paved as it follows the Black River's east fork. The blue-gray and dark purple volcanic, potholed rocks are awash with

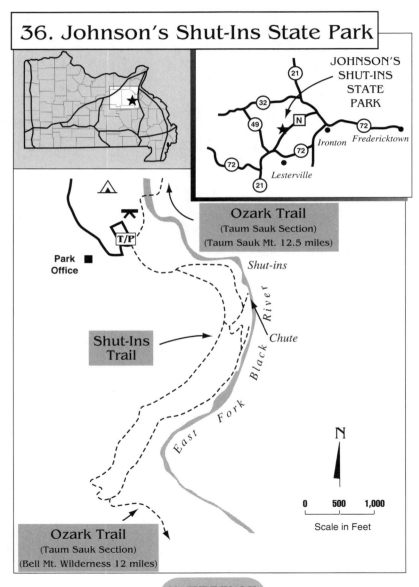

36. Johnson's Shut-Ins State Park

JOHNSON'S SHUT-INS STATE PARK

Ironton   Fredericktown

Lesterville

Ozark Trail
(Taum Sauk Section)
(Taum Sauk Mt. 12.5 miles)

Shut-ins

Park Office

Shut-Ins Trail

Chute

Black River

East Fork

N

0   500   1,000

Scale in Feet

Ozark Trail
(Taum Sauk Section)
(Bell Mt. Wilderness 12 miles)

NATURE WALK
36

swirling waters and during warm weather, swimmers and waders. The dazzling combination of rocks, waterfalls, canyon and pines is intoxicating.

*F*rom the boardwalk observation deck, the trail follows a staircase uphill to the short and long trail loops junction. Those who prefer to cut the trail to a mile-long walk should follow the red arrow-blazed, connector trail, looping back along the rocky ridgeside trail to the trailhead.

*F*or those who enjoy the shut-ins and desire to see more, follow the long main loop of 2.5 miles. Before the connector trail junction, the pine shrouded trail descends close to the stream and the area known as the Chute Shut-ins (a sharp contrast to this wild nature is the Union Electric power station a mile downstream). The trail ascends the ridge, skirting the 1,110 acre East Fork Wild Area, and loops back ridgeside (elev. about 900 ft.) to the trailhead. The Ozark Trail to Bell Mountain Wilderness is 12 miles and to Taum Sauk Mountain State Park 12.5 miles.

*T*o reach Johnson's Shut-Ins State Park from Lesterville, travel west on Mo. 21/72 for 3 miles to Hwy. N and turn right (north). Travel about 6 miles to the park entrance. The park entrance is located 12.5 miles southwest of Mo. 21 near Elephant Rocks State Park and 17 miles from Ironton, less than 90 miles from St. Louis.

Area/Location/County:
Potosi-Salem/Lesterville/Reynolds County

U.S.G.S. Map(s):
1:24,000 Johnson's Shut-Ins

Trail(s) Distance:
2.5 mile trail loop
Ozark Trail: Taum Sauk Section

Acreage:
8,670 acres

Activities:
hiking, backpacking, nature study, naturalist, nature programs, observation deck, natural areas, picnicking, shelters, fishing, swimming, camp store, basic camping, electric camping, group camp

Fee(s):
picnic shelter rental, camping

NATURE WALK
36

TRAIL 37: *Taum Sauk Hydroelectric Plant*

Misty Vista, Upper Reservoir

*M*ain attractions for nature walkers at Union Electric's hydroelectric plant atop Proffit Mountain are the nature center, the upper reservoir walk and vista and the three-quarter mile foot trail spur that leads to the Taum Sauk Section of the Ozark Trail. From the Ozark Trail, the flat topped 55 acre and 1.5 billion gallon upper reservoir looks like a New Mexico mesa. Water from the upper reservoir and the lower reservoir circulate along a 7,000 foot shaft cut through the mountain. The force of the "falling waters" produces electricity through the gravity-fed turbines.

*T*aum Sauk Nature Museum is located at the entrance to the hydroelectric project where parking is available. The museum features exhibits pertaining to the natural resources of the Ozark region. Missouri mammals, geology, tree wood types, prehistoric artifacts, crafts made from wood and other topic items are displayed for easy, informative

NATURE WALK
37

viewing in the well-lit, one floor museum. Outside the entrance door are boulder-sized geological specimens, a spacious, shaded picnic deck and exhibits about the operation of the power plant. The Taum Sauk Nature Museum is open daily from March 1 to December 1, 7:30 a.m. to 5:30 p.m.

*F*rom the nature museum, drive to the upper reservoir at 1,500 feet elevation and park in the areas provided at the end of the drive. Walk about 200 yards up the concrete ramp to the rim overlook of the upper reservoir. The views of the reservoir and the St. Francois Mountains are spectacular.

*A*t the north end of the parking area is the trailhead spur (three-quarters of a mile one way) to the Taum Sauk Section of the Ozark Trail. The trail is blazed by "OT" blazes. Hikers can make a day hike from the upper reservoir to Johnson's Shut-Ins State Park and return (about a 5 mile hike round trip) but remember the main gate of the hydroelectric power plant closes at 5:30 p.m. daily and overnight parking is not permitted.

*T*here are two road approaches to Taum Sauk Hydroelectric Plant which is 5 miles southwest of Taum Sauk Mountain. From the junction of Mo. 49 and Hwy. U, 1 mile east of Lesterville, drive north on Hwy. U 8 miles to the Hwy. AA junction and turn left (west). Continue to the plant's entrance and nature museum.

A second approach is at Hogan and the junction of Hwy. AA and Mo. 49/21/72. Go west 10 miles on Hwy. AA to the plant entrance and the museum. Follow the roadside signs. Primitive camping is provided by the Missouri Department of Conservation at the lower Taum Sauk reservoir.

Area/Location/County:
Potosi-Salem/Lesterville/Reynolds County

U.S.G.S. Map(s):
1:24,000 Johnson's Shut-Ins

Trail(s) Distance:
nature museum
one-quarter mile round trip to Upper Reservoir
three-quarter mile Ozark Trail: Taum Sauk Section access

Activities:
nature walk, hiking, nature study, nature center, picnicking, shelter, self-guided facility tours

Fee(s):
none

NATURE WALK
37

37. Taum Sauk Hydroelectric Plant

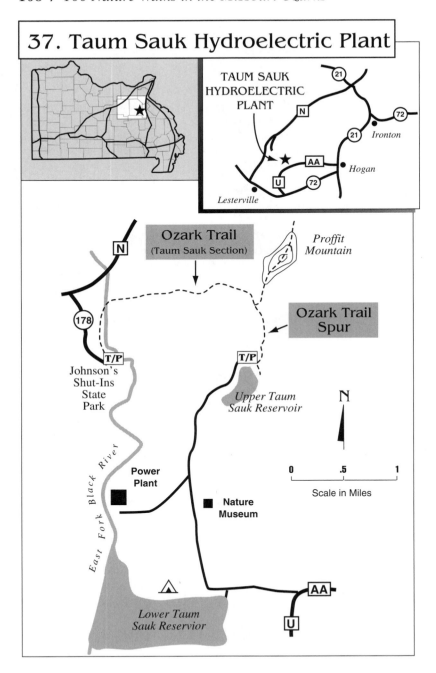

NATURE WALK
37

TRAIL 38: **Sutton Bluff Recreation Area**

View and Sign

Sutton Bluff is a 400-foot-high steep riverbank on the west fork of the Black River. A 1.5 mile rugged U.S. Forest Service trail goes streamside and climbs the cliff above. The Karkaghne Section of the Ozark Trail passes through Sutton Bluff enroute from the Blair Creek Section near Bunker. It heads northeast to eventually link up with the Ottery Creek trailhead on Hwy. A north of Black, and the Trace Creek and the Taum Sauk Sections (not yet completed to Ottery Creek).

There are two trailhead parking areas for Sutton Bluff and the Ozark Trail. One is at the end of the low water bridge, opposite the campground on the Black River. Park along the gravel bottom next to FS 2236 and cross the road to the signed trailhead. The second trailhead parking area is situated half a mile uphill by road from the first trailhead on FS 2236. This mini parking lot is signed for the Ozark Trail.

The forest path moves in a counterclockwise direction from stream bottom to cliff. There are segments of the trail that are narrow "cliff hangers." Wooden footbridges, steps and stairs are part of the trail. Nearly half of the trail follows the narrow edge, or bench, between the river and the

NATURE WALK
38

rock bluff. The trail provides a good opportunity to look at riparian plant life up close, growth that may be overgrown along the trail next to the stream. There is adventure in this short but somewhat challenging hike. A recent tornado has toppled a number of trees along the blufftop.

*S*utton Bluff Recreation Area is located in northwest Reynolds County. From Centerville, drive north on Hwy. 21/72 about 2 miles to FS 2233 and turn left (west). Follow the paved highway 6 miles to FS 2236 and turn left (south). Continue 2 miles on FS 2236 to the recreation area. For a separate return route, follow the river road FS 2324 back to Mo. 21/72 and Centerville.

Area/Location/County:
Potosi-Salem/Centerville/Reynolds County

U.S.G.S. Map(s):
1:24,000 Centerville

Trail(s) Distance:
1.5 mile loop
Ozark Trail: Karkaghne Section

Activities:
hiking, nature study, picnicking, fishing, canoeing, swimming, camping, seasonal hunting

Fee(s):
camping

38. Sutton Bluff Recreation Area

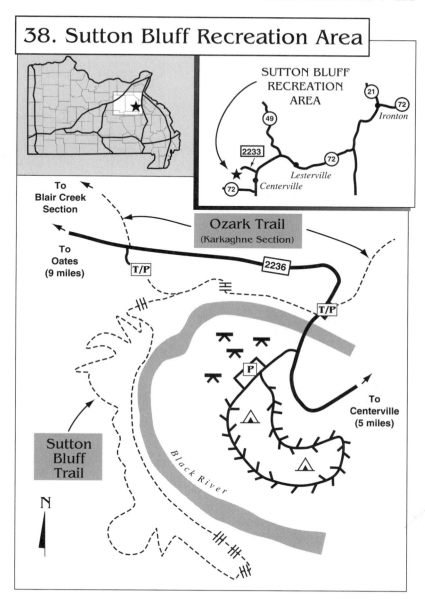

TRAIL 39: **Grasshopper Hollow Natural Area**

Deep Muck Fen

Grasshopper Hollow is a special Ozark place that harbors four types of unique fen communities, including the largest prairie fen in the unglaciated regions of North America. An unmarked old forest road leads north from an abandoned sawmill parking area to the fen wetlands. In addition to the prairie fen, there is a grassy-sedge seep fen, shrubby deep muck fen, and a forest-type fen. The wet, saturated soils are derived from seeps and springs. Rare and endangered plants and animals found here are normally found farther north. Despite a century of logging and grazing, the fens are now protected. The 593 acre area within Grasshopper Hollow is preserved and protected by The Nature Conservancy, U.S. Forest Service, Doe Run Company and the Missouri Department of Conservation.

From the dead end sawmill parking area, walk to the northwest corner and the entry gate. Walk north on the unmarked forest lane slightly above

NATURE WALK
39

39. Grasshopper Hollow Natural Area

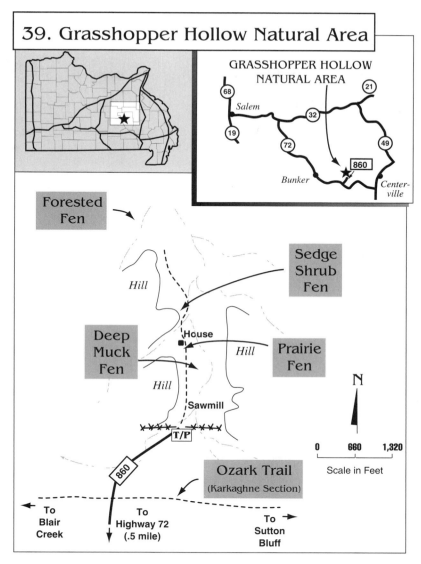

GRASSHOPPER HOLLOW
NATURAL AREA

Salem

Bunker

Center-
ville

Forested
Fen

Sedge
Shrub
Fen

Hill

Deep
Muck
Fen

House

Hill

Prairie
Fen

Hill

N

Sawmill

T/P

860

0   660   1,320

Scale in Feet

Ozark Trail
(Karkaghne Section)

To
Blair
Creek

To
Highway 72
(.5 mile)

To
Sutton
Bluff

and parallel to the deep muck fen. The boggy wetland is carpeted with sedges, bulrushes, royal and marsh ferns, shrubby alders and willows and may contain pockets of "quicksand." The hillside seeps along the old forest road trail will be wet at times, so wear old tennis shoes.

*R*eaching the old abandoned farm house, the forest breaks into a 10 acre prairie fen, a rare Ozark habitat. The wet prairie grows an array of wildflowers in spring. Birding is excellent and there is evidence of beaver and muskrats. Continue on the old road north (can be

NATURE WALK
39

overgrown and wet) past the farm house to the sedge shrub fen and forested fen on the west side of the old lane. Retrace your steps back to the parking area.

*T*o reach Grasshopper Hollow Natural Area from Bunker, take Mo. 72 east 1 mile past the Mo. 72 and Hwy. TT junction to FS 860. Turn left on FS 860 and travel six-tenths of a mile to the old sawmill parking area and trailhead. Enroute look for the Ozark Trail crossing on FS 860. Those who want to day hike the Karkaghne Section of the Ozark Trail west to the Blair Creek Section and east to Sutton Bluff along Bee Fork can park at the old sawmill at Grasshopper Hollow.

*A*nother nearby fen to visit is the three acre Blair Creek Raised Fen Natural Area which is on U.S. Forest Service land along the Blair Creek Section of the Ozark Trail (1:24,000 Midridge). The raised dome-shaped, deep muck fen is the only one of its type in Missouri.

*F*rom Bunker, take Mo. 72 southeast to Hwy. P and turn right. Drive about 2.5 miles to a Shannon County gravel road and turn left. Follow the gravel road 3 miles to the "Y" in the road and bear right. Watch for the Ozark Trail marker on the left and a parking sign on the right. Walk the Ozark Trail south 1 mile looking for an active beaver pond on the left and the boundary signs of the natural area.

Area/Location/County:
Potosi-Salem/Reynolds/Reynolds County

U.S.G.S. Map(s):
1:24,000 Corridon

Trail(s) Distance:
one-half mile one way

Acreage:
593 acres

Activities:
nature walk, nature study

Fee(s):

TRAIL 40: *Loggers Lake Recreation Area*

A 1.5 mile easy loop trail circles 25 acre Loggers Lake, an intact 1930s CCC project. The signed trailhead (a routed wooded trail map) begins and ends near the boat ramp turnaround. The oak and pine woodland path goes clockwise around the lake, crossing Mill Creek at the dam tailwater, then follows the west shore to a spur to Oak Knoll campground and the picnic area. From the shoreside picnic area, the trail continues to the park road and extends right, across the Mill Creek inlet road ford. Across the ford, there is a linear three-tenths mile spur to Rock Spring along Mill Creek. Retrace your steps back to the park road and continue to the trailhead via the developed recreation area at the lakeshore. The marshy inlet area at Loggers Lake offers great birding. The recreation area is about 5 miles west of the Blair Creek Section of the Ozark Trail and about 15 miles east of the Ozark Riverways.

*T*o reach Loggers Lake Recreation Area from Mo. 72 at Bunker, drive west on Hwy. A about half a mile to FS 2221 and turn left (south). Drive about 6 miles southwest (across the Dent-Shannon county line) of Bunker on FS 2221 to FS 2193 and turn left (east). Go 1 mile on FS 2193 to the recreation area.

*A*dditional short walks in the U.S. Forest Service, Potosi/Salem District include Big and Little Scotia Pond (Mo. 72, 10 miles northwest of Bunker) and Huzzah Ponds (Mo. 32, 19 miles east of Salem).

Area/Location/County:
Potosi-Salem/Bunker/Dent and Shannon counties

U.S.G.S. Map(s):
1:24,000 Loggers Lake, Bunker

Trail(s) Distance:
two trails total nearly 2 miles

Acreage:
25 lake acres

Activities:
nature walks, nature study, picnicking, fishing, canoeing, swimming, launch ramp, camping

Fee(s):
camping

NATURE WALK
40

40. Loggers Lake Recreation Area

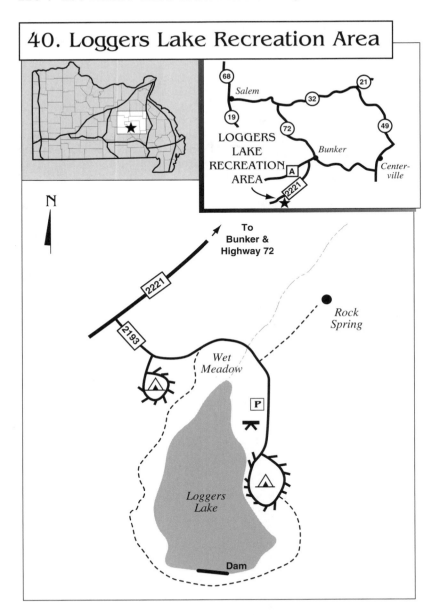

NATURE WALK
40

Ozark Riverways: An Overview

*T*he Current River and Jacks Fork were the first streams in the United States to be protected by the National Park Service (NPS). A combined 134 free-flowing miles of riverways and 52,000 land acres were preserved by the Ozarks National Scenic Riverways Act of 1964. Formally dedicated in 1972, the National Park Service "opened" the clear and inviting rivers to the public for recreational pursuits. Numerous launch slips were developed and primitive campsites were established along with hiking paths and other facilities.

*W*hile most park visitors come to ply the spring-fed rivers with canoes, john and motor boats, some enjoy the terrestrial activity of walking the riparian banks and nearby areas. Overall the nature walks are brief and often lead to picturesque springs such as Montauk, Welch, Pulltite, Round, Blue, Watercress, Alley and Big Spring, one of the largest in the world. Short paths also lead to shut-ins, an underground lake, and historic sites such as Welch Hospital, Alley Mill and the CCC Historic District at Big Spring. During the summer there are naturalist guided "underground hikes" at Round Spring Cave. Nature hikes and history walks are held on summer weekends at Alley Spring. Unfortunately, budget cuts have resulted in cutbacks in programs. For long distance hikers, the Ozark Trail is accessible at three trailhead points: Powder Mill (Mo. 106 east of Eminence at the Current River bridge), Rocky Falls and Creek area (east of Winona on Hwy. NN), and U.S. Hwy. 60 (4 miles west of Van Buren).

*F*or information about seasonal interpretive programs, craft demonstrations, trails and other activities, visit the park headquarters at Van Buren on Business U.S. 60. The park headquarters is open weekdays during regular office hours. An information staff officer is on duty and regional books and topographical maps are offered for sale. For further information write or phone:

Ozark National Scenic Riverways
P. O. Box 490
Van Buren, MO 63965
(573) 323-4236

TRAIL 41: **Montauk State Park**

Rainbow Trout

*B*orn high in the Missouri Ozarks, Montauk State Park is the headwaters source of the Current River. The river is formed from the union of Pigeon Creek and the estimated 40 million-gallon-a-day Montauk Springs. The place name is a transfer by local settlers from Montauk, New York, which is named after an Indian tribe that resided at the eastern tip of Long Island. The state park is one of Missouri's first parks and was established in 1926.

*M*ontauk is primarily a trout anglers' park from March to October, much as are Bennett Spring and Roaring River state parks. A winter catch and release trout season also serves the needs of fly fishermen from throughout the Midwest. The cool waters of the springs flow through the hatchery allowing the rainbow trout to flourish. Canoeists will find no access to the Current River at Montauk State Park, however the first put-in points downstream are at Inman Hollow or Baptist Access, accessible from Mo. YY. Naturalist-led hikes are scheduled and there are tours of the fish hatchery and the 1896 gristmill. Hikers will find the 1.5 mile Pine Ridge Trail and the short walk around Montauk Springs of interest.

NATURE WALK
41

41. Montauk State Park

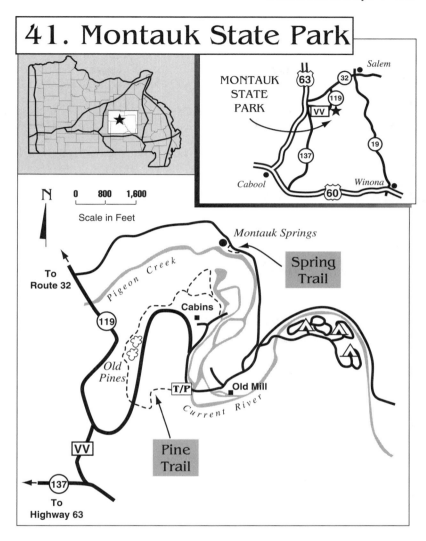

The Pine Ridge Trail begins behind the old CCC picnic shelter (parking is available). The foot trail follows the steep ravine uphill nearly 300 feet through the 40 acre Montauk Upland Forest Natural Area. The forest path emerges at Mo. 19 (park access road north) and crosses it. The trail continues along the shortleaf pine-studded ridgetop to a trail junction. The final half mile offers the options of continuing downridge to the park road at the fish hatchery or following a short loop overlooking Montauk "Lake" and springs. The hill and dale trail concludes at the park road but a loop is completed by walking the road back 300 yards to the trailhead picnic shelter.

NATURE WALK
41

*T*o reach Montauk Springs (possibly 14 springs) from the picnic shelter, go right and cross over the Current River bridge, taking a left before the lodge and park office complex. Drive about a mile north to a small parking lot on the left where interpretive signs describe the springs. A short walk takes visitors to the heart of the sandboil springs.

*T*o reach Montauk State Park from Licking, the nearest sizeable community, drive east on Mo. 32 to Mo. 137 and turn right (south). Proceed 2 miles to Hwy. VV and turn left (east). Go 10 miles to Mo. 119 and the north park entrance. The park is located 22 miles southwest of Salem in Dent County. Montauk State Park is also known for spring wildflowers, warblers and wintering bald eagles.

Area/Location/County:
Ozark Riverways/Salem/Dent County

U.S.G.S. Map(s):
1:24,000 Montauk, Cedar Grove

Trail(s) Distance:
one loop trail totals 1.5 miles
short walk at Montauk Springs

Acreage:
1,353 acres

Activities:
nature walks, nature study, naturalist, nature programs, natural area, picnicking, shelters, historic gristmill tours, trout hatchery, trout fishing, tours, dining lodge, motel, cabins, basic and electric camping, camp store, special events

Fee(s):
shelter rental, gristmill tour, camping, lodging

TRAIL 42: *Welch Spring, Hospital and Landing*

Welch Spring and Hospital Ruins

Welch Spring is downstream on the Current River about 20 miles from Montauk State Park, the river's headwaters, and 7 miles south of Cedar Grove (picnicking, canoe launch, camping). Welch Spring doubles the size of the Current River, the eighth largest spring in the state of Missouri, discharging 78 million gallons daily. Adjacent to Welch

NATURE WALK
42

Spring are the rock and shell block ruins of a sanatorium built by Dr. Christian H. Diehl, who acquired the land from the local Welch family in the 1930s. Both sites have foot trail access.

A well-used trail leads upstream from Welch Landing canoe launch, about half a mile along the spring branch to Welch Spring (adjacent to the Current River's east bank at the base of the bluff). The hospital sits in the shadows of the forested bluff next to the spring. The riparian flora along the gravel path to the spring is of interest. Retrace your steps back to the trailhead landing. Welch Landing is not marked on Hwy. K. The road access (which looks like a driveway) is the first left hand turn (sharp road curve) after Mt. Zion Church north of Akers Ferry.

*T*o reach the historic hospital and spring from the second trail access point, drive north on Hwy. K about half a mile from Welch Landing (about 2 miles north of Akers) along the Devil's Backbone to a locked metal gate on the left (west) side of the highway. Pull in and park in the pullout next to the gate. Walk past the gate and down the service road, which can be steep in places, about half a mile to the hospital ruins (250-foot elev. change). The resort sanatorium was once promoted by Dr. Diehl to be a place where asthmatics could be cured by the "remedial rising vapors" from Welch Spring Cave, now an Indiana bat sanctuary closed to the public. Visitors can get a closer look at the spring and its pool. Retrace your steps uphill to the Hwy. K gate. A third approach to the site, of course, would be via the Current River. Please do not wade or swim in the springs due to their fragile and unique nature.

Area/Location/County:
Ozark Riverways/Akers/Shannon County

U.S.G.S. Map(s):
1:24,000 Cedar Grove, Lewis Hollow

Trail(s) Distance:
two trails total 2 miles

Activities:
nature walks, nature study, historic site, canoeing, launch ramp

Fee(s):
camping at NPS Akers campground, optional ferry toll crossing

NATURE WALK
42

42. Welch Spring, Hospital & Landing

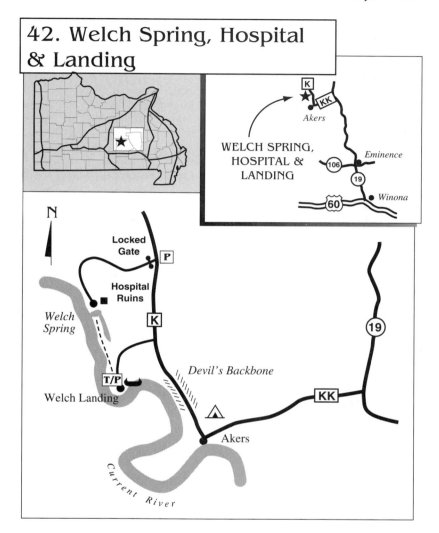

TRAIL 43: *Devils Well*

*T*here are no established trails at this National Park Service site but there is a sunken metal viewing platform and staircase that allows visitors to experience one of the largest underground cave lakes in the United States. One hundred feet below the viewing platform, the underground chamber holds 22 million gallons of water. The subterranean body of water is 100 feet deep at its deepest. Although darkness prevails, the pristine waters are aquamarine. Devils Well flows to Wallace Well Cave lake and the cave spring complex of the Current River, 1 mile south. There is a light button to push just a few steps up the platform that provides about three minutes of light, but bring along a flashlight to check out the depths from the viewing platform. A trail is being planned that will travel about 2 miles from Devils Well to Cave Spring.

*T*he access road to Devils Well can be rough and is not recommended for low-slung vehicles or trailers. Devils Well is reached by taking Hwy. KK west from Mo. 19, between Salem and Eminence. Drive 2 miles west from the Mo. 19 and Hwy. KK junction on Hwy. KK to an unmarked gravel road and turn left (south). Follow this rough gravel road 1.5 miles to Devils Well which is northeast of Akers about 6 miles and 11 miles northwest of Round Spring.

Area/Location/County:
Ozark Riverways/Akers/Shannon County

U.S.G.S. Map(s):
1:24,000 Cedar Grove, Lewis Hollow

Trail(s) Distance:
one-tenth of a mile

Activities:
nature study, picnicking, pond fishing

Fee(s):
none

NATURE WALK
43

43. Devils Well

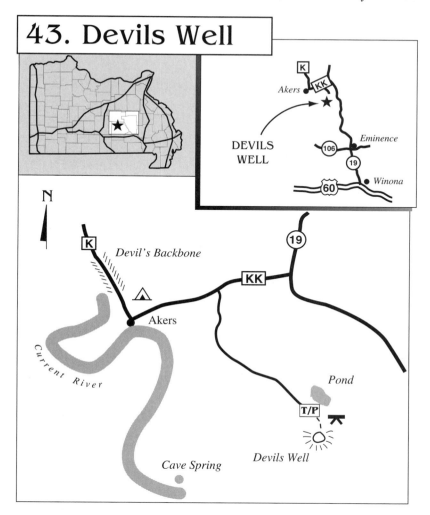

TRAIL 44: *Pulltite*

*P*ulltite is a National Park Service site that offers nature walkers the 1.5 mile Pulltite Trail loop. The place name, Pulltite, refers to the strained harness "pulling tight" as mules labored uphill with a grain load from the former gristmill that operated here years ago.

*T*he Pulltite Trail loop begins and ends at the turnaround and restrooms of Group Camp No. 3. Scenic Pulltite Spring and branch flow freely, emerging from a cave at the base of a cliff bluff. The branch streams half a mile to the Current River, past the historic Pulltite Cabin built in 1903. The spring fluctuates from 20 million to 92 million gallons daily. The trail continues across a footbridge through a farm field and pine forest to loop back along the Current River. The trail follows the floodplain where beavers have been active. Giant sycamores line the stream. The trail crosses a series of footbridges and the Pulltite spring branch to conclude back at the parking lot of Group Camp No. 3. The trail can be overgrown and hard to follow in places.

*P*ulltite lies 4 miles north of Round Spring on Mo. 19 and 4 miles west on Hwy. EE to the dead end at the Current River.

Area/Location/County:
Ozark Riverways/Akers/Shannon County

U.S.G.S. Map(s):
1:24,000 Lewis Hollow, Round Spring

Trail(s) Distance:
1.5 mile loop

Activities:
nature walk, nature study, spring, historic site, picnicking, canoeing, launch site, camping, ranger station

Fee(s):
camping, canoe rental

44. Pulltite

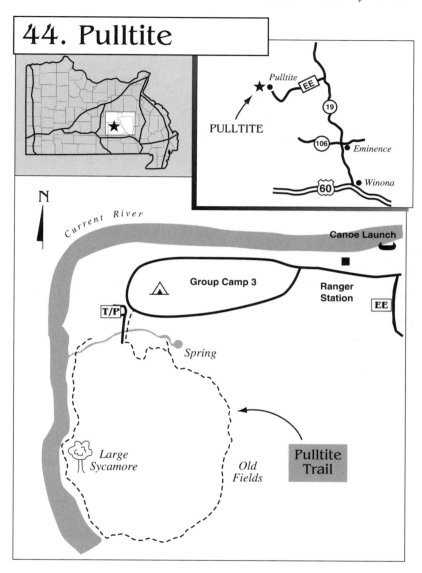

TRAIL 45: **Round Spring**

Round Spring, Ozark Riverways

*R*ound Spring is about 8 river miles downstream and 8 miles down road from Pulltite Spring. Round Spring and Round Spring Cave are situated on opposite sides of Mo. 19. There are two short nature walks to the natural areas.

*R*ound Spring, the Current River and a year around campground are on the east side of Mo. 19. A one-quarter mile easy trail loops about the sinkhole spring pool where 26 million gallons of water a day surfaces quietly. An Osage legend tells of a young warrior causing the spring to appear when he struck the earth with a weapon. The level trail begins enroute to the picnic shelter, north of the campground, close to the river.

*T*he cave is on the west side of Mo. 19 where parking is available near the NPS maintenance building. A short point-to-point path leads across the

NATURE WALK
45

cave spring branch to the gated cave entrance. Scheduled cave tours are given by a naturalist from May to September. Retrace your steps.

*R*ound Spring and Cave are located 13 miles north of Eminence in Shannon County.

Area/Location/County:
Ozark Riverways/Eminence/Shannon County

U.S.G.S. Map(s):
1:24,000 Round Spring

Trail(s) Distance:
two trails total one-half mile

Activities:
nature walks, nature study, seasonal naturalist programs, spring, cave tours, amphitheater, playground, picnicking, shelter, canoeing, camping, group camp, ranger station

Fee(s):
cave tours, canoe rental, camping

NATURE WALK
45

45. Round Spring

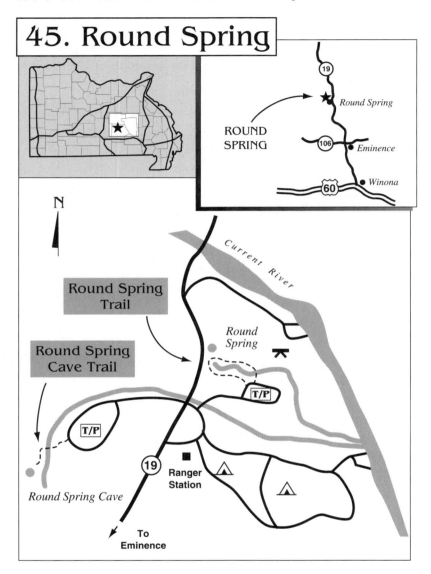

N

Current River

Round Spring
Trail

Round Spring
Cave Trail

Round
Spring

T/P

T/P

19

Ranger
Station

Round Spring Cave

To
Eminence

ROUND
SPRING

19

Round Spring

106

Eminence

60

Winona

TRAIL 46: *Lick Log Hollow Trail and Angeline Conservation Area*

Lick Log Hollow Trail Entrance

*A*lthough the 1 mile-long Lick Log Hollow Trail loop is a few miles from the Current River, the large Angeline Conservation Area borders the river and Jacks Fork. The Missouri Department of Conservation (MDC) maintains the gravel trail for educational purposes. There are old fields, glades and a small shut-in surrounded by a mixed deciduous forest. A 12 page trail booklet for the Lick Log Hollow nature walk is available at the trailhead parking area. The well-kept trail circles the creek banks and there are marked trees and interpretive brochure stops. Some of the woody plants found enroute include flowering dogwood, eastern red cedar, American hornbeam, white and black oaks, shining sumac, poison ivy and even "wolf" trees.

*T*o reach the trailhead from the junction of Mo. 19 and Mo. 106 at Eminence, drive north on M. 19, 2.8 miles to a gravel road on the east side of the highway (first road right, north of scenic overlook, or 1.7 miles north of the MDC forestry office). Turn right and go four-tenths of a mile to a forest gravel road and turn right (south). Proceed one-tenth of a mile to the parking area and trailhead. The forest trail

NATURE WALK
46

area is just south of the Jerkwater Landing Road which leads east to a river camp and launch area.

*W*hile in the Eminence area, consider visiting Prairie Hollow Gorge Natural Area, NPS, near Two Rivers at the confluence of the Current and Jacks Fork rivers (70 miles downstream from Montauk State Park). From the parking lot east to the rim of the gorge is an easy-to-follow old forest road hike of half a mile. There is also a shut-in gorge. Note landmarks enroute since the rocky outcrops near the river make the return trip hard to follow. Great vistas!

*F*rom Lick Log Hollow access road drive south on Mo. 19, 2.8 miles to the junction of Mo. 19 and Mo. 106 at Eminence. Turn left (east) on Mo. 106 and continue 5 miles to Hwy. V and turn left (north). Follow Hwy. V 3 miles to an old road on the right (east) and park at the trailhead, a short distance from the confluence of the two rivers.

Area/Location/County:
Ozark Riverways/Eminence/Shannon County

U.S.G.S. Map(s):
1:24,000 Eminence

Trail(s) Distance:
1 mile easy loop

Acreage:
9,777 acre conservation area

Activities:
nature walk, nature study, picnicking

Fee(s):

46. Lick Log Hollow Trail

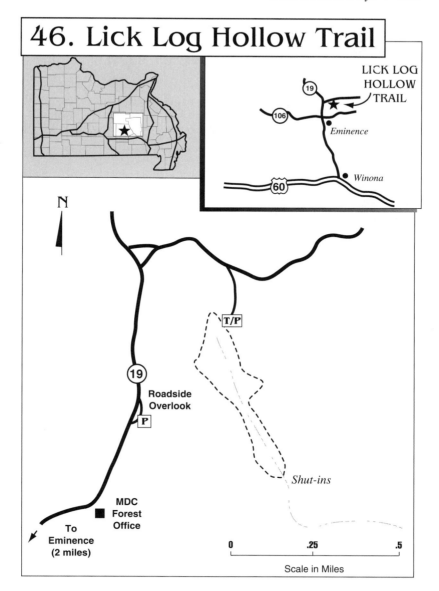

LICK LOG
HOLLOW
TRAIL

19

106

Eminence

60 *Winona*

N

19

Roadside
Overlook

P

T/P

Shut-ins

MDC
Forest
Office

To
Eminence
(2 miles)

0   .25   .5

Scale in Miles

TRAIL 47: **Powder Mill and
Blue Spring Natural Area**

*N*ature walkers will appreciate this 1.5 mile (one way) exceptionally scenic hike along the east bank of the Current River from Powder Mill and Owl's Bend campground downstream to Blue Spring and back.

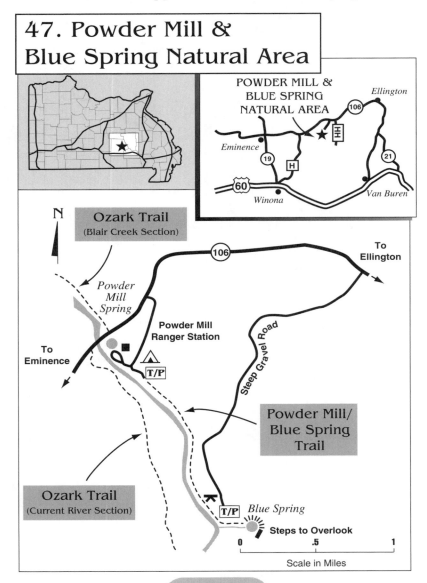

A shorter quarter mile-long stroll to Blue Spring can be made by driving to the second parking area at Blue Spring. Park at the Powder Mill visitor center and ranger station or use the day-use picnic area and walk towards the boat launch ramp which is a former ferry site. A signed trailhead will identify the trail to Blue Spring.

*F*ollow the floodplain forest path south between the river and the bluffs of Booming Shoal Hollow. The trail emerges at the Blue Spring picnic and parking area. Follow the obvious, well-used path along the cascading branch to the spring at the base of the bluff. The deep blue waters rise silently from a depth of 256 feet, the deepest spring in Missouri. Ninety million gallons of water rush to the Current River daily, making Blue Spring the sixth largest spring in Missouri. Steps lead up to a bluff overlook of the spring and the immediate surroundings of the MDC natural area. Not only is Blue Spring physically impressive with its water volume, it is also beautiful. The Osage Indians who had encampments in the area referred to it as the "spring of the summer sky."

*P*owder Mill visitors center and Owl's Bend campground are located 12 miles east of Eminence on Mo. 106, just across the Current River bridge. Blue Spring access may be reached by driving 2.2 miles farther east of the Powder Mill visitors center on Mo. 106, turning south onto an unmarked gravel road. Follow the rough and steep gravel road about 2.5 miles to the parking area dead end and trailhead to Blue Spring or the Powder Mill visitor center.

*T*he Ozark Trail junctions at Powder Mill. The Blair Creek Section heads north and the Current River Section heads south. Some of the best Ozark Trail hiking lies along these two sections.

Area/Location/County:
Ozark Riverways/Eminence/Shannon County

U.S.G.S. Map(s):
1:24,000 Powder Mill Ferry

Trail(s) Distance:
1.5 mile riverside hike (one way)
one-quarter mile springs walk
Ozark Trail: Blair Creek and Current River Sections

Acreage:
77 acre Blue Spring Natural Area

Activities:
hiking, nature study, natural area, picnicking, canoeing, launch ramp, camping, ranger station

Fee(s):
camping

NATURE WALK
47

TRAIL 48: **Rocky Falls and Rocky Creek Shut-Ins**

Rocky Falls and Shut-Ins

Rocky Falls is a 40-foot-long spectacular tumbling display on Rocky Creek, a short 7-mile-long tributary of the Current River. There are paved paths to the falls from the adjacent NPS picnic day-use area. Downstream on lower Rocky Creek are the Rocky Creek Shut-Ins,

NATURE WALK
48

Buzzard Mountain Shut-Ins, Mill Mountain Shut-Ins and the old Klepzig gristmill, all accessible from the Current River Section of the Ozark Trail. Nearby in Wildcat Hollow is The Nature Conservancy's 520 acre Shut-In Mountain Fen Preserve. Shut-ins and narrow boulder-lined canyons are common geological features in the St. Francois Mountains and outlying Shannon County.

*R*ocky Falls is located 11 miles northeast of Winona, and 9 miles southeast of Eminence. From Winona, drive 9 miles on Hwy. H to Hwy. NN and turn right (east). Follow Hwy. NN 2 miles to the second crossing and Shannon County Road 526 and turn right (south). Go three-tenths of a mile and bear left at the road fork to the picnicking parking area. The Ozark Trail intersects Rocky Creek half a mile downstream.

*F*or closer access to lower Rocky Creek sites along the Ozark Trail, follow Rocky Creek downstream to the Ozark Trail. The Ozark Trail crosses Hwy. NN just past the bridge. Walk north about 1.5 miles to the early 1900s Klepzig Mill and Mill Mountain Shut-Ins Natural Area. The best approach to Buzzard Mountain shut-ins is to follow the streambed of Rocky Creek downstream half a mile from the Hwy. NN bridge. Rocky Creek joins the Current River at Roberts Field canoe access at the river end of Hwy. NN. If you follow Rocky Creek you won't get lost.

*T*o reach TNC's Shut-In Mountain Fens, continue north from the junction of Hwy. H and Hwy. NN on Hwy. H, eight-tenths of a mile to Shannon CR 522/Shut-In Mountain Road and turn right (east). Follow the gravel road half a mile and watch for yellow and green TNC signs and park alongside the road. There are no maintained trails but there are old forest roads. The fens are along the draws on the right (south) side of the gravel road.

Area/Location/County:
Ozark Riverways/Winona/Shannon County

U.S.G.S. Map(s):
1:24,000 Stegall Mountain

Trail(s) Distance:
one-quarter mile falls walk
3 mile shut-ins walk along Ozark Trail: Current River Section

Activities:
nature walk, hiking, nature study, historic site, picnicking, fishing

Fee(s):
none

NATURE WALK
48

48. Rocky Falls & Rocky Creek

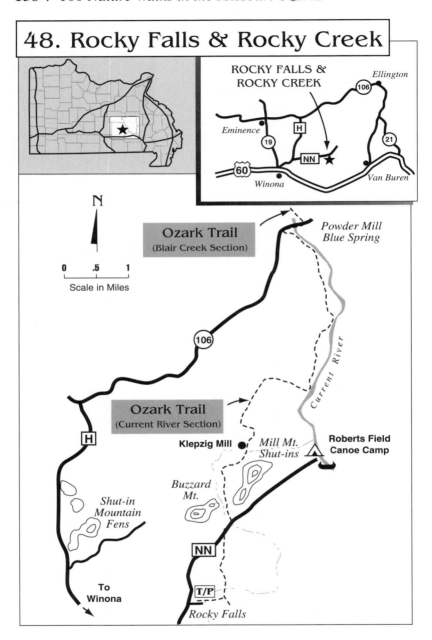

ROCKY FALLS &
ROCKY CREEK

Ellington

Eminence

Winona

Van Buren

N

0   .5   1
Scale in Miles

Ozark Trail
(Blair Creek Section)

Powder Mill
Blue Spring

Ozark Trail
(Current River Section)

Current River

Klepzig Mill

Mill Mt.
Shut-ins

**Roberts Field
Canoe Camp**

Buzzard
Mt.

Shut-in
Mountain
Fens

To
Winona

Rocky Falls

NATURE WALK
48

TRAIL 49: **Watercress Spring Recreation Area**

Watercress Spring

*T*his U.S. Forest Service recreation area is located on the east bank of the Current River at the northwest edge of Van Buren, downhill from the ranger station. The small floodplain "nook" of a recreation area is appreciated by canoeists, picnickers, campers and nature walkers. The biotic diversity of floodplain and upland is also fine for birders and other wildlife watchers.

*S*ongbird Trail forms a 1.2 mile loop beginning at Watercress Spring and is accessible from Group Camp site No. 11. Wooden steps provide easy access to the gently flowing spring which is covered on the surface by a vegetative layer of *Nasturtium officinale,* or watercress, a European freshwater edible herb, a common aquatic plant of nearly all Ozark springs.

*T*he Songbird Trail goes uphill clockwise 100 feet or so along the wooded rocky bluff where a number of migratory bird species such as warblers can be seen. Spring wildflowers light up the shadows of the limestone

NATURE WALK
49

bluff. The peaceful blufftop was once the military entrenchment of Union Army soldiers one winter during the Civil War. Vistas of the Current River can be yours when the leaves of the sycamores and other floodplain forest trees are down. The trail descends the bluff along the park entry road and continues down along the spring branch slough to Watercress Spring and the trailhead. There is also a short, well-used trail that follows along the bank of the Current River.

*V*an Buren, the county seat of Carter County, is accessible from Business Route U.S. Hwy. 60. From Business U.S. 60, turn north onto Watercress Road and drive half a mile to the ranger station and downhill to the recreation area. Van Buren is also the headquarters of the National Park Service Ozark Riverways.

Area/Location/County:
Ozark Riverways/Van Buren/Carter County

U.S.G.S. Map(s):
1:24,000 Van Buren south, Van Buren north

Trail(s) Distance:
one and two-tenths of a mile loop

Activities:
nature walk, nature study, historic site, spring, picnicking, shelter, canoeing, launch site, fishing, camping

Fee(s):
seasonal camping, shelter rental

49. Watercress Spring Recreation Area

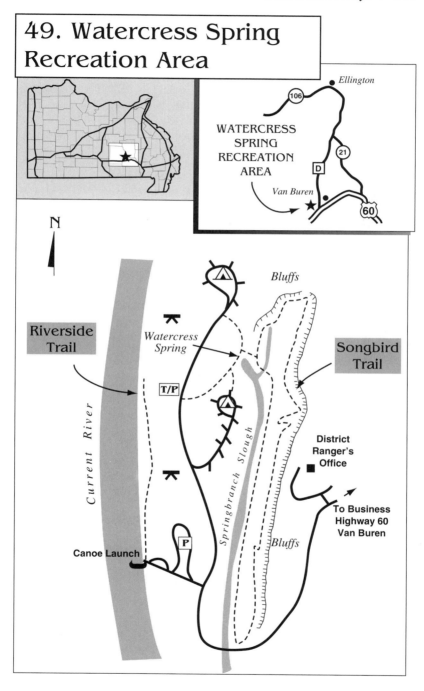

WATERCRESS SPRING RECREATION AREA

Ellington

106

21

D

Van Buren

60

N

Riverside Trail

Watercress Spring

Songbird Trail

Current River

Springbranch Slough

Bluffs

Bluffs

T/P

District Ranger's Office

To Business Highway 60 Van Buren

Canoe Launch

P

NATURE WALK
49

TRAIL 50: *Skyline Trail and Skyline Drive*

Skyline Trail and Skyline Drive (FS 3280) is a scenic side trip enroute to
Big Spring NPS from Van Buren, west of Mo. 103. The Between the
River Section of the Ozark Trail is a few miles away. For great vistas,
the best months to visit are October, November, March and April.
Skyline Trail is a 1.3 mile point-to-point trail. Four mile Skyline Drive
forms a self-guided, paved loop with 15 overlooks.

Skyline Trail begins and ends a quarter mile east of Eagle Lookout Tower,
the second vista on Skyline Drive loop north, and ends and begins at a
roadside pullout on Skyline Drive south. The forest trail surface is earth
with a healthy growth of moss, evidence of little traffic. Skyline Trail
follows the east facing ridge slope down into Sweezie Hollow and
uphill to Skyline Drive south. Retrace your steps.

Skyline Trail and Drive are located about 1 mile south of Van Buren and
the U.S. Hwy. 60 bridge, and 2 miles north of Big Spring at the
junction of Mo. 103.

Area/Location/County:
Ozark Riverways/Van Buren/Carter County

U.S.G.S. Map(s):
1:24,000 Van Buren South

Trail(s) Distance:
1.3 mile trail
one-way 4 mile scenic auto drive loop

Activities:
nature walk, nature study, picnicking, scenic drive

Fee(s):
none

NATURE WALK
50

50. Skyline Trail & Skyline Drive

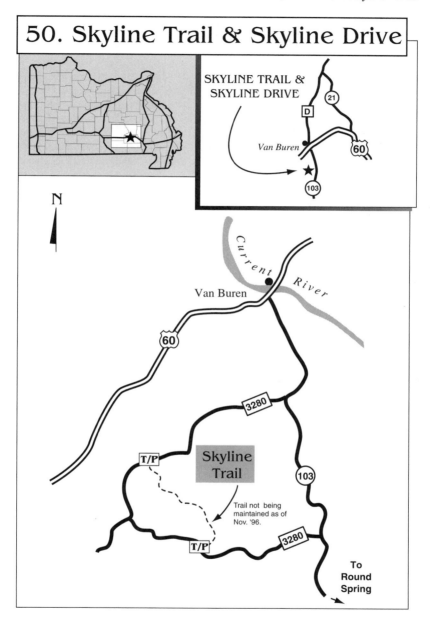

SKYLINE TRAIL &
SKYLINE DRIVE

21

D

Van Buren

60

103

N

Current River

Van Buren

60

3280

T/P

Skyline
Trail

103

Trail not being
maintained as of
Nov. '96.

T/P

3280

To
Round
Spring

NATURE WALK
50

TRAIL 51: *Big Spring*

*B*ig Spring is Missouri's, and one of the world's largest, springs. The awesome boil contributes an estimated 276 million gallons daily to the Current River along a 1,000-foot-long spring branch. Unmaintained nature trails are located near Big Spring, remains of the former days of Big Spring State Park when the CCC developed the park in the late 1930s. Although the trail network has declined, the CCC buildings have been restored into an historic district by the National Park Service. Exhibits about the CCC era are located near Big Spring Lodge.

*I*n 1972, the State of Missouri transferred Big Spring, Alley Spring and Round Spring state parks to the Department of Interior to be included in the nation's first National Scenic Riverway. The 17 acre Big Spring Natural Area includes two caves, a bluff and talus limestone slope.

*B*ig Spring is located 4 miles southeast of Van Buren and the U.S. Hwy. 60 bridge via Mo. 103.

Area/Location/County:
Ozark Riverways/Van Buren/Carter County

U.S.G.S. Map(s):
1:24,000 Big Spring, Van Buren South

Trail(s) Distance:
two-tenths of a mile trail

Acreage:
5,836 acres

Activities:
nature walk, nature study, historic site, amphitheater, spring, picnicking, shelters, fishing, canoeing, launch, john boat tours, cabins, dining lodge, gift shop, camping, walk-in camping, group camping, playgrounds, special events

Fee(s):
shelter rental, camping, lodging, john boat tours

NATURE WALK
51

51. Big Spring

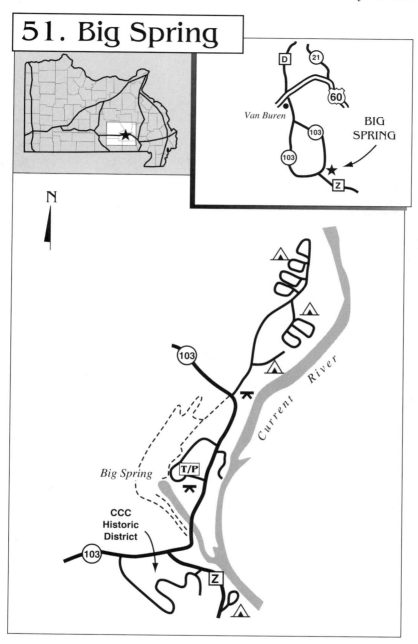

TRAIL 52: *Alley Spring and Mill*

Alley Mill at Alley Spring Branch

*T*he Jacks Fork is a small but swift and beautiful tributary to the Current River. The largest spring in the Jacks Fork basin, Alley Spring is the seventh largest in the state, averaging 81 million gallons daily. The spring and mill are named for a prominent pioneer farmer. Alley Mill is intact and is currently being restored to an operational state. It is one of the most picturesque and most photographed gristmills in the Missouri Ozarks.

NATURE WALK
52

*T*wo interconnecting foot trails originate from Alley Spring and Mill. A 1.5 mile trail loop offers a scenic spring view from the ridge top and a three-tenths of a mile trail circles the spring and follows the branch. The North River Road, which intersects the two nature trails near the spring branch is open to walking but is frequently used by horse riders. From Memorial Day to Labor Day, Alley Mill also serves as an interpretive center and bookstore.

*O*ne-third mile-long Spring Branch Trail begins at the red mill and circles the deep, one acre spring pool at the base of the bluff. The turquoise basin is confined by an old rock dam. Although the mill closed in 1919, its popularity as a social gathering spot continued and it became a state park in 1924. Today the former state park is administered by the National Park Service headquartered in Van Buren.

*T*he 1.5 mile Overlook Trail begins and ends at Alley Mill. The earth path climbs uphill to the overlook 100 feet above the spring and mill. The path follows the ridge south, descending to the spring branch and North River Road (the gravel road leads to the confluence of the spring branch and Jacks Fork). Turn right and continue on the Overlook Trail along the half mile spring branch back to Alley Mill and Spring. Camping is available at Alley Spring as well as other NPS campgrounds at Akers, Pulltite, Round and Big Springs.

*A*lley Spring and Mill are located 6 miles west of Eminence on Mo. 106. Go across the Jacks Fork bridge to the day use parking area on the right side of the highway. Alley Spring and Mill is located 13 miles east of Summersville on Mo. 106.

Area/Location/County:
Ozark Riverways/Eminence/Shannon County

U.S.G.S. Map(s):
1:24,000 Alley Spring

Trail(s) Distance:
two trails total about 2 miles

Activities:
nature walks, nature study, spring, historic sites, mill tours, picnicking, shelters, amphitheater, playgrounds, fishing, canoeing, launch site, interpretive center, seasonal naturalist and programs, camping, walk-in camping, group camping

Fee(s):
canoe rental, shelter rental, camping

NATURE WALK
52

52. Alley Spring & Mill

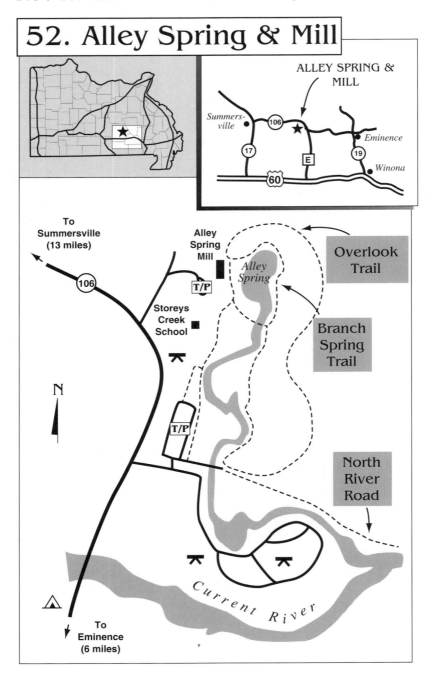

ALLEY SPRING & MILL

Summers-ville
106
Eminence
17
E
19
Winona
60

To Summersville (13 miles)
106
Alley Spring Mill
Alley Spring
T/P
Storeys Creek School
N
T/P
Overlook Trail
Branch Spring Trail
North River Road
Current River
To Eminence (6 miles)

NATURE WALK
52

TRAIL 53: *Float Camp Recreation Area*

Float Camp, White Oak Trail Sign

*T*he U.S. Forest Service recreation area is located 4 miles north of Doniphan on Hwy. Y along the east bank of the Current River. Approximately a mile north and west of Float Camp RA is Deer Leap RA, also maintained and managed by the Forest Service. Although the two recreation areas are not connected by riverside trails, there are two short loop trails at Float Camp. Both foot trails are self-guiding, begin and end in the day use parking area, and are maintained by the Boy Scouts. The half mile Woodchuck Trail includes the Current River floodplain and Malden Spring, crossing the park road twice. The 1.5 mile White Oak Trail is a clockwise directed hike. When White Oak Trail was established, the self-guiding trail educated visitors about the multiple use of forest resources. Today most of the original display stations have been reclaimed by the forest.

*W*oodchuck Trail begins at the southeast corner of the parking area and goes south to the campground along the riparian way and then loops uphill to the woodchuck dens along a south-facing slope. The trail

NATURE WALK
53

crosses the day use area road and then arrives at Malden Spring and Branch where nearly 8,000 gallons of water flows to the Current River every 24 hours. The trail goes left, following a short segment of the White Oak Trail towards the river, crossing the park road to the picnic area parking.

*T*he White Oak Trail begins and ends at the northeast corner of the parking lot near the entry road. The trail is a moderately easy ridge to ravine hike. Ecological multiple-use concepts that were formerly "taught" enroute include the old burn, log display, pine post display, game food plot, wildlife pond and erosion control.

*F*loat Camp Recreation Area and Deer Leap Recreation Area are reached by going north from Doniphan at the junction of Hwy. Y and U.S. Hwy. 160. Follow Hwy. Y, 4 miles to the marked entrance roads on the left (west) side of the highway.

Area/Location/County:
Eleven Point-Doniphan/Doniphan/Ripley County

U.S.G.S. Map(s):
1:24,000 Briar, Doniphan North

Trail(s) Distance:
two loops total 2 miles

Activities:
nature walks, nature study, picnicking, shelter, fishing, swimming, canoeing, boating, launch ramp, camping

Fee(s):
shelter rental, camping

53. Float Camp Recreation Area

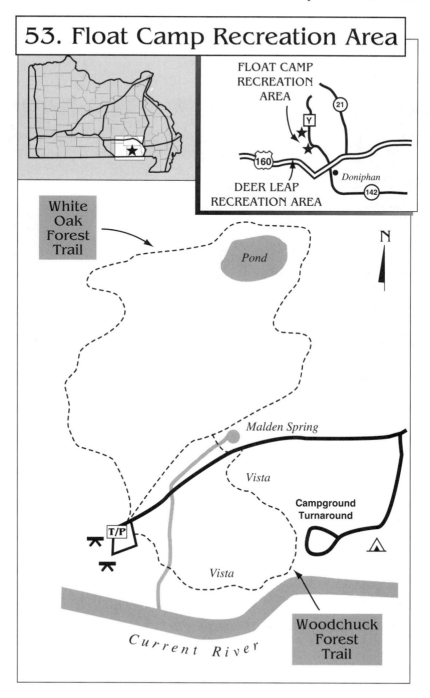

NATURE WALK
53

TRAIL 54: *Big Barren Creek Natural Area and Coward's Hollow Natural Area*

Big Barren Creek

*F*or the adventuresome, the remote natural area of Big Barren Creek, a scenic national forest Ozark headwater stream, is a walk through a narrow valley of shut-ins, glades, cliffs, caves and maturing forest. A warm weather and tennis shoe trail, the old forest road trail crosses and recrosses Big Barren Creek and a tributary, Devil's Run, five times one way. A diverse grouping of plants and animals occur here, including the endangered Carolina phlox and log fern. Camping, collection of plants and animals and vehicular traffic are prohibited in this wild 232 acre oasis.

*T*o reach Big Barren Creek Natural Area from Van Buren, drive west on U.S. Hwy. 60 to Hwy. C junction and turn left (south). Follow Hwy. C south 11 miles, through Eastwood to Carter CR 167, turning right (west) before the bridge over Big Barren Creek. Continue driving 2.3 miles northwest on CR 167 to the first creek crossing where there is parking for two cars in a pullout.

NATURE WALK
54

*P*ark and ford the stream on foot and follow the forest road through the preserve. The nature walk features a boulder-lined stream, bottomland forest, gray limestone bluffs, south-facing glade slopes and dry upland chert forest. Devil's Run joins Big Barren Creek in the middle of the preserve. There are numerous streamside boulders to sit on and enjoy the surroundings. The preserve trail concludes at the fifth and widest stream crossing on Big Barren Creek. Retrace your steps back to the trailhead parking area.

*S*outh a few miles is a second U.S. Forest Service natural area, Cowards Hollow. The 56 acre hiking only preserve is found by continuing south on Hwy. C from the Big Barren Creek NA turnoff, Carter CR 167, 1.5 miles to FS 3142 (at the road curve) and turning right (west). FS 3142 is the first road right (west), south of the Carter-Ripley county line. Proceed 2.5 miles to FS 4875 on the right (north) side of the road. Go three-tenths of a mile on FS 4875 and park at the forest road and walk north to the powerline. Follow the powerline service road and watch for natural area signage on the right (east). A forest path leads to a narrow steep shut-in with cliffs, a rock shelter cave and waterfall.

*C*owards Hollow Natural Area has a number of significant geological features as well as natural plant communities. Instead of limestone or granite, chert is everywhere. Chert shut-ins, chert cliffs and a chert shelter cave are the most outstanding geological features. The cliffs provide habitat for turkey vultures, eastern phoebes and northern rough-winged swallows. A seep-fed fen adds to the biological diversity. The stream is a tributary of Big Barren Creek. Along the south wall is a large chert shelter cave where Civil War draft dodgers and deserters from both sides sought sanctuary in the scenic hollow; hence the place name, Cowards Hollow.

Area/Location/County:
Eleven Point-Doniphan/Van Buren/Carter County

U.S.G.S. Map(s):
1:24,000 Handy

Trail(s) Distance:
1 mile one way on an old forest road

Acreage:
232 acres

Activities:
nature walk, nature study

Fee(s):
none

NATURE WALK
54

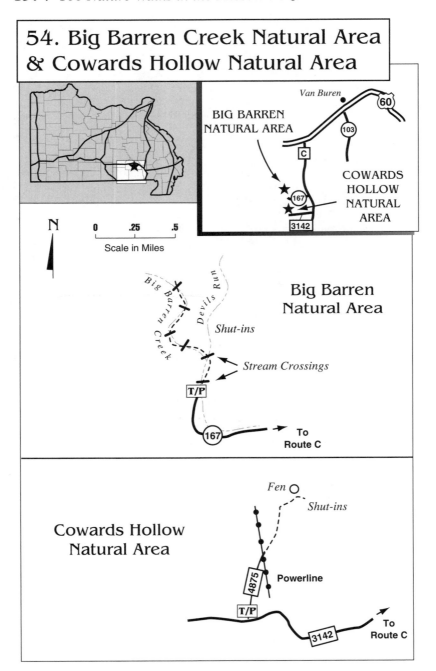

54. Big Barren Creek Natural Area & Cowards Hollow Natural Area

Van Buren

BIG BARREN
NATURAL AREA

60

103

C

COWARDS
HOLLOW
NATURAL
AREA

167

3142

N

0   .25   .5
Scale in Miles

Big Barren Creek

Devils Run

Shut-ins

Big Barren
Natural Area

Stream Crossings

T/P

167   To
Route C

Fen O

Shut-ins

Cowards Hollow
Natural Area

4875

Powerline

T/P

3142   To
Route C

NATURE WALK
54

TRAIL 55: *Irish Wilderness*

Eleven Point River from White's Creek Trail

*T*he Irish Wilderness (elev. 500-900 ft.) is the largest of the U.S. Forest Service wilderness areas in the Missouri Ozarks. The Eleven Point River, shaping the western wilderness boundary, is a National Wild and Scenic River. Father John Joseph Hogan and his "flock" of newly-arrived Old World Irish settlers from St. Louis attempted settlement of the area before the Civil War; hence the derivation of the wilderness place name. The 18.5 mile White's Creek Trail forms a loop through the wilderness and has three trailheads: Camp Five Pond at Hwy. J, Brawley Pond near Wilderness and the river via canoe.

*T*o reach Camp Five Pond, go west on U.S. Hwy. 60 from Van Buren to Fremont and Hwy. J and turn left (south). Drive 16 miles south on Hwy. J to Camp Five Pond on the right (west) side of the highway. From Doniphan, go west on U.S. Hwy. 160 about 13 miles to Hwy. J and turn right (north) and continue 7 miles to Camp Five Pond. The trailhead begins at the southwest corner of the pond.

NATURE WALK
55

55. Irish Wilderness

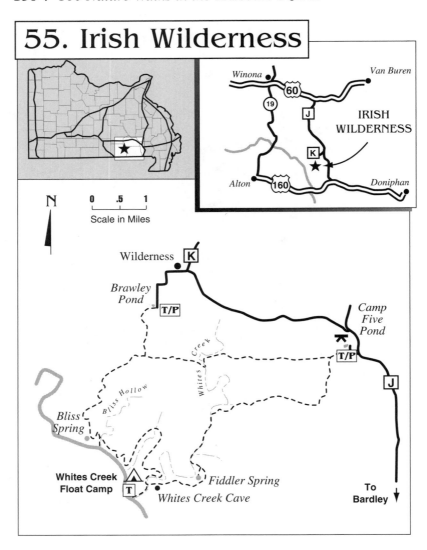

The north section of the loop leaves Camp Five Pond on the west and passes south of Camp Nine Pond (no trail connection to this pond) along ridges to cross White's Creek and continues along ridgetop to junction with the Brawley Pond trail spur (1 mile to trailhead north). The White's Creek Trail continues west and south to descend at Bliss Spring (517,000 gallons daily) and the Eleven Point River.

The south section of the loop leaves Camp Five Pond and follows the fairly level ridgetops to Fiddler's Spring, White's Creek Cave, White's Creek Float Camp, Orchard Hollow and along the Eleven Point River

NATURE WALK
55

bluffs to Bliss Spring. The karst landscape has numerous sinkholes, caves and springs. Although the trail is designed for hiking, horse use is permitted. White's Creek Cave is closed to the public from September 15 to May 1 due to a nesting Indiana bat population.

*T*o reach Brawley Pond trailhead from Camp Five Pond, go north on Hwy. J about 5 miles to the junction with Hwy. K and turn left (south). Follow Hwy. K about 2.5 miles south to Wilderness, turning right (west) at the "T." Continue about four-tenths of a mile to the first road left (south) and turn. Follow the road, jogging right (west), and turn left (south), continuing south about three-quarters of a mile to the Brawley Pond trailhead parking. Follow the spur trail south 1 mile to access White's Creek loop trail.

*A*lways carry a map and compass, even though the single track trail is blazed with white diamonds in both directions. A two day hike is suggested but experienced hikers may hike the entire moderate to rugged route in one day due to the general levelness of the trail surface. Most of the trail along the Eleven Point River is rugged as it clambers along the rocky bluffs. White's Creek float camp along the Eleven Point River is also available for backpackers.

Area/Location/County:
Eleven Point-Doniphan/Wilderness/Oregon County

U.S.G.S. Map(s):
1:24,000 Wilderness, Riverton, Bardley

Trail(s) Distance:
18.5 mile loop

Acreage:
16,500 acres

Activities:
hiking, backpacking, nature study, canoeing, fishing, seasonal hunting, float camps

Fee(s):
none

NATURE WALK
55

TRAIL 56: **Morgan Spring at the Narrows**

*T*he first segment of the old road trail follows a 100-foot-high narrow ridge backbone (The Narrows) that separates the Eleven Point River from Frederick Creek. Blue, Jones, and Sullivan springs lie along the Eleven Point side of the steep ridge and are not easily accessed on foot. Farther north and down the ridge is Morgan Spring, the eighth largest spring in Missouri. These four springs collectively contribute about 100 million gallons daily to the Eleven Point River. At one time Morgan Spring supplied water for the largest aquatic farm in the United States. Aquarium plant materials and mosses were cultivated until the 1960s. A concrete sluice and dam are the remaining evidence of a former gristmill that operated around 1908.

A short loop leads from Morgan Spring along a service road to the streamside canoe camp. A roadside picnic area lies across the river on the east bank of the Eleven Point. The trailhead begins and ends at a locked gate at the Narrows.

*T*o reach the trailhead from the Mo. 142 highway bridge over the Eleven Point River (midway between Doniphan and Thayer) go one-tenth of a mile to the west side of the bridge and turn right (north) on what looks like a private lane. Proceed two-tenths of a mile up the lane to the locked gate and trailhead parking. The service road doubles as a trail.

*T*he east bank of the Eleven Point River has developed recreational facilities. The Eleven Point River is classified as a National Scenic River under the National Wild and Scenic Rivers Act of 1968.

Area/Location/County:
Eleven Point-Doniphan/Doniphan/Oregon

U.S.G.S. Map(s):
1:24,000 Riverton, Billmore

Trail(s) Distance:
one-half mile trail

Activities:
nature walk, nature study, historic site, springs, fishing, canoeing, launch ramp, picnicking, float camp

Fee(s):
none

NATURE WALK
56

56. Morgan Spring at the Narrows

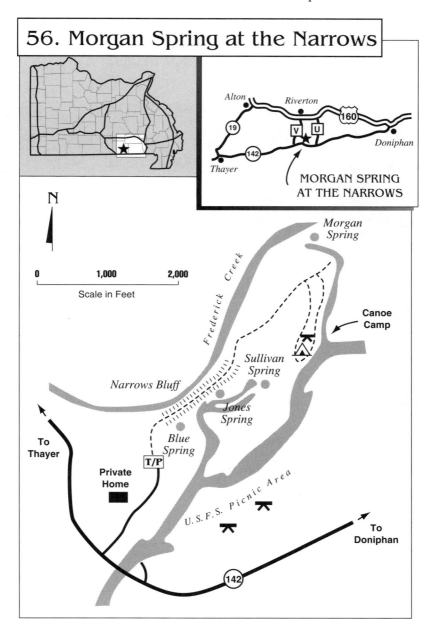

NATURE WALK
56

TRAIL 57: *Greer Spring and Greer Crossing Recreation Area*

Creekbed Boil at Greer Spring

*A*fter Big Spring, the second largest spring in Missouri is Greer Spring. The 222 million gallons of daily flow doubles the stream size of the Eleven Point River. The Eleven Point Section of the Ozark Trail crosses at Greer Crossing Recreation Area and shares the McCormack-Greer Trail for about 3 riverside miles. Greer Spring and Greer Crossing RA are 1 road mile apart via Mo. 19.

*G*reer Spring Trail begins and ends at the well-marked Mo. 19 trailhead parking area, 18 miles south of Winona and 8.5 miles north of Alton on the west side of the highway. The dirt point-to-point trail is in excellent condition and has foot bridges and rest benches as it descends the ridge and ravine to the spring. An observation deck overlooks the impressive spring boil that rises out of the spring branch bed. A second flow emerges upstream 60 yards at the upper cave entrance. The spring

NATURE WALK
57

branch flows through a gorge 1 mile to the Eleven Point River confluence which may be seen from the McCormack-Greer Trail, accessible from Greer Crossing Recreation Area. Retrace your steps uphill nine-tenths of a mile to the Greer Spring trailhead (the benches are appreciated on the uphill return). The spring was purchased by the U.S. Forest Service in 1993.

*G*reer Crossing RA can be reached from Greer Spring by driving north on Mo. 19 1 mile, crossing the Eleven Point River bridge and turning right (east) on FS 3188 into the area. Enroute the remains of Samuel Greer's 1884 gristmill still stand on private property on the west side of the highway.

*G*reer Crossing, once a wagon ford and sorghum cane mill site, is now a forest service recreational area. The 3.7 mile (one way) McCormack-Greer Trail connects a second forest service recreational area at McCormack Lake. A trail brochure is available that points out the natural features and the cultural history. The easy to moderately rugged trail follows riverside, ridgeside, ridgetop and ravine to arrive at the dam spillway at McCormack Lake Recreation Area. Hikers will need to car shuttle or return along the same trail back to Greer Crossing. A shorter 2.1 mile ridge-river loop from Greer Crossing to Duncan Hollow is available. Migratory and nesting warblers include northern parulas, American redstarts and ceruleans.

*T*he Ozark Trail, Eleven Point River Section can be accessed east and west from from both of these recreation areas. The McCormack-Greer Trail and the Ozark Trail share the same tread for about 2.7 miles from Greer Crossing RA west to the trail junction to McCormack Lake RA. From the trail junction, the Ozark Trail continues 18 miles west to terminate at Paty Hollow. From Greer Crossing RA, the Ozark Trail travels northeast to Sinking Creek Lookout Tower and the Between the River Section, south terminus. Future plans call for new trail construction closer to the Eleven Point River, east of Greer Crossing RA.

*D*ownstream from Greer Crossing RA and upstream from the Irish Wilderness, Turner Mill North picnic area is worth visiting while in the vicinity. Drive north of Greer Crossing RA 2.5 miles to FS 3152 and turn right (east). Go 6 miles on FS 3152 to FS 3190 and turn right (south). Drive about 3 miles on FS 3190 to the Turner Mill picnic area (the east terminus of the Eleven Point Section, Ozark Trail is at the junction of FS 3152 and FS 3190). Directly across the Eleven Point River is Turner Mill South.

A short trail leads to the 1.5 million gallons-a-day Turner Spring, which flows from the mouth of a cave. All that remains of the spring-powered Turner Mill is a 26-foot steel overshot wheel that sits in the spring branch. Nothing remains of the ghost town of Surprise which was established by Mr. Turner.

NATURE WALK
57

Area/Location/County:
Eleven Point-Doniphan/Greer/Oregon County

U.S.G.S. Map(s):
1:24,000 Greer

Trail(s) Distance:
1.8 mile spring trail
3.7 mile recreation trail (one-way)
Ozark Trail: Eleven Point Section

Activities:
nature walks, nature study, backpacking, historic sites, picnicking, fishing, canoeing, launch ramp, camping

Fee(s):
developed camping

Old Mill Overshot Wheel, Turner Spring North

NATURE WALK
57

57. Greer Spring & Greer Crossing Recreation Area

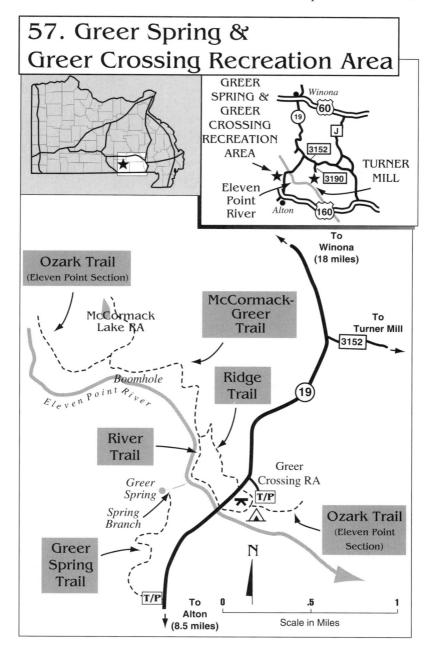

GREER SPRING & GREER CROSSING RECREATION AREA

Winona

60

19

J

3152

3190

TURNER MILL

Eleven Point River

Alton

160

To Winona (18 miles)

Ozark Trail
(Eleven Point Section)

McCormack Lake RA

McCormack-Greer Trail

To Turner Mill
3152

Boomhole

Ridge Trail

19

Eleven Point River

River Trail

Greer Spring

Spring Branch

Greer Crossing RA

T/P

Ozark Trail
(Eleven Point Section)

Greer Spring Trail

N

T/P

To Alton (8.5 miles)

0   .5   1

Scale in Miles

NATURE WALK
57

TRAIL 58: *McCormack Lake Recreation Area*

*S*prings that flow from McCormack Hollow feed the 15 acre lake that was constructed in the 1930s as a bass rearing pond by the CCC. A one-quarter mile loop circles the peaceful body of water where waterfowl and other wildlife gather. From the dam spillway waterfall, the 3.7 mile (one way) McCormack-Greer Trail begins, leading 1 mile south to the junction of the Ozark Trail, and then up bluff and downstream along

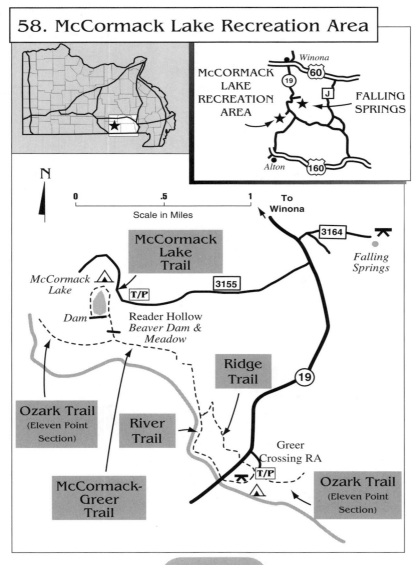

58. McCormack Lake Recreation Area

McCORMACK LAKE RECREATION AREA

Winona
60
19
J
FALLING SPRINGS
Alton 160

N

0   .5   1   To Winona
Scale in Miles

McCormack Lake Trail

McCormack Lake
T/P
3155
3164
Falling Springs

Dam
Reader Hollow
Beaver Dam & Meadow

Ridge Trail
19

Ozark Trail
(Eleven Point Section)

River Trail

Greer Crossing RA
T/P

McCormack-Greer Trail

Ozark Trail
(Eleven Point Section)

NATURE WALK
58

the Eleven Point River to Greer Crossing Recreation Area. The McCormack-Greer Trail shares the same tread with the 30 mile Eleven Point River Section of the Ozark Trail.

*T*he point-to-point McCormack-Greer Trail (and Ozark Trail feeder spur) leads from the McCormack Lake spillway dam across Reader Hollow (beaver dam and meadow) 1 mile to the Ozark Trail junction (east and west). The McCormack-Greer Trail goes left (east) at the fork upridge to the Boom Hole vista, several hundred feet above the Eleven Point River. The trail follows the glade-dotted ridgetop east (downriver), descending to cross Duncan Hollow and Creek, arriving at the loop trail junction of Ridge Trail and River Trail. Both trail routes (same loop) continue to Greer Crossing RA in 1 mile. The confluence of Greer Spring and the Eleven Point River may be seen from the River Trail, about three-quarters of a mile from Greer Crossing RA. Upon reaching Greer Crossing retrace your original route or follow the Ridge Trail back to McCormack Lake RA.

*M*cCormack Lake Recreation Area is located 13 miles south of Winona, on Mo. 19, turning right (west) and driving 2 miles on FS 3155. The day use parking lot on the opposite shore from the campground, is spacious and marked.

*A*nother nearby popular and charming spot is Falling Spring picnic area and mill site. A bluffside spring yields half a million gallons daily, cascading into a spring pool 50 feet below. Ruins of an old mill constructed in the 1920s still stand at the pool's edge and nearby is an original log cabin. The Falling Spring picnic area is located 3 miles north of the McCormack Lake RA turnoff on Mo. 19, 10 miles south of Winona and 2 miles east on FS 3170 and FS 3164 (turning left at the "Y" onto FS 3164 a few yards from Mo. 19 going east).

Area/Location/County:
Eleven Point-Doniphan/Winona/Oregon County

U.S.G.S. Map(s):
1:24,000 Greer

Trail(s) Distance:
one-half mile lake loop
7.5 mile linear trail round trip

Activities:
hiking, backpacking, nature study, fishing, canoeing, launch ramp, camping

Fee(s):
camping

NATURE WALK
58

TRAIL 59: *Ponds: An Overview*

Tupelo Gum Pond

*T*he karst topography of the Eleven Point District is an irregular region with sinks, underground streams and caves that is suggestive of a sponge or Swiss cheese. Sinks or sinkholes will occasionally clog with surface debris and fill with water, creating a pond, a special habitat in the Missouri Ozarks. Eight sinkhole ponds on the Eleven Point District are registered Missouri Natural Areas that are preserved and protected. Unique plants and animals exist in these wetlands, some rare and endangered. Most sinkhole ponds are fishless, thus they are important breeding habitat for amphibians. Trees that are normally found in the Mississippi River bottoms appear as botanical oddities, out of place, thriving in and around the ponds.

*O*nly half of the ponds have marked paths. Some are more scenic and remote than others. All eight ponds are owned and managed by the U.S. Forest Service. With the exception of Grassy Pond, brochures on

NATURE WALK
59

59. Ponds: Wetland Natural Areas (8)

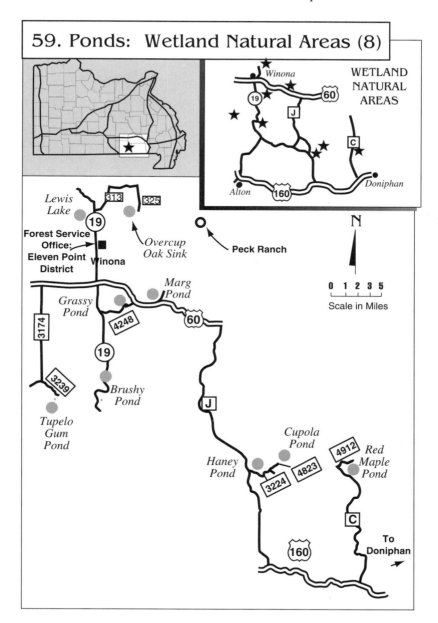

the ponds are available from the Eleven Point ranger offices. The uniqueness of the ponds and special natural beauty of the area are the main attraction to nature walkers. Camping, collecting of plants or animals and vehicular traffic is prohibited.

NATURE WALK
59

TRAIL 59A: *Ponds: Overcup Oak Sink Natural Area*

Overcup Oak Sink Natural Area is a shallow sinkhole wet depression where a grove of overcup oak (*Quercus lyrata*) thrive. The overcup, or swamp post oak, is a tree that is normally confined to swamps and bottomlands associated with water and laurel oaks, swamp bay, tupelo gum, water gum, water ash, river birch and cypress. Amazingly, the overcup oak present here are a persistent remnant of a former flora when the ancient seas retreated and the swamps appeared several thousand years ago. The one acre pure stand of overcup oak has a round crown of drooping branches and the acorn is nearly enclosed by the cap. This water pocket draws wildlife. Watch for summer tanager, black and white warblers and ruffed grouse.

From Winona, go north on Mo. 19 to Shannon CR 513, 1 mile past Lewis Lake, and turn right (east). Travel 1 mile on CR 513 to the junction with MDC 313 at Rocky Creek Conservation Area and turn right (east). Follow MDC 313 3.5 miles to MDC 325 and turn right (south). Go 1 mile on MDC 325 to the natural area boundary on the right (west) side of the road.

Area/Location/County:
Eleven Point-Doniphan/Winona/Shannon County

U.S.G.S. Map(s):
1:24,000 Winona

Trail(s) Distance:
one-quarter mile loop

Acreage:
5 acres

Activities:
nature walk, nature study

Fee(s):
none

NATURE WALK
59A

TRAIL 59B: **Ponds: Marg Pond Natural Area**

Three-Toed Box Turtles

The sinkhole pond marsh is located at ridgetop, an important oasis for wildlife, especially rare and endangered species. The pond marsh has an abundance of herbaceous aquatic plants and is an important breeding site for amphibians. Red maple and even sugar maple grow around Marg Pond.

Marg Pond Natural Area can be reached by driving 4.8 miles east on U.S. Hwy. 60 from the junction of U.S. Hwy. 60 and Mo. 19 at Winona, turning left (north) on Shannon CR 60A. Continue three-tenths of a mile on the gravel road to a roadside pullout and Marg Pond on the left (west) side of the road. A one-quarter mile white diamond foot trail circles the pond.

Area/Location/County:
Eleven Point-Doniphan/Winona/Shannon County

U.S.G.S. Map(s):
1:24,000 Low Wassie

Trail(s) Distance:
one-quarter mile user path

Acreage:
42 acres

Activities:
nature walk, nature study

Fee(s):
none

NATURE WALK
59B

TRAIL 59C: *Ponds: Grassy Pond Natural Area*

Grassy Pond

*G*rassy Pond is reached from the junction of Mo. 19 and U.S Hwy. 60 at Winona by driving east on U.S. Hwy. 60, 3.1 miles to Shannon CR 579 and turning right (south). Bear right (southwest) at the immediate road fork onto FS 4248 and proceed 1.1 mile and park alongside the forest road. Walk west along an old forest lane to the pond.

*T*he nearly circular pond sits in a depression sinkhole with open upland forest on the east and north knolls. A levee-like earthen bank follows the west and south rim where plenty of blackberry canes, rose briars and poison ivy thrives. There is an abundance of water lilies and buttonbush rings the pond's edge. A large dry sinkhole lies adjacent to the west.

Area/Location/County:
Eleven Point-Doniphan/Winona/Shannon County

U.S.G.S. Map(s):
1:24,000 Low Wassie

Trail(s) Distance:
one-quarter mile loop

Activities:
nature walk, nature study

Fee(s):
none

NATURE WALK
59C

TRAIL 59D: *Ponds: Tupelo Gum Pond Natural Area*

*O*ne of the most ancient of Ozark sinkholes is the remote five acre Tupelo Gum Pond. The outstanding natural feature is the pure narrow ring of water tupelo or swamp gum (*Nyssa aquatica*). Essentially southern U.S. in range, the rare tree relic is more likely found growing in the swamps and floodplains of southeast Missouri. The record size tupelo gum, measuring 67 feet tall, thrives in the wetland surrounded by a "sea" of oak and hickory forest. The open understory allows for easy walking around the pond margin. The only other known stand of tupelo gum in the Missouri Ozarks is at Cupola Pond.

*T*o reach Tupelo Gum Pond Natural Area, drive west from the junction of U.S. Hwy. 60 and Mo. 19 at Winona, 4.5 miles to Shannon CR 617 (also signed CR 610 and CR 625) and turn left (south). Continue south on the gravel road which becomes FS 3173, 8.2 miles to the Tupelo Gum Pond turnoff (signed) on the left (east) side of FS 3173 onto FS 3239. Proceed 2.5 miles southwest along the narrow forest road FS 3239 to the pond. The last mile may be difficult when rainwater has filled in the low spots. Go left (east) at the final fork and the pond sits at the base of the hill ridge.

A second highway approach from Winona is to drive south on Mo. 19, 11 miles and turn left (west) on FS 3174. Drive 6 miles west on FS 3174 and turn left (south) on FS 3173. Go 1.2 miles on FS 3173 and turn left (east) on FS 3239. Continue 2.5 miles to the pond.

Area/Location/County:
Eleven Point-Doniphan/Thomasville/Oregon County

U.S.G.S. Map(s):
1:24,000 Birch Tree SW

Trail(s) Distance:
one-quarter mile loop

Acreage:
32 acres

Activities:
nature walk, nature study

Fee(s):
none

NATURE WALK
59D

TRAIL 59E: *Ponds: Brushy Pond Natural Area*

Brushy Pond

Brushy Pond lives up to its place name. The ridgetop sinkhole pond is an outstanding example of a pond marsh with a pond shrub swamp surrounding it. The crater-deep pond (10 to 20 feet) is circled by open oak and hickory forest which allows for easy walking. The preserve lies adjacent to Mo. 19 and is easily accessed.

To reach Brushy Pond Natural Area, drive 11.4 miles south of Winona, from the junction of Mo. 19 and U.S. Hwy. 60 on Mo. 19. The natural area is half a mile south of FS 3174 and 1.5 miles north of McCormack Lake Recreation Area turnoff. The preserve is on the left (east) side of Mo. 19 where FS 4220 allows vehicles to pull in and park.

Area/Location/County:
Eleven Point-Doniphan/Greer/Oregon County

U.S.G.S. Map(s):
1:24,000 Greer

Trail(s) Distance:
one-quarter mile loop

Acreage:
20 acres

Activities:
nature walk, nature study

Fee(s):
none

NATURE WALK
59E

TRAIL 59F: *Ponds: Haney Pond Natural Area*

*H*aney Pond is a rare forest acid seep. The forested sink supports a stand of sweet gum trees (*Liquidambar styraciflua*), a tree that is native to the lowlands of Bootheel Missouri. This member of the witch hazel family has star-shaped, maple-like fragrant leaves and is often planted as a landscaping tree. Tussocks of mosses and royal ferns carpet the sinkhole floor. A white diamond-blazed trail leads downhill from the forest road turnaround parking area to and around the pond buffer.

*F*rom Doniphan, drive west on U.S. Hwy. 160 to Hwy. J and turn right (north). Go north on Hwy. J about 8 miles (passing Camp Five Pond, Irish Wilderness trailhead) to FS 3224 and turn right (east). Travel half a mile on FS 3224 to the Old Bellevue Trail pullout and park on the left (north) side of the gravel road. The trail may be overgrown, but look for the white diamond blazes. Cupola Pond Natural Area is about 2 miles northeast from Haney Pond Natural Area.

Area/Location/County:
Eleven Point-Doniphan/Wilderness/Oregon County

U.S.G.S. Map(s):
1:24,000 Handy

Trail(s) Distance:
approximately half a mile

Acreage:
68 acres

Activities:
nature walk, nature study

Fee(s):
none

NATURE WALK
59F

TRAIL 59G: *Ponds: Cupola Pond Natural Area*

Cupola Pond

*C*upola Pond is one of the most scenic of the sinkhole ponds in the Eleven Point District. The water tupelo surrounding the pond contrasts sharply with the upland oak and hickory forest, reminding one of an oasis in a desert. The ancient sinkhole pond is at least 20,000 years old. The only other known stand of water-loving tupelo in the Missouri Ozarks is at Tupelo Gum Pond Natural Area. A short white diamond-blazed trail leads down from the road's end parking area to the pond's edge. The pond is easy to walk around at a slow pace.

*F*rom Doniphan, go west on U.S. 160 to Hwy. J and turn right (north). Continue on Hwy. J north 8 miles to FS 3224 and turn right (east). Travel 1 mile on FS 3224 (past Haney Pond at Bellevue Trail) to FS 4822 and turn left (north). Continue on FS 4822 about a mile to the dead end and park at the turnaround. The trail heads up at the northwest corner of the parking area.

Area/Location/County:
Eleven Point-Doniphan/Handy/Ripley County

U.S.G.S. Map(s):
1:24,000 Handy

Trail(s) Distance:
one-quarter mile

Acreage:
160 acres

Activities:
nature walk, nature study

Fee(s):
none

NATURE WALK
59G

TRAIL 59H: *Ponds: Red Maple Pond Natural Area*

Red Maple Pond

*T*he short white diamond-blazed trail leads down to Red Maple Pond from the forest ridge. The shallow pond holds water for most of the year and supports a stand of red maple (*Acer rubrum*). At the raised base of the trees are hummocks or "little islands" that provide homes for a variety of plants including wild azaleas. The point-to-point trail requires retracing your steps.

*F*rom Doniphan, take U.S. Hwy. 160 west 20 miles to Hwy. C and turn right (north). Go north on Hwy. C, 10.3 miles to FS 4912 and turn right (east) at the marked sign for Red Maple Pond. Continue a short distance to the parking area and trailhead at the ridgetop.

Area/Location/County:
Eleven Point-Doniphan/Doniphan/Ripley County

U.S.G.S. Map(s):
1:24,000 Grandin

Trail(s) Distance:
six-tenths of a mile

Acreage:
106 acres

Activities:
nature walk, nature study

Fee(s):
none

NATURE WALK
59H

TRAIL 60: *Grand Gulf State Park*

*G*rand Gulf is a premier geological example of an Ozark karst valley. The 159 acre National Natural Landmark features a 450 million-year-old collapsed cave system (collapsed 10,000 years ago) that has left a spectacular three-quarter mile, 130-foot-deep canyon, sometimes referred to as "Missouri's Little Grand Canyon." Bussell Branch flows through the Grand Gulf and after heavy rains, the deep chasm gulf may fill and remain a temporary "lake." Much of the water flows 9 miles southeast to reappear at Mammoth Spring State Park, just across the state line in Arkansas.

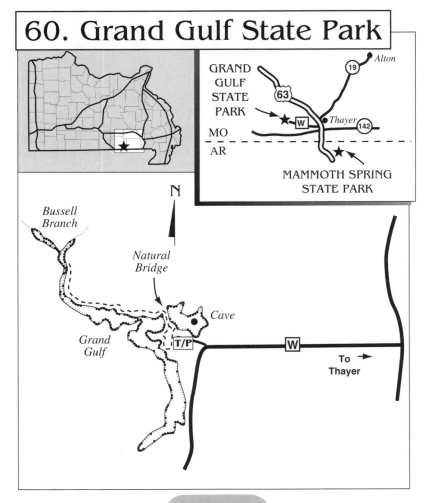

60. Grand Gulf State Park

GRAND
GULF
STATE
PARK

MO

AR

19 Alton

63

W Thayer 142

MAMMOTH SPRING
STATE PARK

N

Bussell
Branch

Natural
Bridge

Cave

Grand
Gulf

T/P

W

To →
Thayer

NATURE WALK
60

*T*he day-use state park makes a great picnic and hike experience. The parking lot trailhead overlook features interpretive geological displays and property maps. A quarter mile loop trail follows the overlook rim with its grand views of the abyss. The three-quarters of a mile (round trip) rimtop trail crosses over a 200-foot expanse of natural bridge (uncollapsed cavern roof) to follow the rim northwest to a dead end at a private property fence. Retrace your steps back to the parking area. Unmarked user paths descend to the Gulf at several points, however entry into the Gulf is discouraged due to the rugged terrain and difficult access. New designated trails are being planned to preserve the landmark.

*G*rand Gulf State Park is located 6 miles west of Thayer and U.S. Hwy. 63 on Hwy. W. Follow Hwy. W to the dead end at the state park.

*M*ammoth Spring State Park, in which is Arkansas' largest spring, is situated across the state line at Mammoth Spring, Arkansas, just south of Thayer on Hwy. 63. Nine million gallons of water spring forth hourly. There is an interpretive trail that circles the spring and its lake. There is also a native fish aquarium at the adjoining National Wildlife Service fish hatchery, plus a museum, mill, playgrounds and playfields.

Area/Location/County:
Eleven Point-Doniphan/Thayer/Oregon County

U.S.G.S. Map(s):
1:24,000 Koshkonong

Trail(s) Distance:
approximately 1 mile

Acreage:
322 acres

Activities:
nature walk, nature study, geology site, picnicking

Fee(s):
none

NATURE WALK
60

Ozark Trail: An Overview

*T*he Ozark Trail is the premier centerpiece of Missouri's hiking trails. Since 1977, public and private agencies, landowners and individuals have been collaborating and constructing a long distance recreational trail that will traverse the Missouri Ozarks from St. Louis southwest to Norfork Lake and the Arkansas state line. Since its conception, the Ozark Trail has about 300 constructed miles of a proposed 500 miles in Missouri. The State of Arkansas is also committed to developing a connecting interstate trail through the Ozark Mountains of northwest Arkansas that will terminate near Fort Smith on the Oklahoma border. When completed, the bi-state, non-motorized path will total nearly 700 miles through the only major highlands in the Central United States between the Rockies and the Appalachian Mountains.

*C*urrently hikers can traverse 12 sections of the Missouri Ozark Trail which runs through mostly state and federal lands. Several sections are interconnecting but long gaps remain. The Courtois and Karkaghne Sections are nearing completion but it may be years before the Meramec Section will be tied in. Some sections permit horses and mountain bikes and others sections are hiking only. Backpackers will find numerous trailside campsites.

*D*ue to the linear point-to-point layout of the trail, car shuttle is recommended, however there are some interconnecting loops and more are planned. Experienced hikers may walk 20 to 25 miles a day but a more leisurely pace is 8 to 12 miles daily. Know your limitations and act accordingly and always be prepared. The trail is blazed by the green and white Ozark Trail symbol with the letters "O" and "T" intertwined. The Ozark Trail is divided into two regional divisions: West Main Trail (eight sections) and the Eastern Loop (four sections).

*T*he public is invited to attend the bi-annual meetings of the Ozark Trail Council. For further information, please contact the Missouri Department of Natural Resources, Ozark Trail Council, at P. O. Box 176, Jefferson City, MO 65102; phone (573) 751-2479.

The Ozark Trail: 61-72 Overview

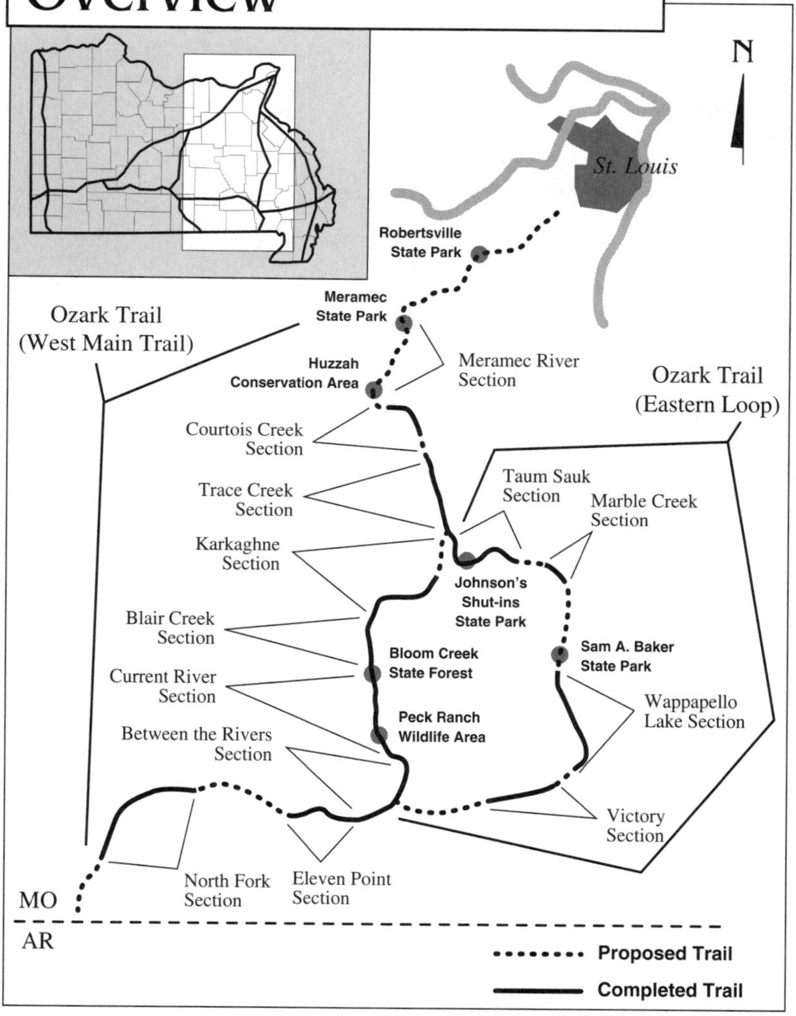

N

St. Louis

Robertsville State Park

Ozark Trail (West Main Trail)

Meramec State Park

Huzzah Conservation Area

Meramec River Section

Ozark Trail (Eastern Loop)

Courtois Creek Section

Trace Creek Section

Taum Sauk Section

Marble Creek Section

Karkaghne Section

Johnson's Shut-ins State Park

Blair Creek Section

Bloom Creek State Forest

Sam A. Baker State Park

Current River Section

Peck Ranch Wildlife Area

Wappapello Lake Section

Between the Rivers Section

Victory Section

MO

AR

North Fork Section

Eleven Point Section

• • • • • • • **Proposed Trail**

————— **Completed Trail**

TRAIL 61: *East Loop Ozark Trail: Taum Sauk Section*

Devil's Toll Gate

*T*he 33 mile Taum Sauk Section is right at the top for St. Francois Mountain adventure. There are six trailheads and parking access points and this Ozark Trail section is open to hiking only. Several day options are available. The moderate to rugged trail crosses U.S. Forest Service (USFS), Department of Natural Resources (DNR), and Missouri Department of Conservation (MDC) lands. Highlights of the trail section include Bell Mountain, Goggins Mountain, Johnson's Shut-Ins, Proffit Mountain, the Upper Reservoir, Mina Sauk Falls, Taum Sauk Mountain and Russell Mountain. Be advised that flash flooding may occur on the Padford Branch, East Fork Black River and Taum Sauk Creek. Backcountry camping is allowed along most sections of the Ozark Trail, however, at Johnson's Shut-Ins State Park, trail camping is prohibited 2 miles east and west of the main parking area. Special rules apply in state parks. Large groups must camp at the developed state park camping sites of Johnson's Shut-Ins and Taum Sauk Mountain.

NATURE WALK
61

Trail Summary:

*W*est terminus Ottery Creek trailhead is a U.S. Forest Service parking lot at the west base of Bell Mountain Wilderness on Hwy. A, 3 miles north of the junction of Mo. 49 and Hwy. A at Edgehill, in Iron County, or half a mile south of the Mo. 32 and Hwy. A junction. The Taum Sauk Section begins 100 feet north of the parking lot across Hwy. A. The Ottery Creek trailhead is also the trail junction of the Trace Creek Section north and the Karkaghne Section south (not yet open).

*I*n brief, the Ozark Trail climbs and follows the seepy open glade ridgeside of Bell Mountain south, descending into the Padfield Branch hollow (5.9 miles), then climbs and follows the west rim of Goggins Mountain (elev. 1,484 ft.), descending into Walker Branch, continuing east to cross Hwy. N (12.7 miles) and on to Johnson's Shut-Ins overlook (15 miles).

*J*ohnson's Shut-Ins State Park trailhead is located about 8 miles west and north of Lesterville on Hwy. N. The park entrance is about 12.5 miles southwest of Mo. 21 near Elephant Rocks State Park at Graniteville.

*F*rom the state park trailhead at the daytime picnic and parking area, the Ozark Trail crosses a low water concrete foot bridge over the East Fork Black River and follows the east bank to a tributary and turns east and heads to Proffit Mountain. At 17.6 miles, 2.6 miles east of Johnson's Shut-Ins, there is a trail junction with a three-quarter mile spur to the upper reservoir of Union Electric's Taum Sauk Mountain Hydroelectric Plant. The visible upper reservoir appears similar to a flat-topped southwestern mesa on the horizon.

*T*he Union Electric hydroelectric plant trailhead is reached by driving 8 miles north on Hwy. U from the junction of Mo. 49 and Hwy. U, 1 mile east of Lesterville. From the junction of Hwy. U and Hwy. AA, turn west and continue the drive to the hydroelectric plant entrance and nature center, and on to the upper reservoir trailhead and parking area. The three-quarter mile-long spur trail is signed and leads to the Ozark Trail.

*F*rom Proffit Mountain (elev. 1,656 ft.), the Ozark Trail continues east following the ridgetop (MDC and DNR lands) to gradually descend to Mossy Creek Hollow and Taum Sauk Creek (24.5 miles). The Ozark Trail follows the creek hollow northeast to and through the Devil's Toll Gate and up along Mina Sauk Falls (the highest waterfall in Missouri), to the top of 1,772-foot-high Taum Sauk Mountain and State Park (26.5 miles). Taum Sauk Mountain State Park trailhead can be reached by traveling south of Ironton on Mo. 21/49 to Hwy. CC and turning right (west). Travel about 3 miles on Hwy. CC to the park entrance and another mile to the trailhead parking area. The Ozark Trail follows a portion of the Mina Sauk Falls Trail loop.

NATURE WALK
61

*A*t Mina Sauk Falls, the Ozark Trail joins with the Mina Sauk Falls Trail loop and bears right, ascending the mountain. The Ozark Trail leaves the Mina Sauk Falls loop after 1 mile (27.5 miles) and switches back down Taum Sauk Mountain's rocky rhyolite surface to the headwater hollow of Claybaugh Creek. Crossing the small stream, the trail goes upridge to Russell Mountain to a trail junction, where a four-tenths of a mile trail access spur leads north to the Hwy. CC pullout where parking is available for two or three vehicles.

*T*he Historic BSA Taum Sauk Trail crosses Hwy. CC a few hundred yards west. The white blazed trail goes north to Shepherd Mountain and Lake and concludes at Ft. Davidson State Historic Site. Information about the Boy Scout trail is available at Taum Sauk Mountain State Park and Ft. Davidson State Historic Site.

*T*he final leg of the Taum Sauk Section of the Ozark Trail (3.2 miles) descends Russell Mountain and drops south through Ketcherside Mountain Conservation Area to the east terminus (33 miles) at Claybaugh Creek trailhead parking area on Mo. 21/72, less than half a mile north of Royal Gorge and south of Hwy. CC. Further trail construction east to Crane Lake and Marble Creek is underway.

Area:
Ozark Trail-Eastern Loop

U.S.G.S. Map(s):
1:24,000 Johnson Mountain, Edgehill, Johnson's Shut-Ins, Ironton

Trail(s) Distance:
approximately 33 mile total

Trailhead(s):
west terminus, Ottery Creek, Hwy. A, Bell Mountain Wilderness
Johnson's Shut-Ins State Park
Upper Reservoir, Taum Sauk Hydroelectric Plant
Taum Sauk Mountain State Park
Russell Mountain, Hwy. CC
east terminus, Hwy. 21 near Royal Gorge

Activities:
hiking only, backpacking, nature study, seasonal hunting

Fee(s):
developed camping available at Johnson's Shut-Ins and Taum Sauk state parks

NATURE WALK
61

61. East Loop Ozark Trail: Taum Sauk Section

Highest point in Missouri– 1,772'

32
21
A
N
Ironton
49
CC
OZARK TRAIL: TAUM SAUK SECTION
49

N

0 .5 1
Scale in Miles

72 21 T/P **Claybaugh Creek Trailhead**
CC
Taum Sauk Mtn. State Park
1,772'
T/P

Devil's Toll Gate

Mina Sauk Falls

PROFFIT MOUNTAIN

Upper Reservoir Taum Sauk Lake

N
T/P **Johnson's Shut-Ins State Park**

Bell Mtn. Wilderness
GOGGINS MOUNTAIN

T/P
A
49

NATURE WALK
61

TRAIL 62: *East Loop Ozark Trail: Marble Creek Section*

Rocky Upland Glades

*T*ying together two U.S. Forest Service recreation areas, the 8 mile-long Marble Creek Section of the Ozark Trail is a point-to-point trail with an optional 5 mile loop around Crane Lake. The moderately difficult hollow to ridgetop trail is also open to equestrians and all-terrain bicycles. The trail surface is fairly smooth tread and mostly single track with numerous gradual climbs and stream crossings (elev. 680-1,100 ft.).

*O*utstanding features include the glades and shut-ins at Crane Pond Creek and Lake, Reader Hollow, rocky upland glades at the trail's mid point (4 miles) and Marble Creek Shut-Ins. An experienced hiker may cover the hike both ways in one day (16 miles) but a car shuttle is usually preferred. The trail is marked with OT blazes and white diamonds. In the future, the completed 21 mile Marble Creek Section will tie in with the Taum Sauk Section at Mo. 21 and the MDC Claybaugh Creek access at Ketcherside Mountain Conservation Area. Future plans also call for construction on the trail to move east and south to and along the St. Francis River.

Trail Summary:

*M*arble Creek Recreation Area trailhead is easily accessed on Hwy. E. From Ironton, drive 2 miles south on Mo. 21 and turn east on Hwy. E.

NATURE WALK
62

Continue 12 miles to Marble Creek Recreation Area (RA) entrance to the left (north) side of the highway. From Fredericktown, at the junction of Hwy. E and U.S. Hwy. 67, drive 18 miles west on Hwy. E to Marble Creek RA on the right (north) side of the highway. The parking area is adjacent to the entrance. The trail begins on the south side of Hwy. E across from the recreational area entrance.

*C*rane Lake Recreation Area trailhead is reached by driving about 4 miles west of Marble Creek RA on Hwy. E to an Iron County gravel road and turning left (west). Go 2.5 miles to a four-way stop junction and turn left (south). Proceed 2 miles south to Crane Lake picnic area parking lot and the trailhead.

*I*n brief, from the Marble Creek RA parking trailhead at the entrance, walk south across Hwy. E and head uphill 200 feet to the ridgetop (elev. 900 ft.) and follow the blazed path southwest, alternating between ridgetop, hollows, cedar glades, forest roads, wildlife ponds, clear cuts and draws to eventually descend to Reader Hollow. The Ozark Trail joins with the South and North Loops of the Crane Pond Creek and Lake trail; following the north trail segment to the glades, shut-ins, dam and spillway site and then along the north shore coves to Crane Lake parking area.

*F*or those who have more time and stamina, follow the double loop trail around Crane Lake and along Crane Pond Creek to loop back with the Ozark Trail at the farm lane. The Ozark Trail will eventually lead northwest from Crane Pond Lake to join Claybaugh Creek access on Mo. 21/49, Ketcherside Mountain Conservation Area and southeast to the St. Francis River.

Area:
Ozark Trail-Eastern Loop

U.S.G.S. Map(s):
1:24,000 Des Arc NE

Trail(s) Distance:
8 miles one way

Trailhead(s):
Marble Creek entrance, Hwy. E, east terminus
Crane Lake picnic area parking, west terminus

Activities:
hiking, backpacking, picnicking, fishing, canoeing, seasonal camping at Marble Creek

Fee(s):
developed seasonal camping at Marble Creek

NATURE WALK
62

62. East Loop Ozark Trail: Marble Creek Section

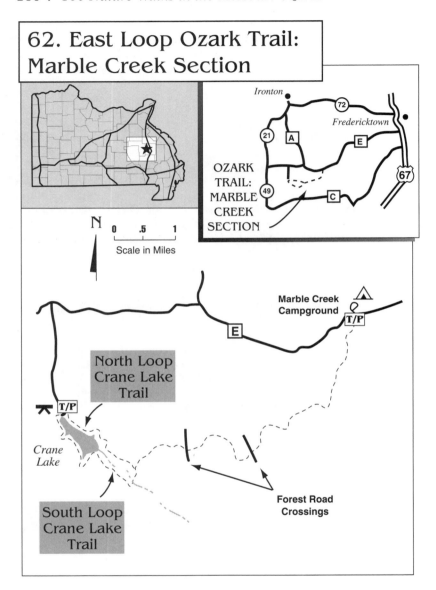

Ironton

Fredericktown

72

21

A

E

67

OZARK
TRAIL:
MARBLE
CREEK
SECTION

49

C

N

0   .5   1

Scale in Miles

Marble Creek
Campground

T/P

E

North Loop
Crane Lake
Trail

T/P

*Crane
Lake*

Forest Road
Crossings

South Loop
Crane Lake
Trail

NATURE WALK
62

TRAIL 63: *East Loop Ozark Trail:*
Wappapello Lake Section

River Otter

Summarizing, the Wappapello Lake Section follows the west bank or shore of the St. Francis River and Lake Wappapello floodplain from the south edge of Sam A. Baker State Park south to Hendrickson, and Hwy. 0, north of the Black River and west of U.S. Hwy. 67. (The Mo. 172 trailhead south to Hendrickson is considered Victory Trail but is placed here for access convenience). The 28 mile trail section crosses Army Corps of Engineers and U.S. Forest Service lands enroute through Wayne and Butler counties. Riparian forest along creek bottoms, old abandoned fields, forested bluffs and ridges, rock formations, ravines and hollows are some of the scenes along the Wappapello Section.

Some trail highlights include Sam A. Baker State Park, St. Francis River, Lake Wappapello, Logan Creek, Rings Creek, Joe Bill Bluff Hole, Lake Creek, Browns Hollow, Historic Greenville, Fox Den Mine, Otter Creek West Fork, Hockenberry Hollow and Caldwell Creek. The easy to moderately difficult trail has few elevation challenges but there are several stream crossings and places for wet feet. There are also a

NATURE WALK
63

number of road crossings including Mo. 34, Hwy. FF, U.S. Hwy. 67 and Mo. 172. Numerous trailhead parking points allow for easy access, hiking and primitive camping. The Wappapello Lake Section is also open to equestrians and all terrain bicycles. Hunting is permitted 500 feet from parking areas and the trail.

Trail Summary:

*S*am A. Baker State Park is located 3 miles north of Patterson, on Mo. 143 in Wayne County. The Wappapello Lake Section north terminus is situated at the south park entrance and is signed. A mini parking lot allows for five or six vehicles. The level floodplain corridor path follows the west bank of the St. Francis River south 4.2 miles to Mo. 34 and crosses the highway. Exercise caution crossing the sometimes busy highway.

*M*o. 34, St. Francis River bridge trailhead parking is located on the east bank and road access from Mo. 34 is on the south side of the highway. The Ozark Trail continues south along the west bank of the St. Francis River and comes to a road where the trail turns left, then continues through the woods to Clarks Creek where it crosses and proceeds south through woodland for 3 miles to the Joe Bluff access at PA 53.

*C*ontinue south from Joe Bill Bluff access through fields, woods and a natural wetlands area called Holmes Bottoms for about 4 miles to the Horhouse access at PA 55.

*F*rom the Horhouse access at PA 55 proceed south for 3.6 miles through woods and fields and one creek crossing to Carlton Place at PA 58 on Mo. Hwy. FF.

*F*rom Carlton Place, the Ozark Trail follows a road for about a half mile to arrive at open fields and into forest for about a mile to climb a steep hill and onto Hwy. FF. Cross the highway and continue through field and forest to U.S. Hwy. 67 and the Pine Tree access, PA 60.

*F*rom Pine Tree access, PA 60, a mile south of the Greenville bridge on Hwy. 67 at the Unknown Soldiers grave, continue south through U.S. Corps and U.S. Forest Service lands through a 3.7 mile section of native pines, natural springs and in general, beautiful scenery, to arrive at Hwy. F.

*F*rom Hwy. F access and Caldwell Creek the trail continues south through hilly forest for 6 miles to Wet Fork access and Fox Den. There is one road crossing.

*F*rom Wet Fork and Fox Den to PA 68 are wetlands, forest, Otter Creek and a pipeline. You will come out at PA 68 at CR 547, approximately 3.5 miles.

NATURE WALK
63

*F*rom PA 68 on CR 547 the Ozark Trail to Mo. 172 is about 3 miles of open fields, forest and a pipeline crossing. Mo. 172 trailhead access is located about 1.5 miles east of U.S. Hwy. 67 on the north side of the road.

*F*rom Mo. 172 south to Hendrickson is actually considered part of the Victory Section of the Ozark Trail but is included here since the trail runs through but disconnects south and west of Hendrickson. The Ozark Trail continues south from Mo. 172 through U.S. Forest Service lands. The trail goes up and down, crossing FS 3704, parallel to FS 3704, and FS 3672, entering Butler County. The Ozark Trail descends into Hockenberry Hollow and upridge to a forest road, less than a quarter mile from Hwy. O and Hendrickson, about 2 miles south of U.S. Hwy. 67. Trailhead parking is being developed.

Area:
Ozark Trail-Eastern Loop

U.S.G.S. Map(s):
1:24,000 Patterson, Greenville, Greenville SW, Hendrickson

Trail(s) Distance:
approximately 28 miles

Trailhead(s):
major trailhead access points includes north terminus, south edge of Sam A. Baker State Park
Mo. 34 - St. Francis River bridge trailhead parking
U.S. Hwy. 67 - Pine Tree Access
Mo. 172 access
south terminus Hwy. O at Hendrickson

Activities:
hiking, backpacking, nature study, fishing, seasonal hunting, equestrians, all-terrain bicycles

Fee(s):
developed camping at Sam A. Baker State Park, Wappapello Lake State Park and Wappapello Lake Corps

63. East Loop Ozark Trail: Wappapello Lake Section

OZARK TRAIL: WAPPAPELLO LAKE SECTION

143

34

● *Greenville*

A

49

172

67 O

● *Poplar Bluff*

SAM A. BAKER STATE PARK

Ozark Trailhead T/P

Hwy 34 Rec. Area

143

T/P 34

T/P

● Silva

67

Hixon Cemetery T/P

Joe Bill Bluff

380

N

FF T/P Horhouse

● Greenville

Carlton Place T/P

Pine Tree T/P

A T/P

F

543

N. Caldwell Creek T/P

546

Wappapello Lake

547 T/P

Wet Fork

172

T/P

T/P Hendrickson Trailhead

Hendrickson ● O

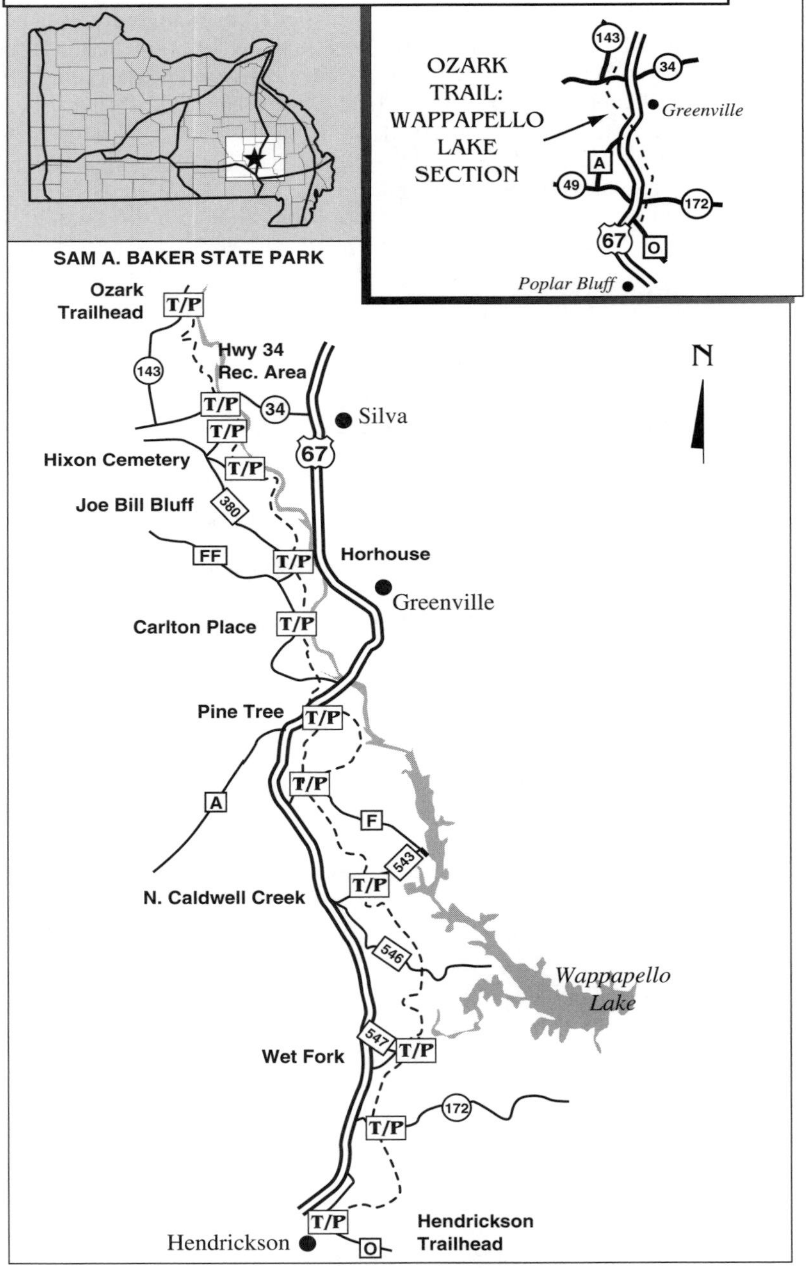

NATURE WALK
63

TRAIL 64: *East Loop Ozark Trail: Victory Section*

Azalea Flower in Early May

*P*rior to its Ozark Trail designation, the Victory Section was designed and listed as the Victory Horse Trail. The trail continues to be popular with equestrians and is also open to mountain bikes. For the sake of geographic convenience, the Victory Trail segment from Mo. 172 south to Hendrickson and Hwy. O, is listed with the Wappapello Section since the trail is connected. No trail has yet been constructed connecting Hendrickson, and Wrangler Trailhead at FS 3110. The trail follows single track and old wood roads entirely within the Poplar Bluff District of the Mark Twain National Forest (Butler, Wayne and Carter counties). There are numerous climbs and declines enroute and several road crossings including Hwy. A and Hwy. V in the west segment. Hikers will find the 6 mile Victory School loop convenient with no backtracking or car shuttle necessary. The Victory Section is not the most scenic Ozark Trail section. There are six trailhead and parking access points.

Trail Summary:

*T*he Victory School trailhead, south terminus, is located 8 miles northwest of Poplar Bluff. Go north on U.S. Hwy. 67 to the junction with U.S. Hwy. 60 and turn left (west). Follow U.S. Hwy. 60 3 miles to Butler CR 410 and turn right (north). Continue 1 mile on CR 410 to FS 3117 and turn right (north). Proceed about 300 feet to the trailhead parking adjacent to FS 3117 near the road fork.

*T*he 6 mile loop begins and ends at the Victory School trailhead. The loop follows, parallels, and crosses several forest service roads in addition to forest single track trails. Turn east at the powerline swath. The trail

NATURE WALK
64

64. East Loop Ozark Trail: Victory Section

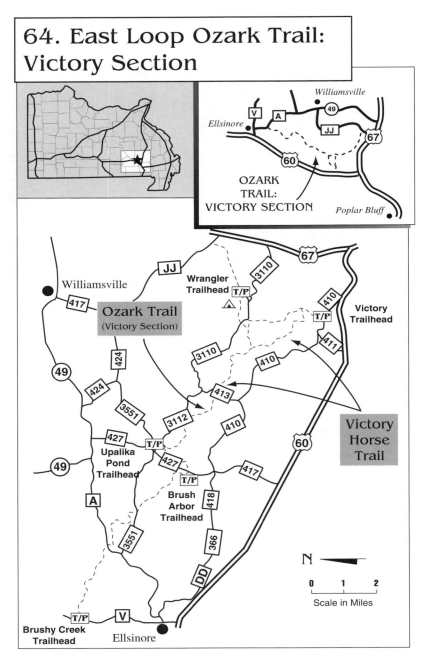

nearly skirts the Wrangler trailhead and camp at FS 3110, about 3 miles from U.S. Hwy. 67 via Butler CR 402 and FS 3140, 3 miles north of the junction of U.S. Hwy. 67 and U.S. Hwy. 60. The Victory School

NATURE WALK
64

trail loop curves south along old woods roads to return to the trailhead at FS 3117.

*W*alton Chapel trailhead and Upalika Pond trailhead are reached by driving about 12 miles west on U.S. Hwy. 60 from the junction of U.S. Hwy. 67 and U.S. Hwy. 60, turning right (north) on Butler CR 415. Follow Butler CR 415 about 1.5 miles and turn left north on Butler CR 417. Continue north on Butler CR 417, crossing Cane Creek, and going about one third mile to Walton Chapel trailhead at the ford on the left (west) side of the county road.

*T*o reach Upalika Pond trailhead continue north on Butler CR 417 and cross the Butler-Wayne county line (the road now becomes Wayne CR 427). Continue about a mile north from the county line to FS 3112 and turn right (east). Upalika Pond, near mid-point of the Victory Section is about a quarter mile east on FS 3112 on the left (north) side of the road and the pond camp area. A trail spur from Upalika Pond goes south about a quarter mile to connect the Victory trail section. Further west at the Hwy. A trail and road crossing in Carter County near Tick Seed Hollow and Orchard Switch is another possible trailhead.

*T*he west terminus is at Brushy Creek trailhead on Hwy. V, 3 miles north of Ellsinore, on the left (west) side of the highway. Sometime "down the trail," the Ozark Trail Council plans to extend the Eastern Loop of the Ozark Trail west to join the Between the River Section and Current River Section of the West Main Ozark Trail near Van Buren.

Area:
Ozark Trail-Eastern Loop

U.S.G.S. Map(s):
1:24,000 Hendrickson, Stringtown, Williamsville, Ellsinore

Trail(s) Distance:
24 miles constructed (30 miles when complete)

Trailhead(s):
Victory School, south terminus, U.S. Hwy. 60 to FS 3117
Wrangler Camp, east terminus, U.S. 67 to FS 3110
Upalika Pond, mid point, Wayne CR 427 to FS 3112
Walton Pond, Butler CR 417
Brushy Creek, Hwy. V, north of Ellsinore

Activities:
hiking, backpacking, nature study, seasonal hunting, equestrians, all-terrain bicycling

Fee(s):
developed camping at Lake Wappapello State Park, Wappapello Lake, Markham Spring RA, Pinewoods RA

NATURE WALK
64

TRAIL 65: *West Main Loop Ozark Trail:*
Courtois Creek Section

"The Keyhole" at Courtois Creek, Huzzah Conservation Area

NATURE WALK
65

*W*hen completed, the 30 mile Courtois (locally pronounced Coat-away) Creek Section of the Ozark Trail, will begin and end at the Huzzah Conservation Area, and run south and east uninterrupted to a south terminus at Hazel Creek campground. Currently there are two major gaps in the Courtois Section. One is between the south boundary of Huzzah CA to the northwest segment of the Berryman Trail (near the Butts area), and from the Berryman Trail south about 5 miles to Hazel Creek campground (now shown as following active roads).

*T*he following three areas are trailhead access points:

*T*he north terminus of the Ozark Main Trail is at Huzzah Conservation Area where 4.5 miles of hiking only pathway has been constructed of the 8.5 miles planned within the conservation area. The trail access is at the Courtois Creek campground at the turnaround by the stream. The Ozark Trail goes north and south at this mid-point trailhead.

*W*alking north, the Ozark Trail follows the scenic bluffside along Courtois Creek about two-tenths of a mile, then goes uphill to an old forest road, following it north about a mile before turning off left (west). Continue another mile, leading through the old Scotia iron furnace area, and ending at the main property gravel access road. Retrace your steps back on this point-to-point trail segment.

A two mile segment continues south from the Courtois Creek campground turnaround trailhead. Cross Courtois Creek from the southeast edge of the campground (Courtois Creek can be too high to cross at times) and follow the trail downstream to the bluff base and go uphill. Follow the ridgetop south to the dead end at the south property at the Narrows. The U.S. Forest Service is planning on connecting from the south. Eventually, an additional 4 miles of Ozark Trail will be constructed north to connect the Meramec Section in Huzzah Conservation Area.

*H*uzzah Conservation Area is accessed from I-44, exit Hwy. H south at Leasburg, in Crawford County. Drive south on Hwy. H to Onondaga Cave State Park and cross the Meramec River, continuing on the gravel road into Huzzah CA. Continue south on the gravel road about 3 miles to MDC 24 and turn left, and go three-tenths of a mile to the campground turnaround at Courtois Creek.

*T*o the south, the next completed segment of the Courtois Creek Section of the Ozark Trail follows a 10 mile west segment of the Berryman Trail. It extends from the Harmon Spring trail camp south and east to the Berryman trailhead and campground. The deeply grooved single track is also open to equestrians and mountain bicyclists. The Ozark Trail will continue north and west from the Berryman Trail, paralleling FS 2265, on to Courtois Creek then north to finally connect at the Narrows of Huzzah CA.

NATURE WALK
65

*T*o reach the Berryman trailhead from Potosi, take Mo. 8 west for about 16 miles to FS 2266, 1 mile east of Berryman. Turn right (north) on FS 2266, and drive 1 mile to the marked trailhead and campground. The trailhead is at the west end of the parking area.

*F*arther south, the south terminus of the Courtois Creek Section begins and ends at Hazel Creek campground and goes north to the Berryman Trail along foot trails and several miles of roadway. From the Berryman trailhead, follow FS 2266 1 mile south to Mo. 8 and turn east. Go four-tenths of a mile on Mo. 8 east to FS 2266 and turn right (south). Follow FS 2266 south 3.5 miles to FS 2247 and go southeast along a forest trail. The foot path descends the ridge from FS 2247 into Boiling Springs Hollow and up and down, into Snapps Branch, and upridge to FS 2540. Cross FS 2540, go downridge to cross Hwy. Z and FS 2392, the entry road to Hazel Creek campground.

*T*o reach Hazel Creek camp and trailhead from Potosi, go southwest on Hwy. P about 14 miles to Hwy. C and turn right (west). Follow Hwy. C about 5 miles to Hwy. Z and turn right (north). Continue on Hwy. Z about 3 miles to the entry road, FS 2392, 1 gravel mile beyond the paved road.

*P*rojected completion of the Courtois Creek Section of the Ozark Trail will be two years, if funding is available.

Area:
Ozark Trail-West Main Trail

U.S.G.S. Map(s):
1:24,000 Huzzah, Courtois, Berryman

Trail(s) Distance:
roughly 16 miles completed (30 miles upon completion)

Trailhead(s):
Huzzah Conservation Area campground, north terminus
Berryman Trailhead
Hazel Creek campground, south terminus

Activities:
hiking, backpacking, nature study, developed camping,
equestrian use, mountain biking

Fee(s):
developed camping at Berryman and Hazel Creek campgrounds

NATURE WALK
65

65. West Main Ozark Trail: Courtois Creek Section

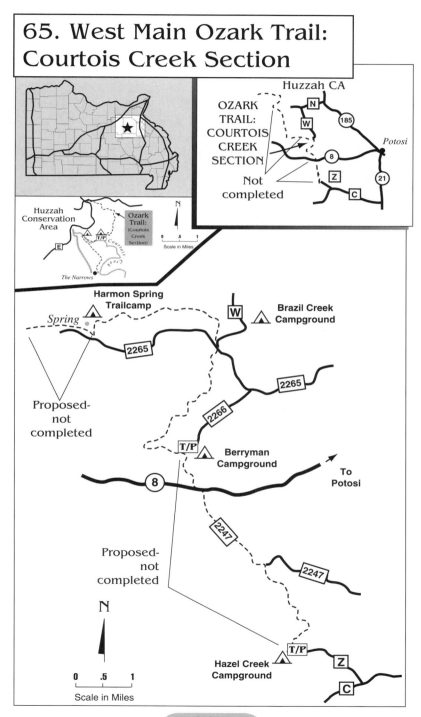

NATURE WALK
65

TRAIL 66: *West Main Ozark Trail: Trace Creek Section*

Bloodroot Awakens From Winter

*T*he 24 miles of the Trace Creek Section of the Ozark Trail lies entirely within U.S. Forest Service lands of the Mark Twain National Forest, Washington and Iron counties (elev. 900-1,350 ft.). The north terminus begins and ends at Hazel Creek campground and the south terminus ends and begins at Ottery Creek trailhead at the west base of Bell Mountain Wilderness. Here the Trace Creek Section junctions with the Eastern Loop, Taum Sauk Section and the incomplete south-bound Karkaghne Section, West Main Trail. The Trace Creek section is open to mountain bikes and equestrians.

*F*rom the Hazel Creek campground, the Ozark Trail follows Hazel Creek valley, crossing Town Branch and a powerline swath, continuing along Hazel Creek, crossing and recrossing, then heading upridge. The trail continues south, descending into Piney Branch, then ascending to cross Hwy. C north of Delbridge. Between Hwy. C and Hwy. DD there are four climbs and declines, two forest road crossings and a segment of trail along the headwaters of Trace Creek. From Hwy. DD (Council

NATURE WALK
66

Bluff Lake RA, three-quarters of a mile north), the Ozark Trail continues south to Mo. 32. This segment has three major ridgetop climbs and stream bottom declines into and along Tellick Branch and Big River Branch that flow to Council Bluff Lake. As yet, no connecting trail runs from Council Bluff Lake to the Ozark Trail.

*F*rom Mo. 32 south to Ottery Creek trailhead at Hwy. A, there are four climbs and declines, two forest road crossings, and three small stream branch crossings. Approximately 2.5 miles from Ottery Creek in Peter Cave Hollow there are two caves near the trail.

*T*o reach Hazel Creek campground and trailhead from Potosi, go southwest on Hwy. P about 14 miles to Hwy. C and turn right (west). Follow Hwy. C about 5 miles to Hwy. Z and turn right (north). Continue on Hwy. Z about 3 miles to the entry road FS 2392, 1 gravel road mile beyond where the paved road ends.

*T*o reach Ottery Creek trailhead at Bell Mountain Wilderness from Potosi, take Mo. 21 south to Mo. 32 and turn left (west). Follow Mo. 32 west 7 miles to Hwy. A and turn left (south). Proceed on Hwy. A south 6.5 miles to the parking area on the right (west) side of the highway.

Area:
Ozark Trail-West Main Trail

U.S.G.S. Map(s):
1:24,000 Courtois, Palmer, Johnson Mountain

Trail(s) Distance:
approximately 24 miles

Trailhead(s):
Hazel Creek Campground, north terminus
Ottery Creek Trailhead, Bell Mtn. Wilderness, south terminus

Activities:
hiking, backpacking, nature study, equestrian use, mountain biking, developed camping, seasonal hunting

Fee(s):
developed camping at Hazel Creek campground and nearby Council Bluff Lake RA

66. West Main Ozark Trail: Trace Creek Section

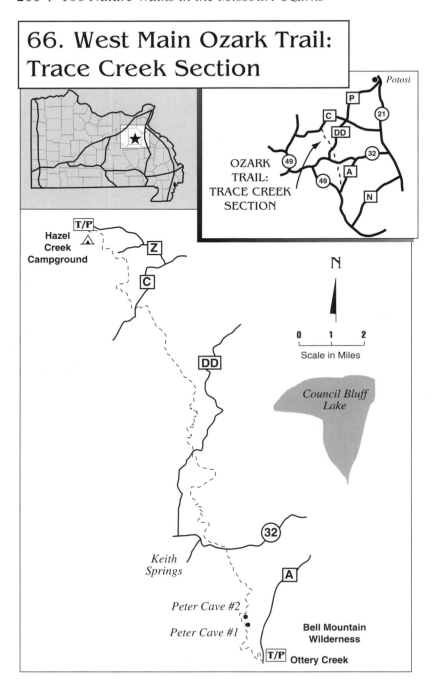

OZARK
TRAIL:
TRACE CREEK
SECTION

Potosi

Hazel
Creek
Campground

N

0   1   2
Scale in Miles

*Council Bluff
Lake*

*Keith
Springs*

Peter Cave #2

Peter Cave #1

**Bell Mountain
Wilderness**

Ottery Creek

NATURE WALK
66

TRAIL 67: *West Main Ozark Trail: Karkaghne Section*

Black River Ford at Sutton Bluff

*L*ocated in the northwest portion of Reynolds County, the Karkaghne Section of the Ozark Trail will eventually run from Ottery Creek trailhead at Bell Mountain Wilderness, 31 miles south and west to join the Blair Creek Section at the Mo. 72 and Hwy. P junction. Currently about 15 miles of the hiking trail have been completed, a few miles north of Sutton Bluff Recreation Area, southwest to Hwy. 72. Depending on funding, the Salem Ranger District is constructing the trail section north to connect with the south terminus of the Trace Creek Section and the Eastern Loop, Taum Sauk Section west terminus at the Ottery Creek, Hwy. A trailhead. Present trailhead and parking access points are located at Sutton Bluff RA, Hwy. TT, and Mo. 72.

*T*o reach Sutton Bluff RA from Centerville, drive north on Mo. 21/72 about 2 miles to FS 2233 (formerly called Karkaghne Scenic Drive) and turn left (west). Follow the paved road 6 miles to FS 2236 and turn left (south). Continue 2 miles on FS 2236 to the recreation area. Trailhead parking is along FS 2236 at the bluff top, up from the Black River west fork bridge ford.

NATURE WALK
67

*F*rom Sutton Bluff to Hwy. TT trailhead, in brief, the Ozark Trail pursues ridgetops, descending to Bee Fork, crossing South Branch, ascending and continuing on ridge tops to Grasshopper Hollow and then up on ridgetops to Hwy. TT parking and trailhead (about 10 miles).

*F*rom Hwy. TT to Mo. 72 southwest terminus, the Ozark Trail descends to Vest Hollow, ascends to ridgetop, then descends again to Jayhawker Hollow, and up, continuing southwest to the Mo. 72 trailhead and parking area (about 5 miles) at the junction with Hwy. P.

*T*he Hwy. TT trailhead is located about 3.5 miles northwest of Reynoldson Mo. 72, turning right (north) on Hwy. TT and continuing about one-quarter mile to the trailhead parking area.

*T*he Mo. 72 trailhead is located about 3 miles southeast of Bunker on the left (north) side of the highway at the junction of Hwy. P.

Area:
Ozark Trail-West Main Trail

U.S.G.S. Map(s):
1:24,000 Oates, Corridon, Bunker

Trail(s) Distance:
approximately 15 miles completed (31 miles when finished)

Trailhead(s):
Sutton Bluff Recreation Area, current north terminus
Hwy. TT, Mo. 72 and Hwy. P junction, southwest terminus

Activities:
hiking, backpacking, nature study, seasonal hunting

Fee(s):
developed camping at Sutton Bluff RA

NATURE WALK
67

67. West Main Ozark Trail: Karkaghne Section

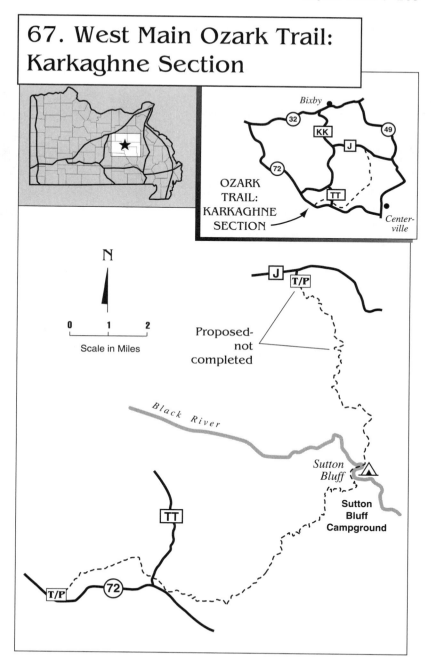

Bixby

OZARK
TRAIL:
KARKAGHNE
SECTION

Center-ville

N

0   1   2
Scale in Miles

J T/P

Proposed-
not
completed

Black River

Sutton
Bluff

Sutton
Bluff
Campground

TT

T/P 72

NATURE WALK
67

TRAIL 68: *West Main Ozark Trail: Blair Creek Section*

Eastern Yellow Bellied Racer

*T*he Blair Creek Section of the Ozark Trail is approximately 26.5 miles long and includes national forest, a privately owned Pioneer Forest (one of the largest private forest lands in Missouri), and lands administered by the Missouri Department of Conservation. The moderate to semi-rugged hiking section was one of the first of Ozark Trail development. The Blair Creek Section is well travelled, especially in the southern segments of Pioneer Forest and Bloom Creek Conservation Area. There are three trailheads and parking areas.

*M*o. 72/Hwy. P junction in west central Reynolds County, 3 miles southeast of Bunker, is the northern terminus of the Blair Creek Section. From the northern terminus, the trail heads south, entering Shannon County along an old railroad bed that follows a ridgetop (elev. 1,270 ft.) paralleling a Shannon County Road 6 miles to the second trailhead on the county road.

NATURE WALK
68

*T*he trailhead is located south of the junction of Mo. 72 and Hwy. P. From the highway junction, drive south on Hwy. P about 2.5 miles to the Shannon County Road. Turn left on the county road taking the right leg of the "Y" for 3 miles to the Ozark Trail parking and trailhead location.

*T*he Ozark Trail travels south along the Blair Creek valley for about the next 13 miles to Holmes Hollow. Enroute trailside are such highlights as Blair Creek Raised Fen (7 miles), Pioneer Forest (8.5 miles), Barton Hollow, Laxton Hollow, Harper Spring (15 miles), Dee Hollow and Holmes Hollow (19 miles).

*F*rom Holmes Hollow, the Ozark Trail continues south to Little Blair Creek (21 miles), and goes upridge to leave Pioneer Forest, and enters the MDC Bloom Creek Conservation Area. The final 5.5 mile segment continues southeast through Bloom Creek CA, along ridgetop and hollow to Bloom Creek, Little Bloom Creek, and the Current River Owls Bend bluffs, eventually reaching the southern trail terminus at Powder Mill NPS and the north terminus of the Current River Section.

*P*owder Mill trailhead and parking area and Owls Bend campground are located 12 miles east of Eminence on Mo. 106, just across the Current River bridge, east side.

Area:
Ozark Trail-West Main Trail

U.S.G.S. Map(s):
1:24,000 Bunker, Midridge, Powder Mill Ferry

Trail(s) Distance:
approximately 26.5 miles

Trailhead(s):
Mo. 72 and Hwy. P junction, north terminus, Reynolds County
Shannon County 2220
Mo. 106, Powder Mill NPS, south terminus

Activities:
hiking, backpacking, nature study, developed camping and ranger station at Powder Mill NPS, seasonal hunting

Fee(s):
developed camping at Powder Mill NPS and Owls Bend campgrounds

NATURE WALK
68

68. West Main Ozark Trail: Blair Creek Section

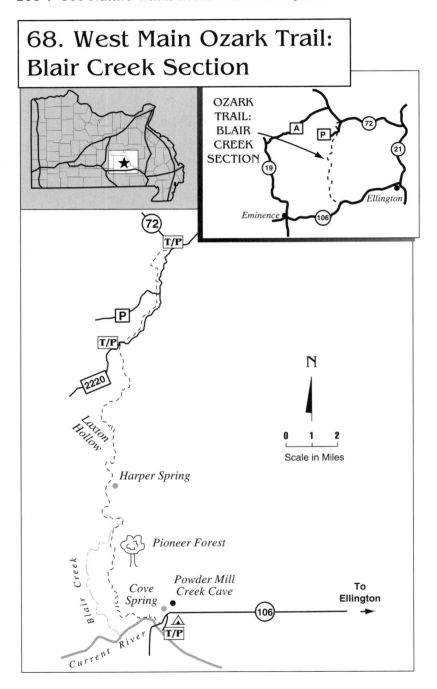

TRAIL 69: **West Main Ozark Trail: Current River Section**

Current River near Owls Bend

The 30 mile stretch of the Current River Section of the Ozark Trail is often considered the most scenic of the entire trail. The hiking only pathway sees light use and is rated easy to moderate. The section crosses Shannon and Carter counties, lands managed by the National Park Service and private landowners. The north terminus is at Powder Mill Ozark Riverways NPS at Owls Bend (Mo. 106) and the south trail terminus is at U.S. Hwy. 60, 4 miles west of Van Buren. There are five trailhead and parking areas.

NATURE WALK
69

*P*owder Mill Ozark Riverways NPS at Owls Bend, the section's north terminus is located east of Eminence on Mo. 106 at the east side of the Current River bridge. Park and walk west across the highway bridge to the trail on the west bank.

*T*he Ozark Trail runs south, paralleling the Current River and a service road to a second parking area at riverside, across the stream from the Blue Spring branch inlet. The riverside parking and trailhead area is accessible from a road on the south side of Mo. 106, about 2 miles west of Powder Mill and the Current River bridge. Follow the paved access road nearly 2 miles northeast from Mo. 106 to the old Powder Mill Ferry landing site at the river, and turn right (south) and continue on a gravel road to the dead end parking area and trailhead, just over a mile.

*O*zark Trail continues south (entering Indian Creek CA), and moves up along a ridge slope about 2 miles to the confluence of Indian Creek and the Current River. The trail turns west and south along Indian Creek, crossing a saddle on the south base of Barnett Mountain, then descends and crosses (wet feet) Rocky Creek (7 miles, re-enter NPS land). The historic Klepzig gristmill is next to Rocky Creek plus the Mill Mountain Shut-Ins. The trail continues south between Mill Mountain and Buzzard Mountain through Denning Hollow to Hwy. NN and crosses (8.5 miles).

*A*bout 1 mile after crossing Hwy. NN is another Rocky Creek crossing. At this point, an old half mile road trail to Rocky Falls intersects the Ozark Trail, and goes left (west) upstream. The Rocky Falls picnic area and trailhead is about 11 miles northeast of Winona on Hwy. H to Hwy. NN east.

*T*he Ozark Trail continues southbound through Kelley Hollow (enter Carter County and Peck Ranch CA), switchbacking uphill to Stegall Mountain (elev. 1,300 ft.) to glade top vistas. The trail switchbacks down Stegall Mountain and enters Wolf Hollow and crosses Rogers Creek, a forest road and a refuge fence stile (14.5 miles). There is no camping allowed between this refuge fence and the next refuge fence on Peck Ranch Conservation Area. The fourth trailhead and parking area is about half a mile south of the Rogers Creek and fence crossing, following a forest road.

*T*o reach the Peck Ranch parking area and trailhead from Winona, drive north on Hwy. H roughly 5 miles and turn right (east) at ridgecrest and the Peck Ranch cantilevered sign. Follow the gravel road east about 5 miles to the parking trailhead area on the left (north) side of the road. Walk north to the Ozark Trail on the service road half a mile to the Rogers Creek crossing and the trail.

NATURE WALK
69

*T*he Ozark Trail continues south through Peck Ranch CA along ridgetops above Mule Hollow, through Pritchard Hollow and Midco Hollow to the second refuge fence crossing and fourth trailhead (20.5 miles) at the southern boundary of Peck Ranch.

*T*he trailhead and parking area are reached by road from U.S Hwy. 60, about two miles west of Fremont, turning north onto Hwy. P and driving to Peck Ranch CA, turning east, following the property road east along the refuge fence.

*T*he final 9.5 miles of the Current River Section continues south and east along Midco Hollow (U.S.F.S. lands), following ridgetops east to Brushy Hollow and Long Hollow, going south, crossing the railroad tracks (private) and U.S.F.S. land, ridgetopping to U.S. Hwy. 60, southern terminus. The U.S. Hwy. 60 trailhead and parking area is located 4 miles west of Van Buren.

Area:
Ozark Trail-West Main Trail

U.S.G.S. Map(s):
1:24,000 Powder Mill Ferry, Stegall Mountain, Fremont, Van Buren South

Trail(s) Distance:
approximately 30 miles

Trailhead(s):
Mo. 106, Powder Mill NPS, north terminus
Mo. 906, Old Powder Mill Ferry site
Hwy. NN at Rocky Falls and Rocky Creek
Peck Ranch CA, north and south fence boundaries
U.S. Hwy. 60, west of Van Buren, Carter County, southern terminus

Activities:
hiking only section, backpacking, nature study, picnicking, canoeing, fishing, developed camping at Powder Mill NPS, seasonal hunting

Fee(s):
developed camping at Powder Mill NPS

NATURE WALK
69

69. West Main Ozark Trail: Current River Section

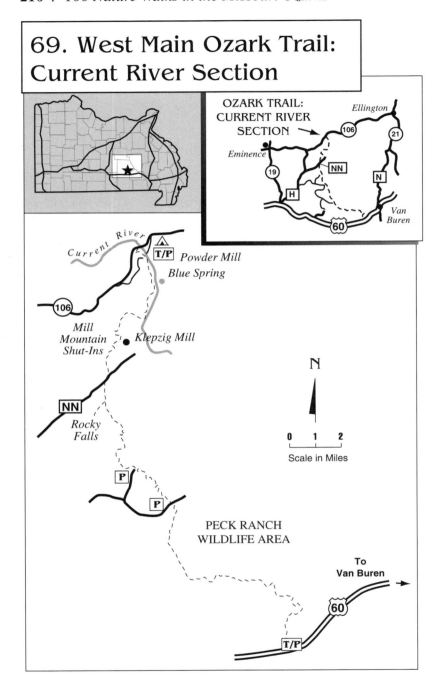

OZARK TRAIL:
CURRENT RIVER
SECTION

Ellington

Eminence

Van
Buren

N

0   1   2
Scale in Miles

Current River

Powder Mill
Blue Spring

Mill
Mountain
Shut-Ins

Klepzig Mill

Rocky
Falls

PECK RANCH
WILDLIFE AREA

To
Van Buren

NATURE WALK
69

TRAIL 70: *West Main Ozark Trail: Between The Rivers Section*

Vista near Skyline Drive

*T*he 30 mile Between The Rivers Section of the Ozark Trail lies entirely within the Eleven Point District of the Mark Twain National Forest in Carter and Oregon counties. The easy to moderate single track trail has light use and moves in a southeast to southwesterly direction from the Current River drainage to the Eleven Point basin (elev. 580-1,025 ft.). The trail is shared with equestrians and mountain bikes. In addition to the Hwy. 60, north terminus and the FS 3152, south terminus, there is a third access point at the Sinking Creek Lookout Tower (22.5 miles).

*F*rom the north terminus at U.S. Hwy. 60, about 4 miles west of Van Buren, the Ozark trail heads southeast, hiking along a level and gentle slope, then uphill, crossing Skyline Drive/FS 3281 and dropping down into Windhorse Hollow (2 miles). The next 4.6 miles the trail drifts southwest up ridges and down bottoms, into Chilton Creek and up to Hwy. C (6.6 miles).

*S*outh of Hwy. C, the Ozark Trail winds through numerous small tributaries that flow to the Current River. These include Devil's Run, Hog Hollow and Big Barren Creek. From Big Barren Creek, the Ozark Trail crosses FS 3145 (13.3 miles) and moves west crossing Deer Pond Hollow, Spring Hollow, Stillhouse Hollow and onto the north prong of Cedar Bluff Creek to Hwy. J (21.3 miles). West of Hwy. J (watershed divide) the drainage flows to the Eleven Point River.

NATURE WALK
70

*H*eading west from Hwy. J about half a mile, the Ozark Trail skirts Cotham Pond meadow and continues another mile to the trail junction spur to Sinking Creek Lookout Tower trailhead and parking area.

*F*rom Sinking Creek Lookout Tower area, the trail continues southwest through Gold Mine Hollow (enter Oregon County) following the ridgeline above Kelly Hollow, dropping into Wilderness Hollow, upridge and down into Fox Hollow, and upridge to the southern terminus of the Between The River Section at FS 3152.

*T*o reach FS 3152 trailhead and parking area, drive south from the junction of Hwy. 60 and Mo. 19, 14 miles on Mo. 19 (about 2 miles south of McCormack Lake RA, FS 3155 turnoff) to FS 3152 and and turn left (east). Follow FS 3152 east 6 miles to the trailhead, about 1.5 miles east of the Hurricane Creek ford. Roadside parking is limited. The north terminus of the Eleven Point Section is at FS 3152.

Area:
Ozark Trail-West Main Trail

U.S.G.S. Map(s):
1:24,000 Van Buren South, Handy, Wilderness, Greer

Trail(s) Distance:
approximately 30 miles

Trailhead(s):
Hwy. 60, 4 miles west of Van Buren, Carter County
Sinking Creek Lookout Tower, FS 3152
FS 3152, Oregon County

Activities:
hiking, backpacking, nature study, equestrian use, mountain biking, seasonal hunting

Fee(s):
developed camping at Big Spring NPS and Watercress Spring RA at and near Van Buren

NATURE WALK
70

70. West Main Ozark Trail: Between The Rivers Section

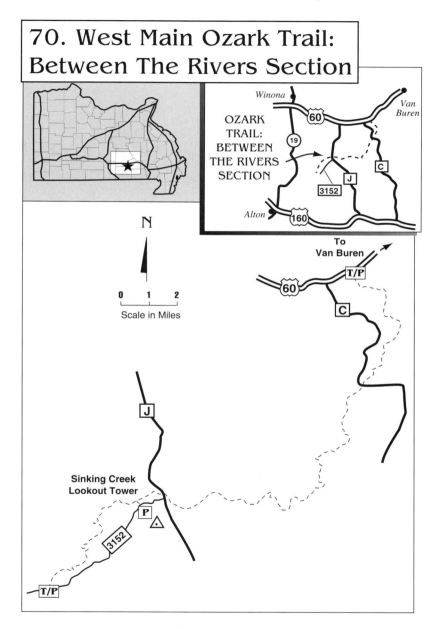

NATURE WALK
70

TRAIL 71: *West Main Ozark Trail: Eleven Point Section*

Boomhole Vista, Eleven Point River

Pristine Eleven Point River, dramatic river bluffs and entrenched hollows make this remote 30 mile section special. The blufftop and ridgetop views are especially outstanding at Lefler Overlook near Hurricane Creek (3 miles), the Boomhole area near McCormack Lake RA (12 miles), and Spring Creek (26 miles). Bockman Spring and Cave (20 miles) is a trailside highlight, (rest stop or camp) and the confluence of Greer Spring Branch and the Eleven Point River are scenic. There are many steep climbs and descents. The entire section runs through Oregon County and National Forest Service lands. The trail is open to equestrians and mountain bikes. Future plans call for rerouting the Ozark Trail closer to the Eleven Point River from Hurricane Creek west to Greer Crossing RA. There are four trailheads and parking areas.

FS 3152, the northeastern terminus of the Eleven Point Section, is reached by road by driving 14 miles south of the U.S. Hwy. 60 and Mo. 19 junction at Winona, and turning left (east) on FS 3152. Continue

NATURE WALK
71

6 miles to the parking area on the left (north) side of the road, just over a mile beyond the Hurricane Creek ford.

*T*he Ozark Trail descends from the ridgetop trailhead through forest to and across Hurricane Creek (1.5 miles, expect wet feet). From Hurricane Creek, the trail climbs up the 400-foot-high bluff to Lefler Overlook (3 miles). The trail continues west on a level ridge (4 miles) and then switchbacks down into a river cove hollow and then up along the pine studded river bluff slope (5 miles) and drops into Hackleton Hollow. The Ozark Trail rises to the ridgetop and continues west, descending into the not-so-deep or so-steep Graveyard Hollow (8 miles). Continuing west above the river, the trail proceeds to Greer Crossing Recreation Area trailhead and parking (10 miles).

*G*reer Crossing RA is reached by road by driving 18 miles south of the junction of U.S. Hwy. 60 and Mo.19 at Winona, on Mo.19. The recreation area entrance is on the east side of the highway, just before the Eleven Point bridge crossing.

*F*rom Greer Crossing RA, the Ozark Trail runs west under the Mo.19 bridge and along the Eleven Point River, sharing the McCormack-Greer Trail. Across the river, Greer Spring Branch joins the Eleven Point about four-tenths of a mile west of the Mo. 19 bridge. The trail goes up a bluff at Duncan Hollow to a blufftop overlook area known as the "Boomhole," a former logging drop chute (12 miles). The Ozark Trail descends the Boomhole bluff to a trail junction (13 miles), a 1 mile spur to McCormack Lake Recreation Area.

*M*cCormack Lake RA trailhead and parking area is reached by driving south 13 miles from the junction of U.S. Hwy. 60 and Mo. 19 on Mo. 19, turning right (west) on FS 3155. Proceed 2 miles on FS 3155 to the trailhead parking area overlooking McCormack Lake. Follow the lakeside trail south to the dam and spillway and continue along the marked path through Reader Hollow 1 mile to the Ozark Trail junction.

*F*rom the Ozark Trail-McCormack Lake spur junction (13 miles) continue west following the river, going up bluff 400 feet and descending to Becky Hollow (16.9 miles). The trail leaves the river and proceeds up Becky Hollow, then goes upridge, down and across to Three Mile Hollow, to a saddle crossing at Devil's Backbone and to Bockman Spring and Cave (20 miles). The spring and cave once served as a refrigerator and a present-day "doorway" serves as an entry point to the cave.

*T*he Ozark Trail continues west on old farm lanes through abandoned fields and forest, gradually going upridge to FS 3238 (22.3 miles). From FS 3238, the trail keeps heading southwest via ridge and ravine to the bluffs overlooking Spring Creek, following the bluffs northwest, descending to Betsy Hollow (26.9 miles), FS 3173 and Spring Creek.

NATURE WALK
71

The trail crosses Spring Creek and proceeds along the north facing ridge slopes above Spring Creek to conclude at the western trailhead terminus at Paty Hollow and FS 4155.

*P*aty Hollow and FS 4155 trailhead and parking area is accessed by driving north from Thomasville half a mile on Mo. 99, turning right (east) on FS 3173. Follow FS 3173 east half a mile to FS 4155 and turn left (north). Continue on FS 4155 north one-quarter mile to a parking area in an old field on the left (west). Park and walk north on FS 4155 about 200 yards to the signed trailhead. The Blue Ridge Horse Trail also starts here but continues on a separate path.

Area:
Ozark Trail-West Main Trail

U.S.G.S. Map(s):
1:24,000 Greer, Piedmont, Thomasville

Trail(s) Distance:
approximately 30 miles

Trailhead(s):
FS 3152, east of Hurricane Creek, north terminus
Greer Crossing Recreation Area, Mo. 19
McCormack Lake Recreation Area, FS 3155
FS 4155, Paty Hollow, west terminus

Activities:
hiking, backpacking, nature study, equestrian use, mountain biking, fishing, canoeing, developed camping

Fee(s):
developed camping at Greer Crossing RA and McCormack Lake RA

NATURE WALK
71

71. West Main Ozark Trail: Eleven Point Section

OZARK
TRAIL:
ELEVEN
POINT
SECTION

Winona

60

19

99

4155

3152

J

Alton

160

N

0   1   2
Scale in Miles

T/P

Lester
Look

Greer
Crossing
Recreation
Area

3152

To
Winona

T/P

T/P

McCormack
Lake

Greer
Spring

19

To
Alton

Bockman
Spring

Cooper
Spring

Paty
Spring

4155

T/P

3173

99

NATURE WALK
71

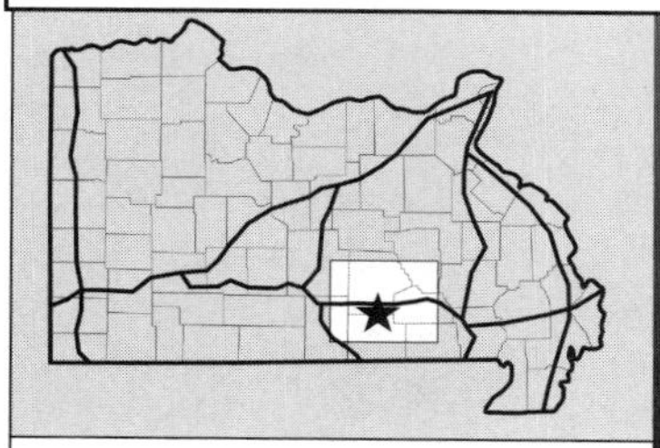

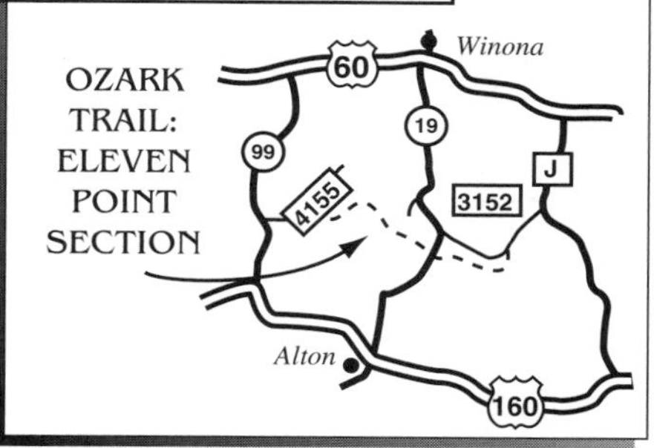

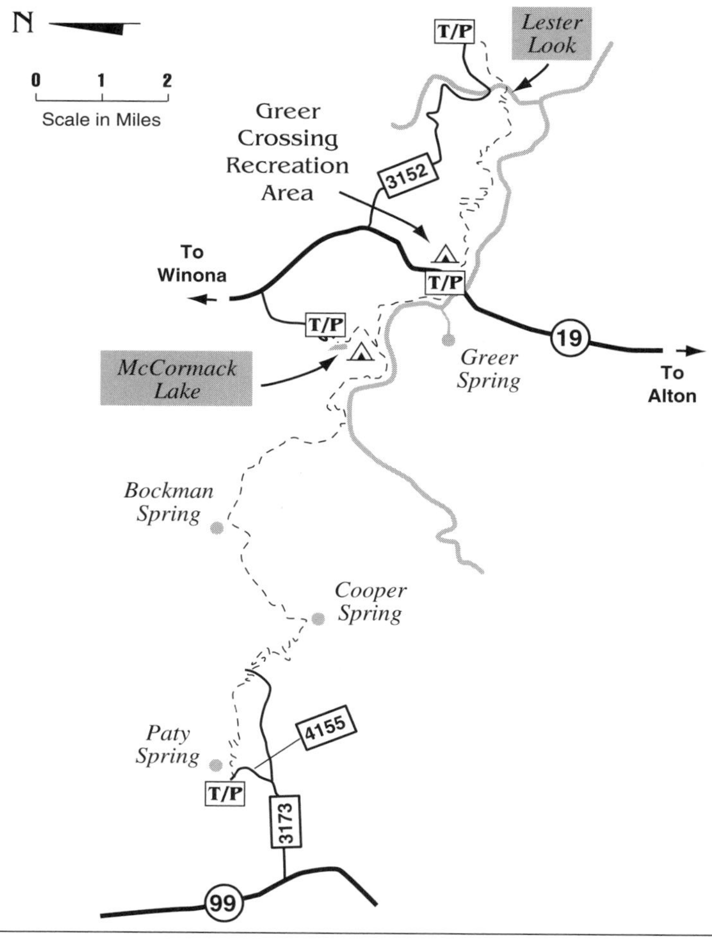

TRAIL 72: *West Main Ozark Trail: North Fork River Section*

Lovers Leap

*T*he 11-mile-long North Fork River Section of the Ozark Trail was recently developed on U.S. Forest Service lands in the Willow Springs District. The rugged section lies entirely in Howell County. At Blue Hole western terminus, the Ozark Trail continues west to connect with the Ridge Runner Trail, sharing the tread south to the North Fork Recreation Area, and along McGarr Ridge of the Devils Backbone Wilderness Area (approximately 17 miles). Eventual plans include connecting the North Fork Section with the Eleven Point Section east, and the Arkansas Ozark Highlands Trail south. The two trailheads and parking areas of the North Fork River Section are near Pomona and Blue Hole on Mo. 14.

NATURE WALK
72

*P*omona trailhead and parking area is found by driving 1 mile west of Pomona, and the U.S. Hwy. 63 and Hwy. P junction and turning left (south) from Hwy. P onto a gravel forest road. Follow the gravel road about 200 yards to a turnout loop and park. Walk west a few yards to the trailhead registration box and map shelter.

*T*he Ozark trail heads west, with numerous ridge climbs and bottom declines, small stream and forest road crossings (elev. 850-1,200 ft.). The streams are usually dry and drain to Dry Creek, the main stream of the section. Occasionally the trail will follows or parallels forest roads.

*A*pproximately 2.5 miles east of the Blue Hole trailhead parking area, the Ozark Trail leads through south through the old growth portion of Kenyon Hollow. About a mile east of Blue Hole is a Lovers Leap, a fine vista point that looks over Dry Fork and a great blue heron rookery in a giant sycamore.

*B*lue Hole trailhead and parking area is located on Hwy. AP, south of the Dry Creek bridge, and about 2 miles north of the Mo. 14 and Hwy. AP junction. From Pomona, go west on Hwy. P to Hwy. AP and turn left (south). Follow Hwy. AP south about 2.5 miles to Blue Hole.

*F*rom West Plains, drive north on U.S. Hwy. 63 to Mo. 14 and turn left (west). Go west on Mo. 14 about 9 miles to the junction with Hwy. AP and turn right (north). Continue about 2 miles to Blue Hole and the parking area and trailhead.

Area:
Ozark Trail-West Main Trail

U.S.G.S. Map(s):
1:24,000 Willow Spring SW, Siloam Springs

Trail(s) Distance:
11 miles

Trailhead(s):
Pomona, east terminus, Hwy. P
Blue Hole, west terminus, Mo. 14
Note: Ozark Trail shares a 14 mile segment of Ridge Runner Trail south plus a 3 mile segment of McGarr Ridge, Devils Backbone Wilderness south

Activities:
hiking, backpacking, nature study, equestrian use, mountain biking, seasonal hunting

Fee(s):
developed camping at Noblett RA, North Fork RA

NATURE WALK
72

72. West Main Ozark Trail: North Fork. River Section

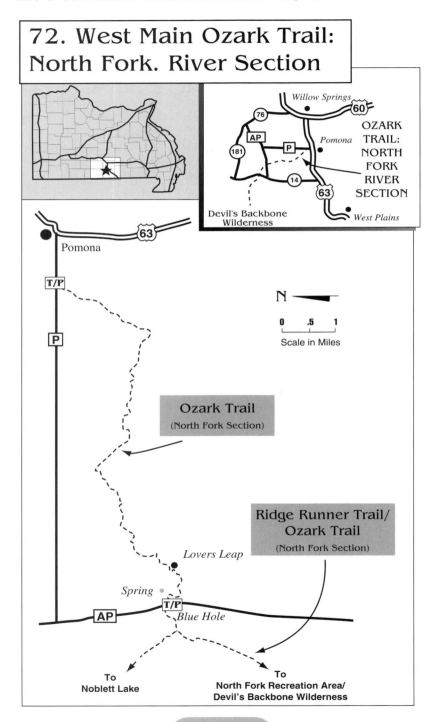

Willow Springs

76

60

OZARK
TRAIL:
NORTH
FORK
RIVER
SECTION

AP

Pomona

181

P

14

63

Devil's Backbone
Wilderness

West Plains

Pomona

63

T/P

P

N

0   .5   1

Scale in Miles

Ozark Trail
(North Fork Section)

Ridge Runner Trail/
Ozark Trail
(North Fork Section)

Lovers Leap

Spring

AP

T/P

Blue Hole

To
Noblett Lake

To
North Fork Recreation Area/
Devil's Backbone Wilderness

NATURE WALK
72

TRAIL 73: *Clifty Creek Natural Area and Conservation Area*

Clifty Creek Natural Bridge

*P*icturesque Clifty Creek natural bridge is probably one of the most photogenic in all of the Missouri Ozarks. The stream-carved, dolomite arch is 13 feet high and spans 40 feet over Little Clifty Creek at the confluence with Clifty Creek. The natural area was designated in 1971 by the Missouri Department of Conservation from land leased from the L.A.D. Foundation. The natural habitats include upland and bottomland forests, cliffs, glades, a headwater stream and a natural bridge. Old tennis shoes are good enough for this leisurely streambed hike of a mile, one way.

*T*he trailhead begins at an MDC parking area just beyond where the Hwy. W. pavement ends. A posted sign at the northwest corner identifies the trailhead. The narrow worn path leads down the oak- and hickory-covered slope to the floodplain forest and Clifty Creek. Continue walking

NATURE WALK
73

downstream in the streambed channel at a slow safe pace (it's easy to slip and fall). The unmarked streambed "path" is lined with half canyons of sheer Gasconade dolomite white limestone.

*T*he natural bridge is easily spotted and will be on the left at the Little Clifty Creek confluence after hiking 1 rugged mile. The creeks are normally dry in the fall, but running water adds to the natural beauty of the place. Retrace your steps back to the parking area.

*A*nother approach of about the same distance is from the downstream, low water crossing on Clifty Creek. To reach the road ford, continue east from the original parking trailhead along the gravel road about 1.1 mile to the Clifty Creek ford and the picnicking and camping area. Walk upstream to the natural bridge and retrace your steps. Stay in the streambed about a third of the way since the streambanks are private property.

*C*lifty Creek Natural Area and Conservation Area is located 10 miles north and east of Dixon (Pulaski County) at the end of Hwy. W (Maries County). From I-44, exit 163 north on Mo. 28 and drive to Dixon. Continue north on Mo. 28, 3.9 miles to Hwy. W and turn right (east). Proceed about 4.5 miles to the parking lot and the trailhead on the left (north) side of the gravel road. It is 5.6 miles to the Clifty Creek ford and picnic area on the left side of the road.

Area/Location/County:
Rolla-Houston/Dixon/Maries County

U.S.G.S. Map(s):
1:24,000 Nagogami Lodge

Trail(s) Distance:
approximately 1 mile one way

Acreage:
230 acre conservation area
230 acre natural area

Activities:
nature walk, nature study in natural area,
picnicking, camping in conservation area

Fee(s):
none

NATURE WALK
73

73. Clifty Creek Natural Area & Conservation Area

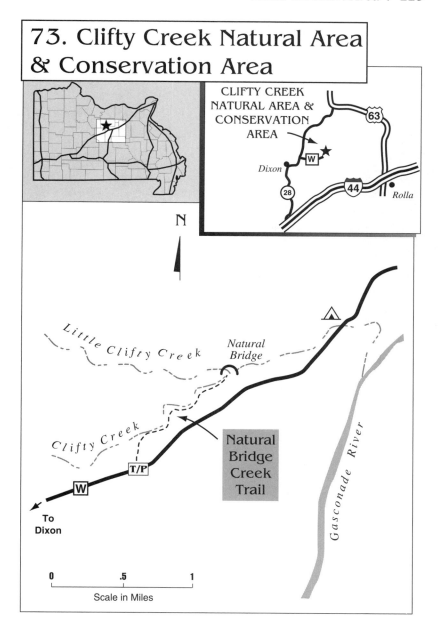

CLIFTY CREEK
NATURAL AREA &
CONSERVATION
AREA

Dixon

Rolla

N

Little Clifty Creek

Natural
Bridge

Clifty Creek

Natural
Bridge
Creek
Trail

Gasconade River

T/P

W

To
Dixon

0   .5   1

Scale in Miles

NATURE WALK
73

TRAIL 74: *Mill Creek Recreation Area*

Entrance to Natural Bridge Tunnel, Kaintuck Trail

*M*ill Creek is a U.S. Forest Service Recreation Area located in a scenic upper Ozark area southwest of Rolla. Special features to see on foot include a hollow bottom, a perennially flowing Ozark stream, springs, a pond, caves and a natural bridge tunnel. Mill Creek is a wild rainbow trout stream that flows north to Little Piney Creek. The picnic area and campground are separated by Mill Creek which may flood at times and make the bridge crossing impossible. There are three hiking areas.

*T*he seven-tenths of a mile Cave Trail begins and ends at the picnic area near the west bank of Mill Creek. The rugged path begins adjacent to the flowing artesian well pump. The rocky path goes ridgeside uphill to a gated cave and descends the ridgeslope to a gravel-covered CR 245 about 100 yards north of the flowing spring pump.

A second area, located 3 miles south of the Mill Creek picnic area, is Wilkens Spring and Pond, where 3 million gallons of water flow freely to Mill Creek every day. The setting, with an attractive spring, two acre pond and thousand foot branch, is also a trailhead parking area for the

NATURE WALK
74

2 mile Deer Track loop of the Kaintuck Hollow Trail. The trail loop is single track, with steep ridge slopes and level open fields near the springs. Kaintuck Trail is also popular with equestrians.

A suggested third hiking area leads to a natural bridge tunnel along a segment of the Oak Leaf section of the Kaintuck Trail. This area is located about 2 miles southeast of Mill Creek Recreation Area. The signed trailhead and parking area is just off FS 1576. Park and cross Kaintuck Hollow ford and walk several hundred yards southeast along the level narrow path to the natural tunnel cave. The tunnel is open at both ends and is 175 feet long, 30 feet wide, and 10 feet high with a wet weather stream passing through. Retrace your steps or consider hiking the additional loop trails off the Oak Leaf section (Pine Tree, Mushroom, Squirrel, Butterfly, Cardinal and Deer Track).

*T*o reach Mill Creek Recreation Area from I-44, exit 179 south on Hwy. T and drive about 3 miles to and through Newburg to Hwy. P, located just across the Little Piney River bridge. Turn right (west) on Hwy. P and drive 2.8 miles and turn left (south) on Phelps CR 245. Follow CR 245 2.3 miles to the recreation area.

*T*o reach Wilkins Spring and Pond from Mill Creek Recreation Area, drive south 3 miles on CR 245 and Hwy. AA. Turn left (east) on a forest road located about half a mile past Mill Creek church, and drive to the spring.

*T*o reach Kaintuck Hollow natural bridge tunnel from Mill Creek RA and CR 245, drive across the bridge over Mill Creek and follow FS 1576/Kaintuck Road southeast about 2 miles to the marked trailhead parking area for the natural bridge (signed). The FS 1576 road may be closed at times due to high water at Mill Creek and Kaintuck Hollow Creek.

Area/Location/County:
Rolla-Houston/Newburg/Phelps County

U.S.G.S. Map(s):
1:24,000 Kaintuck Hollow

Trail(s) Distance:
three trails total approximately 4 miles

Activities:
nature walks, nature study, picnicking, fishing, camping

Fee(s):
developed camping

NATURE WALK
74

74. Mill Creek Recreation Area

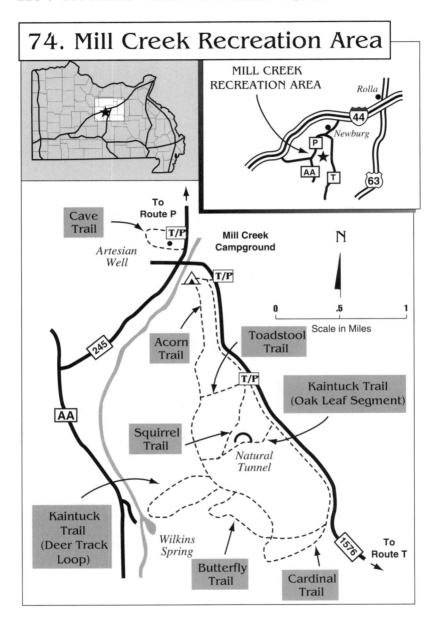

MILL CREEK
RECREATION AREA

Rolla

44

Newburg

P

AA T

63

Cave
Trail

To
Route P

T/P

Mill Creek
Campground

Artesian
Well

N

T/P

0   .5   1

Scale in Miles

245

Acorn
Trail

Toadstool
Trail

T/P

Kaintuck Trail
(Oak Leaf Segment)

AA

Squirrel
Trail

Natural
Tunnel

Kaintuck
Trail
(Deer Track
Loop)

Wilkins
Spring

1576

To
Route T

Butterfly
Trail

Cardinal
Trail

NATURE WALK
74

TRAIL 75: *Lane Spring Recreation Area*

Lane Spring Pool and Branch, Lane Spring Recreation Area

*E*asily accessed from a main highway, Lane Spring is a popular National Forest Service recreation area, located 11 miles south of Rolla. The recently renovated picnicking and camping areas are situated along the level forested floodplain on the north bank of Little Piney Creek. Lane Spring Pool and Branch are near the creek just west of the day use parking and picnic area. Constructed by the Boy Scouts, two loop trails traverse the floodplain and the bluffs above (elev. 850-950 ft.).

*T*he 1.5 mile Cedar Bluff Trail loop begins and ends at the day use picnic parking area and moves counterclockwise. The signed trailhead is east of the parking lot near the junction with the forest entry road. The first half of the trail climbs a ridge to a rocky red cedar dolomite glade where there are excellent views of the valley. The second half descends and follows the riparian plain. A short loop is formed in the floodplain by walking the service road and the trail, both concluding at the locked

NATURE WALK
75

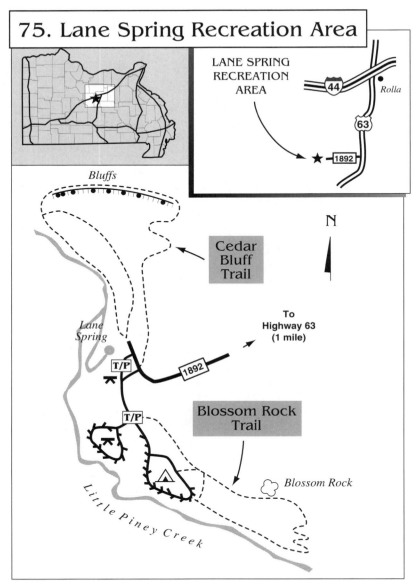

75. Lane Spring Recreation Area

LANE SPRING
RECREATION
AREA

Rolla

1892

Bluffs

Cedar
Bluff
Trail

N

To
Highway 63
(1 mile)

Lane
Spring

T/P

1892

T/P

Blossom Rock
Trail

Blossom Rock

Little Piney Creek

metal gate in the day-use parking area. Lane Spring is near the trail's end, just upstream from the day use picnic area. This nature walk takes a leisurely hour or longer.

*T*he mile-long Blossom Rock Trail loop is located in the campground area. The trailhead for day users begins at the fee entry station to the campground. The trail skirts the campground along the densely wooded base of a bluff, interconnecting with campground feeder spurs.

NATURE WALK
75

The trail ascends the bluff from the Little Piney bottoms to a large mass of sandstone called Blossom Rock. Up close the 50-foot-high and 125-foot in diameter rock appears to "blossom" due to fracture lines caused by weathering. The trail switchbacks down the bluff to follow the sandy floodplain back to the campground and the trailhead. This is a 45 minute walk that is somewhat trying.

*L*ane Spring Recreation Area may be reached by driving U.S. Hwy. 63 south from I-44 at Rolla. Drive 12 miles and turn right (west) on FS 1892. Follow FS 1892 for 1.2 miles to the day use parking area.

Area/Location/County:
Rolla-Houston/Rolla/Phelps County

U.S.G.S. Map(s):
1:24,000 Yancy Mills

Trail(s) Distance:
two trails total 2.5 miles

Acreage:
397 acres

Activities:
nature walks, nature study, picnicking, shelters, fishing, canoeing, camping

Fee(s):
camping, shelter rental

Blossom Rock at Lane Spring Recreation Area

NATURE WALK
75

TRAIL 76: *Slabtown Bluff Recreation Area*

Slabtown Bluff Recreation Area is about a mile or so by road from Paddy Creek Wilderness but to date, there is no connecting trail. The recreation area occupies level, open floodplain and high river bluffs along the Big Piney River. Across an open grassy field near the entrance, a cave opening can be seen, high on the opposite river bluff. The picnic area, walk-in campground, boat launch ramp and parking area are at the riverfront, where the 1.5 mile Slabtown Bluff Trail loop begins (elev. 900-1,100 ft.).

The moderately rugged trail follows a narrow path between the river and the bluff six-tenths of a mile before ascending the switchbacks to the blufftop (Slabtown Natural Arch is upstream about another half mile, a short distance upstream from the confluence of Paddy Creek and Big Piney Creek). At the 300-foot-high, cedar-coated ridgetop, there are distant vistas of the Slabtown Natural Arch bluff (bring binoculars). The trail descends the backsides of the forested bluff to eventually return to the trailhead riverside parking area.

Slabtown Bluff RA is located 13 miles west of Licking. From the junction of U.S. Hwy. 63 and Mo. 32, go west on Mo. 32, 4 miles and turn right (northwest) on Hwy. N. Follow Hwy. N 2.5 miles and turn left (southwest) onto Hwy. AF. Continue on Hwy. AF 6.5 miles to Slabtown Recreation Area entrance on the left side of the highway before the Big Piney River bridge.

Area/Location/County:
Rolla-Houston/Licking/Texas County

U.S.G.S. Map(s):
1:24,000 Slabtown Spring

Trail(s) Distance:
1.5 mile loop

Activities:
nature walk, picnicking, fishing, canoeing, boat launch ramp, tent camping

Fee(s):

76. Slabtown Bluff Recreation Area

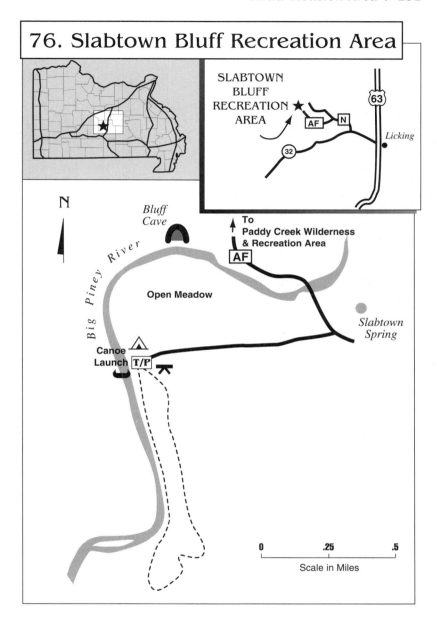

NATURE WALK
76

TRAIL 77: **Paddy Creek Wilderness and Recreation Area**

Big Piney Trail, Big Paddy Creek Vista

Established in 1983, Paddy Creek Wilderness in northwest Texas County is composed of thousands of acres of ridges, ravines, hollows and streams of the Salem Plateau (elev. 800-1,290 ft.). Deeply carved by water drainage, the Big Paddy and Little Paddy creeks are the major streams. The 19 mile Big Piney Trail forms a double loop and trail

NATURE WALK
77

access is from three trailheads. The trail is also a favorite of equestrians. Paddy Creek Recreation Area is at the northeast edge of the wilderness and has a short 1 mile trail along Paddy Creek plus picnicking and camping.

*P*addy Creek Wilderness is accessed on foot via Piney Creek Trail at the following three trailheads.

*P*addy Creek Recreation Area is nestled in a hollow along Paddy Creek where the trailhead is marked at the day use picnic area. To reach the area from Roby, take Mo. 17 north 2 miles and turn right (north) on Slabtown Road. Continue north on Slabtown Road 6 miles and turn right on FS 220. Proceed 2 miles downhill to the recreation area. The recreation area is also accessible from Licking and the junction of U.S. Hwy. 63 by driving west 16 miles on Mo. 32 and Hwy. AF.

*B*ig Piney Trail Camp is designed to accommodate horses and their riders, but hikers can also use the trailhead. Instead of turning on FS 220 and continuing downhill to Paddy Creek RA, continue another 1.3 miles on Slabtown Road to Big Piney Trail Camp on the right (south) side of the gravel road.

*R*oby Lake Recreation Area features picnicking, camping, fishing, launch ramp, canoeing and drinking water. To reach the recreation area drive 1 mile north on Mo. 17 from Roby to FS 274, the entrance road. Parking is available at the entrance or continue six-tenths of a mile on FS 274 to five acre Roby Lake and the trailhead. The trail goes nine-tenths of a mile north to connect with the Piney Creek Trail.

*A*lthough there are steep climbs, most of the Piney Creek Trail is fairly level. The levelness allows for a quicker stride and less exertion, however, expect erosion on the ascents and descents and a compacted trail surface. Hikers often can hear military maneuvers at nearby Fort Leonard Wood. Watch for confusing renegade horse trails. FS 220 is crossed twice. The 2 mile-long connecting spur near the trail's mid-point cuts the trail into two day hikes, a north and a south loop. There are scenic shortleaf pine bluff overlooks of Little Paddy Creek on the south loop's south segment, northeast from Roby Lake. Scenic vistas predominate on the north loop from Big Piney Trail Camp south through Paddy Creek RA, and farther south above Big Piney Creek. Experienced hikers can walk the entire 19 mile loop in one day.

*P*addy Creek Trail at the Paddy Creek Recreation Area is a 1 mile, clockwise loop along and above Paddy Creek, just downstream from the confluence of Little and Big Paddy Creeks (high water may discourage crossing). Spur trails offshoot from the designated Paddy Creek Trail loop making its course confusing. The trail crosses FS 220 twice. Two vista points overlook the stream from pine-coated bluffs. The trail starts and ends in the picnic area. The Paddy Creek Natural

NATURE WALK

77

Arch is visible from the first picnic site upon entering the area via the road. Walk down to Paddy Creek from the picnic table and look downstream on the high north bluff (elev. 150-200 ft.). In addition, follow the service road to the campground turnaround and a cabled gate. Cross the gate and walk the old forest road to the confluence of Paddy Creek and Big Piney River. The Slabtown Natural Arch is upstream a short distance at the confluence, however, it is 200 feet up and difficult to see.

Area/Location/County:
Rolla-Houston/Licking/Texas County

U.S.G.S. Map(s):
1:24,000 Slabtown Spring, Roby

Trail(s) Distance:
1 mile trail loop
19 mile wilderness double loop

Acreage:
7,060 acres

Activities:
hiking, backpacking, nature study, picnicking, fishing, developed camping, seasonal hunting

Fee(s):
developed camping

NATURE WALK
77

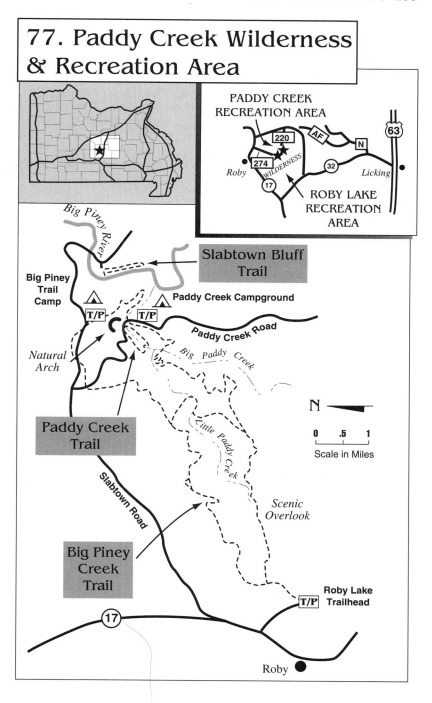

77. Paddy Creek Wilderness & Recreation Area

PADDY CREEK RECREATION AREA

Roby

Licking

ROBY LAKE RECREATION AREA

Big Piney River

Slabtown Bluff Trail

Big Piney Trail Camp

Paddy Creek Campground

Natural Arch

Paddy Creek Road

Big Paddy Creek

Paddy Creek Trail

Little Paddy Creek

N

0   .5   1

Scale in Miles

Slabtown Road

Scenic Overlook

Big Piney Creek Trail

Roby Lake Trailhead

17

Roby

NATURE WALK
77

TRAIL 78: *Horseshoe Bend Natural Area*

*H*orseshoe Bend is a designated natural area managed by the Missouri Department of Conservation and owned by the L.A.D. Foundation. The preserve rises above a hairpin bend in the Big Piney River. A former forest road leads from the parking lot along and down the backbone ridge to the stream below. There are several small caves in the riverside limestone bluffs below the ridge. Vistas of the surrounding farm land appear in the open breaks. This is a good place to explore after the leaves fall.

*H*orseshoe Bend is located about 3 miles northwest of the Texas County Courthouse in Houston. From the courthouse, go north on Grand Avenue four-tenths of a mile, curving around Brushy Creek and continue south on Texas CR 2100. Continue 1 mile to Texas CR 2120 and turn left (west). Proceed 1.5 mile to the dead end and the MDC parking area. While near Houston, visit the Piney River Narrows Natural Area a few miles west of town.

Area/Location/County:
Rolla-Houston/Houston/Texas County

U.S.G.S. Map(s):
1:24,000 Houston

Trail(s) Distance:
no established trails; old wood road

Acreage:
215 acres

Activities:
nature walk, nature study

Fee(s):
none

NATURE WALK
78

78. Horseshoe Bend Natural Area

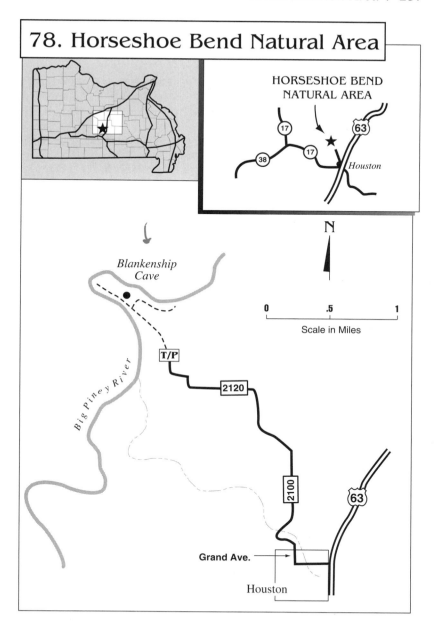

HORSESHOE BEND
NATURAL AREA

Houston

N

Blankenship
Cave

Big Piney River

T/P

2120

2100

63

Grand Ave.

Houston

0   .5   1
Scale in Miles

NATURE WALK
78

TRAIL 79: *Piney River Narrows Natural Area*

*T*he Piney River Narrows is noted for its limestone-pinnacled crest and its narrow hogback ridge situated between two upper Ozark streams. Big Piney River and West Piney Creek have water-carved the bluff a few miles upstream from Horseshoe Bend Natural Area. The 258 acre Narrows harbors a 17 acre natural area at the pinnacles and the 33 acre Piney Creek Natural Area at streamside. The Missouri Department of Conservation manages the area which is leased from L.A.D. Foundation of St. Louis.

*T*here are two trailheads to the Piney River Narrows. The main trailhead parking area is located 3 miles west of the U.S. Hwy. 63 and Mo. 17 junction at Houston. The parking area is on the left (west) side of Mo. 17 just before the river bridge over Big Piney River and Dogs Bluff boat access. From the Mo. 17 parking area, a service road heads straight towards the river and the road narrows to fisherman-user paths that follow the river bank across from the Narrows. At this point, wading the river would be required to access the Narrows on the opposite bank.

A second and more direct approach to the pinnacled crest is from the Hwy. Z pullout. From the Big Piney River bridge and Dogs Bluff, drive half a mile south and east to the junction of Mo. 17 and Hwy. Z and turn right (south). Follow Hwy. Z a short distance to the south side of the Big Piney River bridge and park. Follow the user paths into the cedar-topped preserve about 200 yards or so to arrive at the pinnacle known as Balancing Rock. More pinnacles are along the Narrows ridge. Late fall, winter and early spring would be the best times to walk and view the geological features.

Area/Location/County:
Rolla-Houston/Houston/Texas County

U.S.G.S. Map(s):
1:24,000 Bucyrus

Trail(s) Distance:
approximately half a mile of user paths

Acreage:
258 acres total
50 acres natural area

Activities:
nature walk, nature study

Fee(s):
none

NATURE WALK
79

79. Piney River Narrows Natural Area

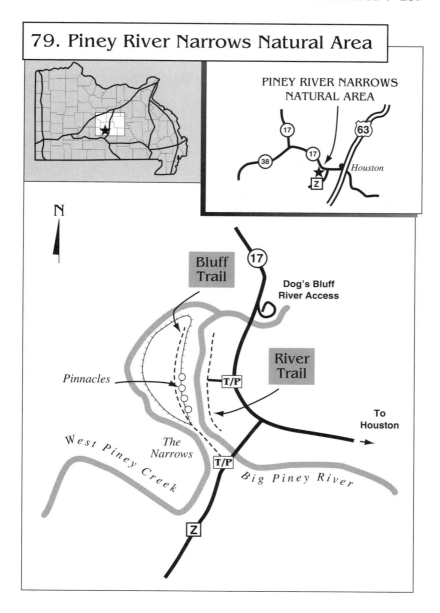

TRAIL 80: *Lake of the Ozarks State Park*

Early Spring Harbinger, Hepatica

Situated in the Osage River hills of the northern Ozarks, Lake of the Ozarks is Missouri's largest state park. The 17,265 acres are centered around the Grand Glaize arm of the vast Lake of the Ozarks. Following creation of the lake by building a dam, the land, developed by the National Park Service, became a state park in 1946. Upland oak and hickory forest, savanna, glades, old fields, bottomland forest, marsh, fen, shoreline and bluffs of Grand Glaize Arm comprise the park's natural areas.

There are 10 foot trails of varying distances and conditions that total about 25 miles. Trails are found in three separate areas of the state park: Main Park north (Mo. 134 access), Grand Glaize Beach west (Mo. 54 access) and Coakley Hollow south (A-33 access). The 10 trails are summarized by area.

Main Park north is located south of the junction of Mo. 42 and Mo. 134, 5 miles west of Brumley and 5 miles east of the junction of Mo. 42 and Mo. 54 at Osage Beach. It is the most developed area of the state park.

NATURE WALK
80

*T*he Woodland Trail begins and ends half a mile south of the park office on Mo. 134, behind the trail center. The 6 mile loop meanders through the 1,275 acre Patterson Hollow Wild Area. The trail experience is a composite of abandoned wild oat-filled meadows, young forest, streambeds, seeps, ridges and ravines. There is a backpacking camp near Patterson Hollow at the southwestern end of the loop. The trail moves counterclockwise and is blazed with blue arrows. There are two connector trails that allow for shorter hikes of 2 miles (orange arrow blaze) and 4 miles (yellow arrow blaze).

*L*azy Hollow Trail is a good introductory hike to the state park. The half mile loop is short and easy, passing through a young upland oak and hickory forest savanna. The trail direction is clockwise and is blazed with green arrows. The trailhead lies directly across Mo. 134 from the trail center, half a mile south of the park office near the entrance.

*D*ouble loop, 6-mile-long Trail of the Four Winds is open to hikers and all-terrain bicycles, however the well-worn trail receives most use from equestrians from the adjacent riding stables. The trailhead is 2 miles south of the park office entrance on the right (west) side of Mo. 134, across from the airport. There is a 3.2 mile blue blazed loop and a 4.1 mile yellow blazed loop. Both move counterclockwise. It is 1.3 miles from the trailhead to the lake cove overlook via the yellow loop.

*S*quaw's Revenge Trail is primarily a horse trail but it is open to hikers. The trailhead is at the horse rental stable (open year around). The 2 mile loop is marked with green arrows and circulates clockwise. Best to hike (if at all) in late fall to early spring.

*F*awn Ridge Trail is a 2.5 mile double loop that moves counterclockwise. The trail has two trailheads, one at the campground registration booth down Lake View Bend Trail, and the second across Mo. 134 from the picnic area south of the riding stables. The north loop is blazed with blue arrows, the south loop with yellow arrows. This is a hiking only trail with good lake vistas when the leaves are down.

*P*oint-to-point, 1-mile-long Lake View Bend Trail begins at the campground registration booth and ends at camping area No. 4 at lake's edge. The semi-difficult, narrow bluffside path follows the boulder base of steep limestone cliffs overlooking the lake. Birding and spring wildflowers are excellent. This is one of the best hikes in the main north park, so take your time.

*G*rand Glaize Recreation Area west is easily accessed from dual lane Mo. 54. The entry road is located 1 mile west of the Grand Glaize bridge in Osage Beach on the south side of Mo. 54. There are separate trailheads for the two trails.

NATURE WALK
80

80. Lake of the Ozarks State Park

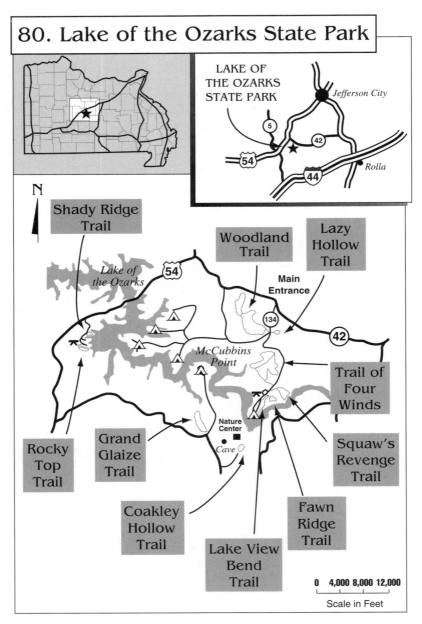

LAKE OF THE OZARKS STATE PARK

Jefferson City

Rolla

N

Shady Ridge Trail

Woodland Trail

Lazy Hollow Trail

Lake of the Ozarks

Main Entrance

McCubbins Point

Trail of Four Winds

Rocky Top Trail

Grand Glaize Trail

Nature Center

Cave

Squaw's Revenge Trail

Coakley Hollow Trail

Fawn Ridge Trail

Lake View Bend Trail

0 4,000 8,000 12,000

Scale in Feet

*R*ocky Top Trail begins and ends at the southwest corner of the picnic area parking lot. The 3 mile double loop trail is equally divided in distance. The first loop features an excellent five acre glade with an array of prairie plants and scenic lake overlooks. The second loop has lake coves and a north facing 100-foot-high bluff.

NATURE WALK
80

*S*hady Ridge Trail begins and ends at the Grand Glaize boat launch and beach parking area. The half mile easy loop flows counterclockwise along the lakeshore, curving back along a glade and old road to the parking lot.

*C*oakley Hollow south is accessed along A-33. From Mo. 54 south of Osage Beach, go west on Hwy. A, 8.5 miles to A-33 and turn left (north). A-33 north accesses Coakley Hollow, the Grand Glaize Trail and McCubbins Point (camping).

*C*oakley Hollow Trail is a 1 mile, self-guiding interpretive loop that begins at the Ozark Caverns and Visitors Nature Center (seasonal March to Labor Day). The 45 minute, yellow-blazed walk has eight posted stations that correspond to a trail brochure. A 200 foot boardwalk accesses Coakley Hollow Fen, a designated Missouri Natural Area. The walk also features a glade, spring branch, dam and mill site. This hollow makes a cool summer retreat. The area's access road is gated in winter and occasionally at other times.

*N*orth on A-33 from the Coakley Hollow turnoff about 1.5 miles is the trailhead parking area of the Grand Glaize Trail, adjacent north of the service area. The 2.5 mile forest loop is signed with yellow arrows in a counterclockwise direction and is one of the park's most remote trails. This is essentially a ridgetop to Honey Run Hollow and back to ridgetop hike.

Area/Location/County:
Rolla-Houston/Osage Beach/Camden, Morgan, Miller counties

U.S.G.S. Map(s):
1:24,000 Bagnell, Lake Ozark, Toronto, Camdenton

Trail(s) Distance:
10 trails total 25 miles

Acreage:
17,265 acres

Activities:
hiking, backpacking, nature study, seasonal naturalist, seasonal cave tours, picnicking, shelters, equestrian use, biking, canoeing, boating, launch ramps, horse stable, airport, camp store, basic and electric camping, group camping, cabins

Fee(s):
camping, cave tours, boat launch fee at Grand Glaize, rentals include shelters, cabins, boats and horses

NATURE WALK
80

TRAIL 81: *Ha Ha Tonka State Park*

Devil's Promenade, Devil's Kitchen Trail

*H*a Ha Tonka is a popular day use hiker's park. Eight hiking-only trails, many interconnecting, traverse the banks and bluffs above the Niangua Arm of the Lake of the Ozarks. At the center of the nearly 3,000 acre property is a remarkable number of karst features and formations including collapsed caverns, pinnacles, promenades, caves, canyons, a giant chasm, a natural bridge, sinkholes and springs. One of the most outstanding examples of a Missouri oak savanna is found within the park. There are cultural historical sites such as the ruins of a 1922 castle (built as a retreat for a wealthy Kansas City businessman), and an old post office (1872-1937). All of the unique natural and cultural features can be accessed on foot from one of the eight foot trails.

NATURE WALK
81

The captivating beauty and charm of the surroundings makes Ha Ha Tonka a repeat park, one you will want to return to again and again.

Trail Summary:

*T*he 1.5 mile Quarry Trail forms a triple loop to the north of the castle. A white arrow-marked connecting loop shortens the trail to a 1 mile hike. The trailhead is at the northwest corner of the castle and is marked clockwise with green arrows. Highlights of the trail include lakeviews, glades and an old abandoned quarry that was exploited to build the castle. Park at the castle parking lot at the base of the hill near Hwy. D and the park's north entrance.

*R*ed arrows blaze the Dell Rim Trail, a half mile, point-to-point boardwalk trail along the vista-rich bluff rim to Whispering Dell sinkhole. The trailhead begins at the castle parking area. A boardwalk spur leads up to the former water tower of the castle. The second half of the wooden trail descends to an overlook in the saddle between the rim and the spring below. Dell Rim Trail interconnects with Spring Trail.

*S*pring Trail's 1.5 mile loop is marked with blue arrows and goes clockwise. The two trailheads are found across Hwy. D from the historic post office and at the spring-lakeside parking area. The trail is actually a double loop with a dividing white connector trail. The path along the spring branch is mostly paved and boardwalk. Ha Ha Tonka Spring yields 48 million gallons daily. Spring Trail interconnects with Whispering Dell Rim boardwalk trail and Island Trail.

*I*sland Trail is an adventure for all ages. The three-quarter mile double loop is accessed from Spring Trail at the mill race and causeway. The Island Trail is signed with green arrows in a counter clockwise direction. There is a gated cave, spring waterfall and a balanced rock. A white arrow-blazed connecting trail cuts the trail distance in half. The blufftop trails are several feet above the lake waters.

*B*oulder Ridge Trail follows the slopes of a high ridge to the southwest of the spring area parking. The trailhead is west of the junction of Spring Road and Hwy. D. Boulder outcrops at ridgecrest add to the enchantment of the overlooks.

*O*ne-half mile-long Colosseum Trail loop begins and ends at the natural bridge parking area just southeast of the castle parking area near the north park entrance. The yellow-blazed path goes clockwise. The trail hikes under the natural bridge through the colosseum sinkhole and up along the Whispering Dell Rim and across the 50 foot span of natural bridge, back to the start. The natural bridge was once used as a vehicle access road bridge to the castle.

*T*urkey Pen Hollow Trail is a three-quarter mile loop moving clockwise with blazed green arrows. Trailhead parking is adjacent to Hwy. D, a half mile from the north entrance on the east side of the highway. Available at the trailhead, a self-guiding booklet interprets the spectacular savanna. There are eight stations or stops to interpret the savanna's heritage enroute along the path. The Devil's Kitchen Trail shares the same path for about 400 feet before the two separate.

*T*he 1 mile-long Devil's Kitchen Trail is signed with brown arrows and walks clockwise. The Kitchen area is a small cave with an open "chimney" shaft. The Devil's Promenade or Walk follows the base of a shelter overhang bluff just beyond the Devil's Kitchen. The trail loops across Hwy. D near the historic post office and shares the same trail along the rim with Colosseum Trail and the Dell Rim Trail. The last segment crosses the natural bridge and Hwy. D back to the trailhead parking area.

*H*a Ha Tonka State Park is day-use only and is gated at sunset. To reach the park from the Mo. 5 and U.S. Hwy. 54 intersection in Camdenton, follow U.S. Hwy. 54 2 miles southwest to Hwy. D and turn left (east). Follow Hwy. D 2.25 miles to and through the park. Parking areas are adjacent to Hwy. D.

Area/Location/County:
Rolla-Houston/Camdenton/Camden County

U.S.G.S. Map(s):
1:24,000 Ha Ha Tonka, Decaturville

Trail(s) Distance:
eight trails total 7.5 miles

Acreage:
2,993 acres

Activities:
nature walks, nature study, natural areas, historic sites, picnicking, shelters, amphitheater, fishing, boating, canoeing

Fee(s):
shelter rental

NATURE WALK
81

81. Ha Ha Tonka State Park

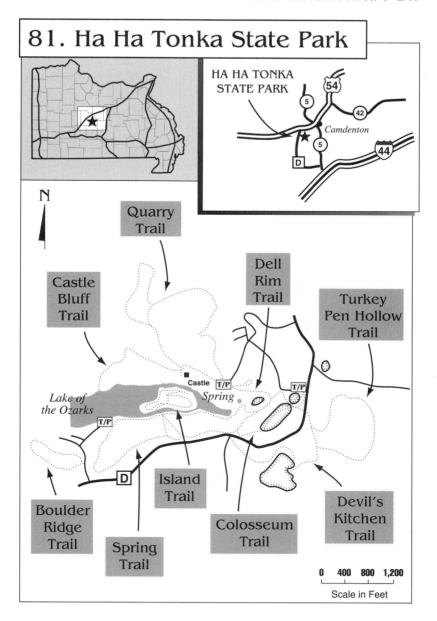

HA HA TONKA
STATE PARK

Camdenton

N

Quarry
Trail

Castle
Bluff
Trail

Dell
Rim
Trail

Turkey
Pen Hollow
Trail

Castle T/P

Lake of
the Ozarks

Spring

T/P

T/P

D

Island
Trail

Boulder
Ridge
Trail

Spring
Trail

Colosseum
Trail

Devil's
Kitchen
Trail

0   400   800 1,200

Scale in Feet

NATURE WALK
81

TRAIL 82: *Bennett Spring State Park*

*B*ennett Spring is one of the oldest and most popular state parks in the Show Me State. The Osage who were the last of many Native American groups to inhabit the land, knew Bennett Spring as the "eye of the sacred one." After Big Spring and Greer Spring, Bennett Spring is the third largest spring in Missouri. Emerging from the spring bed of Spring Hollow Creek, an average 100 million gallons flow daily from the circular emerald pool. The spring branch rushes to the Niangua River, 1.5 miles downstream. Enroute the cool, fresh waters pass over a dam and through the rainbow trout-rearing pools of a fish hatchery. From March to October the park is inundated with fishermen much as are Montauk and Roaring River state parks, however hikers will find their "niche" exploring the park's trails.

*D*o explore the nature center and view the many exhibits about Missouri springs, their flora and fauna and the Ozarks in general. Check with the park naturalist for scheduled hikes and programs. The nature center is open daily in summer and Wednesdays through Sundays from September to May.

*F*ive of the park's seven nature trails are laid out along the spring branch (about 3 miles) or near the nature center. The two other trails are more remote and are longer hikes: one leading to a savanna ridgetop and the second to a natural tunnel.

Trail Summary:

*T*he Oak-Hickory Trail is a quarter mile self-guiding, interpretive loop that begins and ends at the back door of the nature center. The clockwise loop goes uphill and downhill and has 13 forest ecology interpretive stops that correspond to a handout available at the nature center. The short informative path through upland and bottomland forest interconnects with the three-quarter mile Bridge Trail at the top of the hill.

*T*he Bridge Trail is a three-quarter mile, point-to-point connecting trail, extending from the Oak-Hickory Trail loop to the 1 mile-long Bluff Trail on the east bank of the spring branch. The entire trail is shaded by upland forest.

*B*luff Trail follows alongside the spring branch on the east bank, a linear half mile. A half mile return loop ascends and descends a bluff and overlooks the branch stream, rejoining near the trail's junction with the Bridge Trail. This trail travels by a variety of habitats, including streams, bluffs, forest and glades. Bluffside seeps support fen plant communities.

NATURE WALK
82

*T*he Whistle Trail picks up where the Bluff Trail begins its return loop and continues for half a mile along the east bank of the spring branch, ending near the Niangua River. In the middle, it travels by a large picnic area with restroom facilities before resuming its streamside journey. Retrace your steps back to the nature center, or return by the park roads along the west side of the stream. For all practical hiking purposes, the first four trails are interconnecting and may be considered as one hike.

*S*pring Trail begins on the opposite west bank at Bennett Spring and follows the bank two-thirds of a mile to the dam and fish hatchery. This trail offers great fishing and viewing of wildlife and wildflowers throughout the year. Bald eagles make the park their winter home and are often seen in search of dinner near the dam. Part of the trail travels along the downhill side of the Bennett Spring Hanging Fen Natural Area where bluffside seeps support the rich fen plant communities. Retrace your steps, or return on the park road along the east bank.

*S*avanna Ridge Trail is a 2.5 mile loop that begins and ends upstream from the spring along Spring Hollow Creek near the cabin area at the trailhead for the Natural Tunnel Trail. From the trailhead shelter and parking area, cross the park road to the west bank of Spring Hollow Creek and turn left along the marked trail. For about half a mile, the green arrow-blazed Savanna Ridge Trail shares the streamside path with the blue arrow-blazed Natural Tunnel Trail.

*A*fter a half mile hike along the grassy riparian trail, the Savanna Trail turns right and heads up the the first of two hills supporting an oak savanna ecosystem. The counterclockwise shady path crosses a small stream which divides the two hills and a white arrow marked path bypasses the second hill and cuts short the distance to 1.5 miles. The path loops up and around the ridge of the second hill and travels back along the top of the bluff which offers excellent overlooks of Spring Hollow. As the trails descends, it rejoins the Natural Tunnel Trail. Turn left and go back along Spring Hollow Creek to the road bridge crossing right and the trailhead.

*N*atural Tunnel Trail is a 7.5 mile round trip hike and is considered a great morning hike. The trailhead is the same as for the Savanna Ridge Trail. Blue arrow-marked trails travel along the east and west sides of Spring Hollow. This "losing" stream above Bennett Spring normally has little or no water in the streambed but often runs full after heavy rains. Hikers should exercise caution before crossing during flood conditions.

*T*he more level eastside trail travels through bottomland floodplain forest, ascends and descends a forested hill and crosses old farm lands and several large washes. The more rugged westside trail shares a streamside path with the Savanna Ridge Trail for three-quarters of a

NATURE WALK
82

mile, then travels through bottomland forest, crossing Spring Hollow several times. At about the first mile, a half mile trail marked with white arrows connects the east and west sides, offering a small loop hike of 2.5 miles.

*T*he west side then ascends slowly through old farmland and into upland forest. It travels along the top of a high bluff and offers beautiful vistas of the valley below. The east and west side blue-marked trails join at about 2 miles, offering a second loop trail of about 1.75 miles. From farm lane to forest trail, the path crosses Spring Hollow Creek three more times before reaching a tributary of Spring Hollow Creek. Continue along the small stream half a mile, crossing three times to reach the 16-foot-high and 50-foot-wide tunnel, where hikers are able to rock hop through the tunnel. The setting is tranquil, so allow plenty of time to enjoy the trip. Retrace your steps back to the trail junction 1.75 miles and take either the east or west side blue-marked trail back to the trailhead.

*T*o reach Bennett Spring State Park from I-44, exit 129 at Lebanon and drive through the city 3 miles and then west on Mo. 64 about 12 miles to Mo. 64A and turn left (south). Continue on Mo. 64A about 2 miles to the park. Follow the signs.

*S*ix miles south of Bennett Spring State Park on Hwy. 00 is the 160 acre Bennett Spring Savanna, owned by The Nature Conservancy and managed jointly with the Missouri Department of Natural Resources. This prime savanna is open to foot traffic but there are no established trails. An old, gated dirt road appears on the left (east) side of Hwy. 00 and may serve as a foot trail. Park at the gate.

Area/Location/County:
Rolla-Houston/Lebanon/Laclede and Dallas counties

U.S.G.S. Map(s):
1:24,000 Bennett Spring, Windyville

Trail(s) Distance:
 seven trails total approximately 14 miles

Acreage:
3,099 acres

Activities:
nature walks, hiking, nature study, naturalist, nature center, spring, picnicking, shelters, trout fish hatchery, fishing, canoeing, launch ramp, swimming pool, bathhouse, camp store, concessions, dining lodge, camping, cabins, motel

Fee(s):
camping, lodging, shelter rental, canoe rental

NATURE WALK
82

82. Bennett Spring State Park

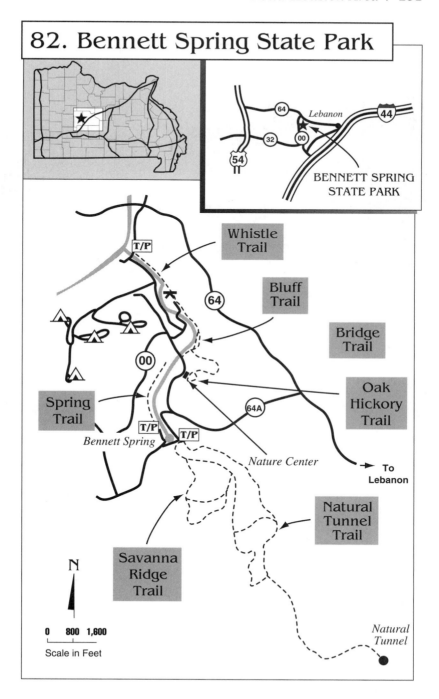

Whistle Trail

Bluff Trail

Bridge Trail

Oak Hickory Trail

Spring Trail

Bennett Spring

Nature Center

To Lebanon

Natural Tunnel Trail

Savanna Ridge Trail

Natural Tunnel

N

0   800   1,600
Scale in Feet

NATURE WALK
82

TRAIL 83: *Pomme de Terre State Park*

Shoreline at Pomme de Terre State Park, Cedar Bluff Trail

Within the Springfield Plateau of the Missouri Ozarks, Pomme de Terre State Park is located on Lake Pomme de Terre which was formed from the waters of the Pomme de Terre River. Legend has it that LaSalle or other French fur traders named the river in the late 1600s for the potato bean (*Apios americana*) whose edible tubers resemble the more familiar pomme or apple to the Frenchmen (literally "apple of the earth").

This Missouri DNR state park occupies two separate lakeside tracts of land leased since the 1960s from the U.S. Army Corps of Engineers: the Hermitage north tract and the Pittsburg south tract. Divided by Lake Pomme de Terre, both tracts offer outdoor recreation opportunities and facilities plus hiking paths. However the savanna landscape of the Pittsburg south tract is more appealing and makes the best hike.

Reach the Pittsburg south tract by road from Pittsburg by driving north on Mo. 64 to Mo. 64B and turning left (west). Follow Mo. 64B to the park and office entrance and the trailhead, a distance of 3 miles.

The 3-mile-long Indian Point Trail begins and ends at the campground entrance parking area but it is also accessible from the north picnic and beach area with a little walking. Through controlled burning, an open oak savanna landscape of prairie grasses and wildflowers have emerged. Big and little bluestem, Indian grass, purple coneflower, rose verbena and Missouri evening primrose are some of the flora found beneath the scattered post and chinquapin oaks and red cedars.

NATURE WALK
83

*G*oing clockwise, the chert rock trail follows the ridge parallel to the park road and down to the picnic and beach area, crossing the park road twice. The path continues to Indian Point peninsula with great lake vistas. From Indian Point the trail loops back along the coves to the ridge, crossing the road to end at the trailhead. The trail is blue blazed. Shorter hikes of 1.5 miles and 2.5 miles are possible by using the red blazed connector trails (elev. 850-940 ft.).

*H*ermitage north tract is reached by driving 3 miles southeast of Hermitage on Mo. 254 to Mo. 64 and and turning right (south) on RD Road. From Pittsburg, drive north on Mo. 64 across the causeway to Nemo and turn left (west). Follow Mo. 64 west to RD Road and turn left, following the signs to the park entrance.

*T*he 2 mile Cedar Bluff Trail loop begins either at the beach or the campground. By using the connector trail, a shorter hike of 1 mile distance is possible. The main loop is signed in a counterclockwise direction with blue arrows; the connector trail has red arrows. The rocky trail straddles the park road on both sides of the finger-like peninsula. High water has obscured the trail in places. Red cedar trees are dominant on the cherty slopes and there is little understory due to high water and periodic controlled burns.

*A*lthough the Corps and MDC do not maintain any trails on their properties surrounding the vast lake, they do offer old roads and fishing paths.

Area/Location/County:
Rolla-Houston/Pittsburg and Hermitage/Hickory and Polk counties

U.S.G.S. Map(s):
1:24,000 Hermitage, Sentinel

Trail(s) Distance:
two trails total 5 miles

Acreage:
734 acres land
7,800 acres reservoir lake

Activities:
nature walks, nature study, picnicking, playgrounds, beaches, swimming, pier, fishing, boating, launch ramps, waterskiing, camping
Pittsburg side: shelter, marina, concessions
Hermitage side: camp store, youth camp

Fee(s):
camping, shelter rental, boat rentals and dock space rental available at marina

NATURE WALK
83

83. Pomme de Terre State Park

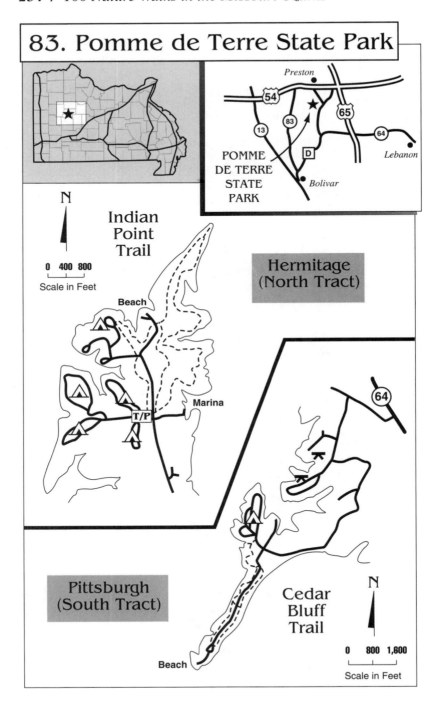

TRAIL 84: *Dean Davis Conservation Area*

Dean Davis Trail

*D*ean Davis Conservation Area is easily accessed and features a pleasant one hour walk that circles a dry lake bed that is undergoing succession. The site was originally intended to be a community lake for the Pomona area. In 1959 the lake bed, dam and spillway were constructed but the would-be lake never held water due to unexpected sinks and seepages. Now nature has reclaimed the man-made basin.

*A*n easy 2 mile loop trail leads northwest from the parking area through a mix of Ozark oak and hickory forest to the open lake bed where instead of water there are cattails, willows, cottonwoods and big bluestem grass. Several educational and surprisingly witty signs are posted along the path, such as "Moss Hills" and "Frog Pond." Reforestation trees of black walnut and shortleaf pine have been planted along the shore uplands. The trail is overgrown in places with thorny wild rose and blackberry canes, especially near and along the dam. The conservation area drains to Camp Creek, a tributary of the Eleven Point River.

*D*ean Davis Conservation Area is located 10 miles north of West Plains, and 2 miles north of Pomona, on U.S. Hwy. 60. From U.S. Hwy. 60, turn right (east) on Howell CR 242 and drive half a mile to the parking area trailhead on the left (north) side of the gravel road. The trail begins at the northwest corner of the parking lot and returns at its east end.

NATURE WALK
84

84. Dean Davis Conservation Area

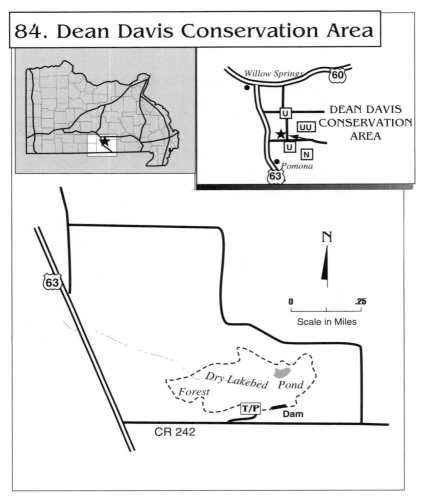

Area/Location/County:
Willow Springs/Pomona/Howell County

U.S.G.S. Map(s):
1:24,000 Willow Springs South

Trail(s) Distance:
2 mile loop

Acreage:
177 acres

Activities:
nature walk, nature study, seasonal hunting

Fee(s):
none

NATURE WALK
84

TRAIL 85: *Tingler Lake Conservation Area*

Tingler Lake

*T*he Missouri Department of Conservation acquired the Tingler Lake property in 1988, thanks to the efforts of The Nature Conservancy. Purchasing of the area preserved a wet mesic prairie, a shallow marsh and Tingler Lake, a five acre sinkhole pond. One hundred sixty acres of open space are being managed as a restored tallgrass prairie community with controlled seasonal burns and native seed plantings. Sixty-five acres are upland oak and hickory forest savanna. Half a mile of the south fork of the Spring River meanders through the east bottomland perimeter of the area on its way to the Missouri Arkansas border, 8 miles south.

NATURE WALK
85

*F*rom the roadside mini-parking lot, the vehicle-wide, grassy trail goes directly to and around the sinkhole pond making for an easy half mile loop. The main loop heads uphill through the oak and hickory forest, then down along the riparian forest of the south fork Spring River. The path curves back through the tallgrass prairie to the parking area. Diverse habitats make for rich birding. A new trail loop is being developed in the prairie portion at the property's southwest corner. The state's endangered green orchid (*Habenaria*) thrives in the wet prairie swales.

*T*ingler Lake Conservation Area is located in south Howell County approximately 8 miles south of West Plains. From the junction of Mo. 17 and U.S. Hwy. 63, drive south on Mo. 17 about 6 miles to the junction with Howell CR 9100 and turn right (west). Continue west on CR 9100 seven-tenths of a mile to CR 8100 and turn left (south). Drive 1.4 miles to the marked parking lot on the left (east) side of the gravel road.

*A*nother MDC day use area to visit close by is Vanderhoef Memorial State Forest. The 140 acre forest has a segment of the Spring River running through it. An eight-tenths of a mile trail loop traverses upland and bottomland forest. A wildlife observation deck overlooks the Spring River, just upstream from a beaver dam.

*T*o reach Vanderhoef Memorial State Forest (MDC) from Tingler Lake Conservation Area parking lot, drive south 4.7 miles on gravel CR 8110, jogging west three times, to the marked spacious parking area on the east side of the road.

Area/Location/County:
Willow Springs/West Plains/Howell County

U.S.G.S. Map(s):
1:24,000 Lanton

Trail(s) Distance:
2 mile loop with shorter options

Acreage:
240 acres

Activities:
nature walk, nature study, picnicking, seasonal hunting

Fee(s):
none

NATURE WALK
85

85. Tingler Lake Conservation Area

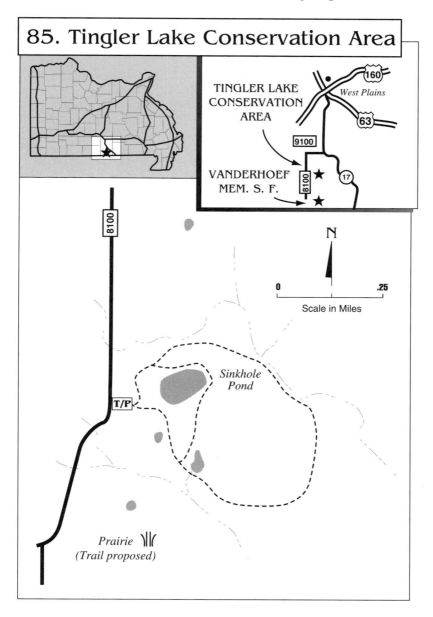

TINGLER LAKE
CONSERVATION
AREA

West Plains

160

63

9100

VANDERHOEF
MEM. S. F.

8100

17

N

0   .25

Scale in Miles

8100

*Sinkhole
Pond*

T/P

Prairie
(Trail proposed)

NATURE WALK
85

TRAIL 86: *Ridge Runner Trail*

*D*esignated a National Recreation Trail, the Ridge Runner Trail is a point-to-point, 23 mile easy to rugged trail that begins and ends at Noblett Lake Recreation Area at the north terminus and ends and begins at North Fork Recreation Area at the south terminus, traversing exclusively through U.S. Forest Service lands of the Willow Springs District. Aside from the Ozark Trail, the Ridge Runner Trail is one of the longest maintained trails in the Missouri Ozarks. In addition to the linear Ridge Runner Trail there are two hiking loops that branch off from the main trail: 8 mile-long Noblett Lake loop and 12.1 mile-long North Fork loop. The North Fork River Section of the Ozark Trail shares the same path from Blue Hole to North Fork RA, a distance of 14 miles.

*T*he Ridge Runner is mostly single track but does follow segments of old forest roads, sometimes as reroutes after burns such as in the Blue Hole area. There are long and difficult ascents and descents from streams to forest ridges. The Ridge Runner can be overgrown and extremely rocky in places. There are several forest road crossings and one major highway crossing, Mo. 14, near Blue Hole. White diamonds mark the trail in both directions. Be advised that the trail is shared with equestrians and mountain bikers. Early spring and mid-fall are the best times to be on foot. There are two backpack camps at Dry Creek and Tabor Creek trail camps. Car shuttling is a possible option. Only the most experienced hikers could make the 23 mile trek in one day due to the many climbs and declines, many steep. There are four trailheads and parking areas.

Trail Summary:

*N*oblett Lake Recreation Area is located 12 miles west of Willow Springs. To get there, take Mo. 76 west to Mo. 181 south. Continue on Mo. 181, 1.5 miles to Hwy. AP and go 3 miles to the recreation area entrance on the right side of the road. The northern trailhead and parking area of the Ridge Runner National Recreation Trail begins and ends across from the Sugar Hill campground. The Noblett Lake loop also begins and ends at the same trailhead.

*T*he main trail goes south 23 miles to the North Fork RA, the southern terminus. The path follows ridgetops and crosses Spring Creek and one of its tributaries enroute to Horton trailhead, the second trailhead south (3.3 miles one way). There are also two trail junctions enroute with the Noblett Lake loop trail.

*H*orton trailhead is reached by driving 3 miles south from the Noblett Lake RA road entrance on Hwy. AP to FS 107, turning right (west). Drive west on gravel FS 107 about 2 miles to the signed trailhead parking area just past the road junction.

NATURE WALK
86

Between Horton and Blue Hole trailheads (4.7 miles), the Ridge Runner follows ridge slopes and ridge tops, crossing Dry Creek and its tributaries. A trail camp area has been established in the upland at Dry Creek. Between Dry Creek and Blue Hole, forest fires have reduced the trail surface down to the chert rock, making hiking rough going.

Blue Hole trailhead is reached by following Hwy. AP about 7 miles south from Noblett Lake RA to the roadside marked trailhead. Park and walk west, following the old paved Children's Forest loop. Blue Hole is also an east-west junction on the Ozark Trail, North Fork River Section. From Blue Hole south, the Ridge Runner Trail shares the same track with the Ozark Trail and "OT" trail markers will appear. A 10 mile segment of the Ozark Trail goes east from Blue Hole to near Pomona.

Condition of the Ridge Runner Trail in the Blue Hole area has been disrupted by fire. South of Mo. 14, the trail resumes good tread along the forested ridges and hollows to Tabor Creek, upridge to Tabor Cave and Tabor trail camp. The final segment of the Ridge Runner Trail heads south along ridge and through ravine to Steamboat Hollow and on to North Fork Recreation Area.

North Fork Recreation Area is about 16 miles west of West Plains, just south off Hwy. CC. The signed trailhead and registration box and parking area is just before the campground entrance.

Area/Location/County:
Willow Springs/Willow Springs/Howell, Douglas, Ozark counties

U.S.G.S. Map(s):
1:24,000 Dyestone Mountain, Siloam Springs, Dora

Trail(s) Distance:
23 miles one way
Ozark Trail: North Fork River Section

Activities:
hiking, backpacking, trail campsites, nature study, developed recreation areas at Noblett Lake north terminus and North Fork south terminus

Fee(s):
developed camping at Noblett Lake and North Fork RA's, shelter rental at Noblett Lake

NATURE WALK
86

86. Ridge Runner Trail

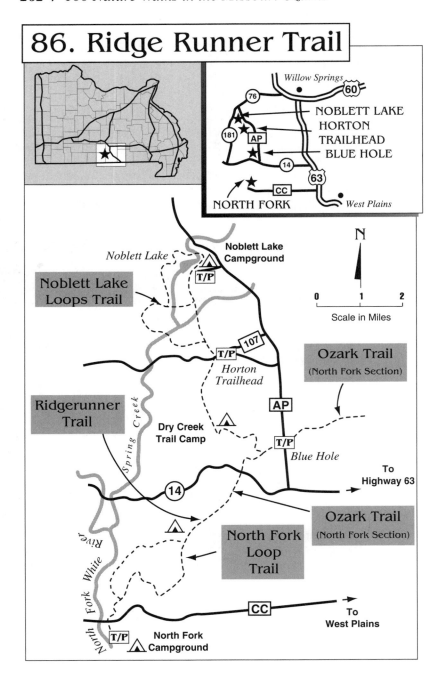

Willow Springs
60
76
NOBLETT LAKE
HORTON
181   AP   TRAILHEAD
BLUE HOLE
14
63
CC
NORTH FORK   West Plains

N

Noblett Lake   Noblett Lake
Campground
T/P

Noblett Lake
Loops Trail

0   1   2
Scale in Miles

T/P   107
Horton
Trailhead

Ozark Trail
(North Fork Section)

Ridgerunner
Trail

Spring Creek

Dry Creek
Trail Camp

AP

T/P
Blue Hole

To
Highway 63

14

North Fork
Loop
Trail

Ozark Trail
(North Fork Section)

North Fork White River

CC   To
West Plains

T/P   North Fork
Campground

NATURE WALK
86

TRAIL 87: *Noblett Lake Loop, Ridge Runner Trail*

Noblett Lake at Sunset

*P*icturesque Noblett Lake Recreation Area was developed by the young men of CCC Camp Willow (2 miles northeast on FS 108) in the 1930s and their efforts are still in place today. The south shore lakeside trail (one-quarter mile) along the former Clearwater Beach was constructed by the CCC, as were the historic buildings in the picnic area and the dam and spillway. Interconnecting trails tie the recreation area together – the two campgrounds, dam, lake, picnic area – and lead to the trailhead for the Ridge Runner Trail and Noblett Lake Loop.

*N*oblett Lake Loop is actually a double loop off of the Ridge Runner Trail. The trailhead begins and ends near the entrance to the Sugar Hill campground, the same trailhead for the Ridge Runner Trail. The 4 mile loop jogs right (west) after about half a mile while the 8 mile loop continues another 2.3 miles (two deep stream crossings) and loops right (half mile north of Horton trailhead) at a signed trail junction.

*C*ontinuing on the 4 mile loop trail west from the main 8 mile loop and Ridge Runner Trail, the short loop goes three-quarters of a mile before

NATURE WALK
87

reconnecting with the 8 mile loop. On the way the path crosses FS 486, follows ridgetops, descends into a beaver meadow and crosses knee-deep Noblett Creek to rejoin the main 8 mile loop where hikers should turn right.

*F*rom the trail junction near Horton trailhead, the 8 mile loop traverses a ridgetop to Cord Hollow and crosses a small stream (1.5 miles). The trail continues, following the base of a bluff about a quarter mile and rejoins the 4 mile loop at the Noblett Creek crossing. Both loop trails share the next 2.75 miles north, curving east back to the point of origin.

*F*rom the Noblett Creek trail junction, the loop follows the ridge (few lake views) and descends to a small hollow near Hellroaring Spring. The trail continues, crossing Noblett Creek again, this time as a tributary stream to Noblett Lake. The trail goes upridge and follows the slope high above Noblett Creek and Lake back to the lakeside picnic area. From the southeast corner of the picnic area with its historic CCC buildings, the trail heads uphill, skirting the Sugar Hill campground and back to the trailhead. Noblett Lake makes a great day hike on either the short or long loop.

*T*o reach Noblett Lake Recreation Area from Willow Springs, and the junction of U.S. Hwys 60/63, drive west about 7 miles on Mo. 76 to Mo. 181 and turn south. Follow Mo. 181 south 1.5 miles (make a vista stop at Blue Buck Tower) to Hwy. AP and turn left. Continue about 3 miles to the entrance of the recreation area on the right (south) side of the road. Continue to the trailhead just beyond the Sugar Hill campground entrance on the left side of the paved road.

Area/Location/County:
Willow Springs/Willow Springs/Douglas, Howell counties

U.S.G.S. Map(s):
1:24,000 Dyestone Mountain

Trail(s) Distance:
short hikes in the developed Noblett Lake Recreation Area
double loop of 4 and 8 miles
Ridge Runner Trail

Acreage:
27 acre Noblett Lake

Activities:
hiking, nature walks, nature study, picnicking, shelter, fishing, canoeing, camping

Fee(s):
summer camping, shelter rental

NATURE WALK
87

87. Noblett Lake Loop, Ridge Runner Trail

NOBLETT LAKE LOOP/ RIDGE RUNNER TRAIL

Willow Springs

West Plains

N

0   .5   1
Scale in Miles

Noblett Lake Loops

Noblett Lake
Dam

857

AP

T/P **Noblett Trailhead**

Ridge Runner Trail

Noblett Creek

To Horton Trailhead

NATURE WALK
87

TRAIL 88: *North Fork Loop, Ridge Runner Trail*

Shortleaf Pine

NATURE WALK
88

*T*he North Fork of the White River and the Ridge Runner Trail, south terminus, provide a full day's hiking excursion with the option of overnight backpacking at the Tabor Creek trail camp. Along the loop, there are six major ravine to ridge climbs and descents (elev. 700-1,050 ft.) along the single track trail and there are few stream and road crossings. Overall the loop trail is fairly level and has minimal overgrowth, allowing hikers to cover ground rapidly if they desire.

*T*he first half of the loop follows the same tread as the Ridge Runner Trail. The North Fork Section of the Ozark Trail also shares the same trail from the North Fork Recreation Area north to Tabor Cave and Camp and on north to Blue Hole, where it turns east to the Pomona trailhead.

*N*orth Fork Loop heads up near the campground entrance at the North Fork Recreation Area where there is convenient shady parking adjacent to the Ridge Runner trailhead registration box. From the trailhead registration box, the trail heads north, crossing Hwy. CC, then follows ridge slopes and ravines to the bluffs of the North Fork of the White River. The trail follows the riverside slope north and descends into Steam Mill Hollow and moves uphill to the ridgetop, heading northeast to Tabor Creek trail camp.

*F*rom the Tabor Creek trail camp, the forest trail loops south along the ridges and descends into Steam Mill Hollow once again, following the hollow for about 1.5 miles before climbing the ridge and reconnecting with the original main loop. Walk left (south) 1.5 miles, recrossing Hwy. CC to the trailhead at the North Fork Recreation Area.

*N*orth Fork Recreation Area is located about 16 miles west of West Plains and U.S. Hwy. 63 on Hwy. CC. The nearest town is Dora, 4 miles west on Hwy. CC to Mo. 181 north.

Area/Location/County:
Willow Springs/Dora/Ozark and Howell counties

U.S.G.S. Map(s):
1:24,000 Dora, Siloam Springs

Trail(s) Distance:
14 mile loop

Activities:
hiking, backpacking, nature study, picnicking, fishing, canoeing, launch ramp, camping, seasonal hunting

Fee(s):
seasonal developed camping

NATURE WALK
88

88. North Fork Loop, Ridge Runner Trail

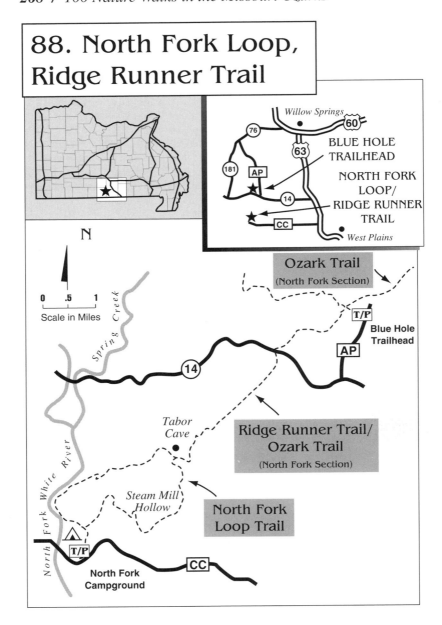

TRAIL 89: *North Fork Recreation Area*

Blue Spring

*I*n addition to the Ridge Runner Trail and its offshoot, North Fork Loop, the North Fork Recreation Area has its own short trail that leads to one of the larger springs in the North Fork River basin. It also offers foot trail access to the Devil's Backbone Wilderness via McGarr Ridge. At this time, the North Fork River Section of the Ozark Trail shares the same track with all four trails.

*T*he half-mile-long trail loop to Blue Spring (one of at least nine in the Missouri Ozarks named "Blue" due to their color) begins at the campground turnaround. The trail crosses a footbridge and follows the floodplain path along the White River's north fork to the spring. Blue Spring rises calmly with no boil at the base of a limestone bluff adjacent to the stream. The spring is often covered by backwater when the river floods. The deep circular pool yields 7 million gallons daily.

NATURE WALK
89

The pool's depth and minerals in the water deflect the light's rays, influencing its aquamarine or turquoise color.

*C*arved stone steps lead to the top of the bluff flanking the spring. At the trail junction, go left and loop back along the bluff, past a small trailside cave. Going right at the trail junction leads uphill to McGarr Ridge and the Devil's Backbone Wilderness (one-third mile). The Blue Springs Trail loop descends to the floodplain and recrosses the footbridge to the parking turnaround. In addition, a half mile (one way) trail follows the White River North Fork from the campground to the canoe launch and picnic area.

*T*he U.S. Forest Service Recreation Area is located on Hwy. CC, 16 miles west of West Plains. The nearest community is Dora, located 4 miles west at Mo. 181 at Hwy. CC.

Area/Location/County:
Willow Springs/Dora/Ozark County

U.S.G.S. Map(s):
1:24,000 Dora

Trail(s) Distance:
half mile spring loop
trailhead access to Ridge Runner Trail
trailhead access to North Fork Loop
trailhead access to Devil's Backbone Wilderness
Ozark Trail: North Fork Section

Activities:
nature walk, hiking, nature study, picnicking, fishing, canoeing, launch ramp, camping

Fee(s):
seasonal camping

NATURE WALK
89

89. North Fork Recreation Area

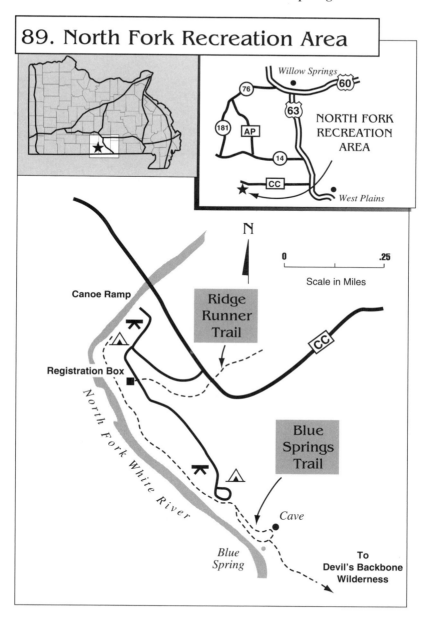

NORTH FORK
RECREATION
AREA

Willow Springs

West Plains

N

0   .25

Scale in Miles

Canoe Ramp

Ridge
Runner
Trail

Registration Box

North Fork White River

Blue
Springs
Trail

Cave

*Blue
Spring*

To
Devil's Backbone
Wilderness

NATURE WALK
89

TRAIL 90: *Devil's Backbone Wilderness*

Flowering Dogwood

*D*esignated in 1980, Devil's Backbone Wilderness encompasses 6,595 acres of rugged Ozark topography (elev. 680-1,020 ft.), characterized by narrow ridges and hollows separated by long steep slopes and bluffs. The swift and clear North Fork of the White River bisects the wilderness and Crooked Creek is its main tributary. The place name is derived from a narrow 900-foot-high "backbone" ridge that was formed by a tight meander loop along Crooked Creek (foot trail accessible). The wilderness is readily accessible and relatively small in size, making day trips feasible.

*T*here are four designated trailheads that access 13 miles of maintained but unmarked trails.They are Raccoon Hollow, McGarr Ridge and Collins Ridge, plus foot access from the Blue Spring Trail in the North Fork Recreation Area. Devil's Backbone Wilderness is located 15 to 17 miles west of West Plains, on the south side of Hwy. CC, flanking the North Fork Recreation Area.

NATURE WALK
90

90. Devil's Backbone Wilderness

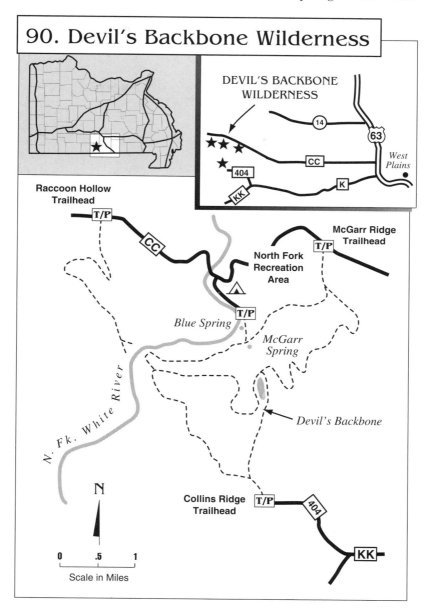

DEVIL'S BACKBONE
WILDERNESS

14

63

CC

West
Plains

404

K

KK

Raccoon Hollow
Trailhead

T/P

CC

McGarr Ridge
Trailhead

T/P

North Fork
Recreation
Area

Blue Spring

McGarr
Spring

Devil's Backbone

N. Fk. White River

N

Collins Ridge
Trailhead

T/P

404

KK

0   .5   1

Scale in Miles

***R**accoon* Hollow trailhead and parking area are located 1.5 miles west of the North Fork Recreation Area on the south side of Hwy. CC. A 2.5 mile linear trail (one way) follows the old fields, young forest ridgetops to a 900-foot-high bluff above Raccoon Hollow and the north fork of the White River. An overgrown trail leads to the bottom of the hollow and stream. Retrace your steps back to the trailhead.

NATURE WALK
90

*M*cGarr Ridge trailhead is also located on the south side of Hwy. CC, 2 miles east from the North Fork Recreation Area entrance. A loop trail of about 7 miles follows McGarr Ridge southwest, looping back along the narrow streambed of Crooked Creek. The Crooked Creek segment can be brushy, wet and slightly confusing in the bottoms, the most challenging and remote part of the loop hike.

*T*hree mile McGarr Ridge trail segment (old forest road) is shared by the North Fork Section of the Ozark Trail. A half mile linear access spur from the Blue Spring Trail, North Fork RA junctions with McGarr Ridge at mid-ridge. The loop trail continues downridge to the North Fork and Crooked Creek confluence and then follows the 4 mile Crooked Creek stream segment back to the Hwy. CC trailhead.

*A*ccess trail spurs from Collins Ridge trailhead also feed into the Crooked Creek trail segment near the confluence with the North Fork River and at the Devil's Backbone. Horse use can be high in the east wilderness area.

*C*ollins Ridge trailhead is the least accessible of the four Devil's Backbone Wilderness trailheads. From West Plains, drive west on Hwy. K from U.S. Hwy. 63 about 11 miles, through Pottersville to the junction of Hwy. KK. Turn right (north) on Hwy. KK and drive about 5 miles to the junction with FS 404. Turn right (north) and proceed on FS 404 about 2 miles to the marked trailhead.

A loop trail of about 7 miles is formed by following the old forest road trail north, turning right at the trail junction along Devil's Backbone, descending into Crooked Creek and turning left to go downstream. The trail follows the stream bottom forest to the nearby confluence with North Fork and turns left, going uphill along Collins Ridge back to the trailhead.

Area/Location/County:
Willow Springs/Dora/Ozark County

U.S.G.S. Map(s):
1:24,000 Dora, Siloam Springs, Cureall NW, Pottersville

Trail(s) Distance:
approximately 16 miles of loop and linear trail

Acreage:
6,595 acres

Activities:
hiking, backpacking, nature study, seasonal hunting, developed facilities at North Fork Recreation Area

Fee(s):
developed camping at North Fork RA

NATURE WALK
90

TRAIL 91: *Caney Mountain Conservation Area*

Black Gum State Champion Tree

*C*aney Mountain Conservation Area was acquired as a wild turkey refuge in 1940 when the native population reached a low of 40 birds. The property includes a range of steep mountains and knobs (elev. 1,200-1,400 ft.) and stream-carved deep hollows. Oak and hickory forest, dolomite glades, chert savannas, spring-fed creeks and remote caves are what hikers can expect. The rare black bear is occasionally seen in this wild remote area. There are two designated trails, both within the 1,330-acre Caney Mountain Natural Area. The point-to-point Sprout Spring Nature Trail heads uphill about 1.75 miles northwest of the property headquarters along Main Forest Road 1. There is limited roadside parking for one or two vehicles. The 1.5 mile, vehicle wide trail (one way) goes north, upstream along Caney Creek. Sprout Spring is trailside, about 1 mile in where the trail dead ends in a hollow. Retrace your steps back to the Main FR 1 trailhead.

*A*long the ridgetop, the Long Bald Trail loops through savanna, glade and upland forest. To reach the trailhead parking area, continue west on

NATURE WALK
91

Main FR 1 from the Sprout Spring trailhead past the signed state champion black gum tree, turning right, going upridge to junction with FR 2. Follow FR 2 about half a mile curving south, downridge to the trailhead and parking area. The three-eighths of a mile path leads through the open scenic glades filled with prairie wildflowers. The open space has a mountainside quality. The trail crosses FR 2 twice as the trail enters and leaves a post oak savanna on the east side of the road back to the trailhead.

*T*here are also several service roads on the property that double as trails. From the Main FR 1, service road trails go south to 1,400-foot Big Acorn Knob and a cave at the base of 1,400-foot Bear Cave Mountain.

*C*aney Mountain Conservation Area entrance lies 5 miles north of Gainesville on Mo. 181. At the cantilevered sign, turn west and drive half a mile on the gravel road to the property headquarters. Seasonal hunting is allowed only in the south portion of the conservation area.

Area/Location/County:
Willow Springs/Gainesville/Ozark County

U.S.G.S. Map(s):
1:24,000 Gainesville NW

Trail(s) Distance:
two trails total about 3.5 miles

Acreage:
6,694 acres

Activities:
nature walks, nature study, picnicking, archery range, camping, equestrian trail, seasonal hunting

Fee(s):
none

NATURE WALK
91

91. Caney Mountain Conservation Area

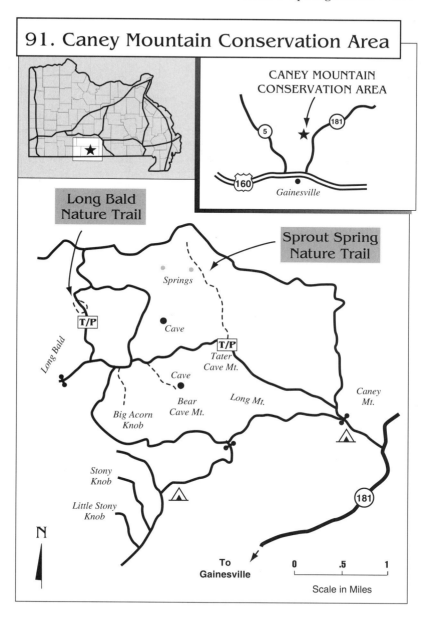

CANEY MOUNTAIN
CONSERVATION AREA

5   181

160   •
Gainesville

Long Bald
Nature Trail

Sprout Spring
Nature Trail

Springs

T/P

Cave

T/P
Tater
Cave Mt.

Long Bald

Cave

Bear
Cave Mt.

Long Mt.

Caney
Mt.

Big Acorn
Knob

Stony
Knob

Little Stony
Knob

181

N

To
Gainesville

0   .5   1

Scale in Miles

NATURE WALK
91

TRAIL 92: **Swan Creek Territory**

*S*wan Creek Territory occupies the northwest section of the U.S. Forest Service's Ava Ranger District. Although the trails are popular with equestrians, adventuresome hikers can also enjoy the 12 ridge-to-ravine-to-stream interconnecting maze of trails. The forested ridges are interspersed with savanna and cedar glades. The main stream, Swan Creek, and its tributaries, Math Branch and Turkey Creek, drain the 8,488 acre watershed. The territory is best visited during the week on a pleasant fall or spring day. Experienced hikers have plenty of trail options with three trailhead access points and a network of short and longer loops. However it is easy to become confused in the maze. Efforts have been made to identify the trails by signage but many of the trails are unidentified, so trail and topo maps and a compass are recommended.

Trail Summary:

*B*ar K Wrangler Camp trailhead is located 6 miles southeast of Chadwick, and 2 miles north of Garrison on Mo. 125. Turn east on FS 533 and continue half a mile to the campsite along the west bank of Swan Creek. Horseshoe Falls, one of the most scenic natural features in the Territory, is streamwide across Swan Creek about a half a mile north of the campsite on the Tin Top Trail/6107. Hikers who are seeking a longer distance loop may combine the 4 mile-long Tin Top Trail/6107 with the 2.5 mile-long Math Branch/6101. If deciding to cut short the suggested hike and head back to the trailhead, there are several trail route options.

*T*wo additional trailheads are located along the ridgecrest of Hwy. UU, 4.7 miles north of the junction of Hwy. UU and Mo. 125 (Whoopin' Willie Ridge trailhead), and 4.8 miles (Tin Top Hill trailhead). From Whoopin' Willie Ridge trailhead, the 2.8 mile linear Patterson Hollow Trail/6114 follows the ridge down to Patterson Hollow and upridge to arrive at Tin Top Trail/6107, just west of the Tin Top trailhead. A 6.5 mile loop may be formed by combining the 4 mile Tin Top Trail/6107 with the 2.5 Math Branch/6101, which will allow hikers to visit Horseshoe Falls. Once again, there are plenty of trail options if deciding to bail out sooner.

NATURE WALK
92

92. Swan Creek Territory

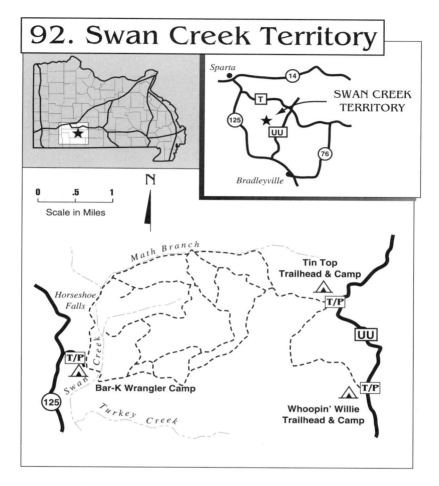

Area/Location/County:
Willow Springs/Garrison/Christian County

U.S.G.S. Map(s):
1:24,000 Garrison, Chadwick, Keltner, Bradleyville

Trail(s) Distance:
20 miles of interconnecting trails

Acreage:
8,488 acres

Activities:
hiking, backpacking, nature study, swimming, fishing, equestrian trails, seasonal hunting

Fee(s):
none

NATURE WALK
92

TRAIL 93: *Hercules Glades Wilderness*

Missouri Tarantula

*H*ercules Glades became the first designated wilderness area in Missouri in 1976. The seemingly vast open spaces along the glade top ridges with their views of the Pilot Knobs makes spectacular hiking. The Time-Life Wilderness Series, *The Ozarks*, devoted a chapter to Long Creek, the principal stream of the wilderness. The extensive rocky dolomite glades or "balds" support a distinct flora and an uncommon fauna such as smoke tree, Ashe juniper, Missouri primrose, Bachman's sparrow, eastern collared lizard, scorpions, roadrunners, long-tailed weasel, Missouri tarantula, western pygmy rattlesnake, Osage copperhead, mountain lion and bald eagle. In addition, for the "foot weary," there is the nearby 23-mile-long Glade Top Trail, Missouri's only National Forest Scenic Byway. (The byway entrance is about 2.5 miles south of Hercules Glades Lookout Tower entrance road on Hwy. 125.)

NATURE WALK
93

*A*s far as hiking is concerned, the trails are shared with equestrians. The trail surface is fairly smooth and level on the ridges but sections along the creeks are rocky, as are the descents and ascents. Experienced walkers can cover ground fairly quickly especially on the open glade top ridges. Climbs are few but steep (elev. 700-1,382 ft.). The trails are unmarked but old signs still persist. Although the trail network is not confusing, a map and compass are beneficial. The openness allows for landmarks to help guide hikers, such as the Pilot Knobs and the lookout tower. Backpacking groups are limited to 10 individuals. Occasionally escaped cows will be encountered. There are three trailheads that allow access to Hercules Glades Wilderness.

Trail Summary:

*H*ercules Glades Lookout Tower is the most easily accessible trailhead and parking area. From Bradleyville at the junction of Mo. 76 and Mo. 125, go south 8 miles on Mo. 125 to the signed Hercules Glades Lookout Tower entry road on the right side of the highway. The lookout tower site may also be reached from the junction of U.S. Hwy. 160 and Mo. 125 at Ruetter, by driving north about 8 miles on Mo. 125 (past Glade Top Trail Byway entrance) to the entrance on the left (west) side of the highway. The trailhead has five developed campsites, picnic tables and a pit toilet but no water. There are two trailheads that provide access and return routes.

*A*bout 60 yards to the west of the lookout tower is a registration box and trailhead for the 12 mile Long Creek-Pilot Knobs loop (suggested hike). Basically the 12 mile loop heads west, descending to Long Creek, and follows the rocky stream about 3 miles to a trail junction that leads steeply uphill to the glade tops. At the streamside junction there is a spur trail that follows the south bank of Long Creek a short distance to a spectacular waterfalls. This spot is popular with backpackers who camp along the banks. In addition, a 2.5 mile feeder spur from Blair Road trailhead and parking area junctions at Long Creek with the 12 mile suggested loop and the waterfalls spur.

*C*ontinue on the 12 mile loop uphill from Long Creek to the glade top where open space vistas of the knobs and balds to the west and north have a far western U.S. flavor. Looping west and north along the cedar dotted glade ridge, the trail arrives at the third trailhead, Coy Bald. At the Coy Bald trailhead, the 12 mile loop continues north and descends to and across Long Creek. The loop trail continues, heading upridge to the glades, continuing north between Lower Pilot Knob and Upper Pilot Knob. At the trail "T," go right (east) and follow the ridge toward Upper Pilot Knob. The loop trail follows the ridge for about 4 miles to return back to Hercules Glades Lookout Tower. Enroute at a rock shelf and seasonal stream crossing will be what looks like fossilized elephant tracks locally known as the Elephant Walk (actually fossilized algae colonies).

NATURE WALK
93

A second trail that originates and ends at Hercules Glades Lookout Tower is the 4 mile Pees Hollow loop. The trailhead begins to the north of the lookout tower. Follow the ridge trail about 200 yards west from the registration box and turn right (north) and follow a somewhat obscure forest trail downridge to Pees Hollow, crossing the seasonal streamlet.

*W*atch for and follow the stone-stacked cairns uphill on this southwest-facing glade, where it is easy to lose track of the trail. The trail follows the base of a 1,100-foot knob southeast and gradually climbs upridge back to the trailhead. The views are worth the possibility of losing the trail but in the open space, the lookout tower is in view and becomes a landmark to follow if losing the trail loop.

*T*o reach the Blair Road trailhead from Hercules Glade Lookout Tower, go south on Mo. 125, just over 1 mile and turn right (west) on Blair Road. Continue on Blair Road 1.5 miles to the trailhead.

*T*o reach Coy Bald trailhead at Hilda on U.S. Hwy. 160, turn northeast on Cross Timbers Road/Broken Back Bridge Road and follow the gravel road across a tributary of Beaver Creek to a "T" and turn right. Follow the rough going, narrow road uphill through grazelands and cattle guards to Coy Bald and the trailhead. There are two developed campsites.

Area/Location/County:
Willow Springs/Bradleyville/Taney County

U.S.G.S. Map(s):
1:24,000 Hilda, Protem NE

Trail(s) Distance:
two suggested loop hikes total approximately 16 miles

Acreage:
12,315 acres

Activities:
hiking, backpacking, nature study, camping, seasonal hunting

Fee(s):
none

NATURE WALK
93

93. Hercules Glades Wilderness

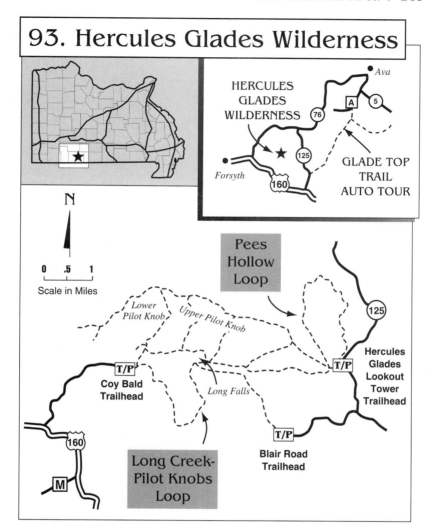

HERCULES
GLADES
WILDERNESS

Ava

76

A

5

125

GLADE TOP
TRAIL
AUTO TOUR

Forsyth

160

N

0   .5   1

Scale in Miles

Pees
Hollow
Loop

Lower
Pilot Knob

Upper Pilot Knob

125

Hercules
Glades
Lookout
Tower
Trailhead

T/P

Coy Bald
Trailhead

Long Falls

T/P

160

M

T/P

Blair Road
Trailhead

Long Creek-
Pilot Knobs
Loop

NATURE WALK
93

Native Ozark Timber Rattlesnake
Dickerson Park Zoo, Reptile House

Winter Hikers
Springfield Nature Center

Union Cannon, Bloody Hill
Wilson Creek National Battlefield

Bass Pro Shops Outdoor World,
Museum Entrance

Non-Native Flamingos,
Dickerson Park Zoo

Missouri Black Bear,
Missouri Habitats, Dickerson Park Zoo

TRAIL 94: *Springfield Nature Places*

*S*pringfield, the "Queen City of the Ozarks," is Missouri's third largest city. The 140,000 population makes it the largest city in the Missouri Ozarks. Although it has its share of theme parks, the "Gateway City" to the Ozarks has a few easily-accessed, nature-oriented parks worth visiting within the metropolitan area.

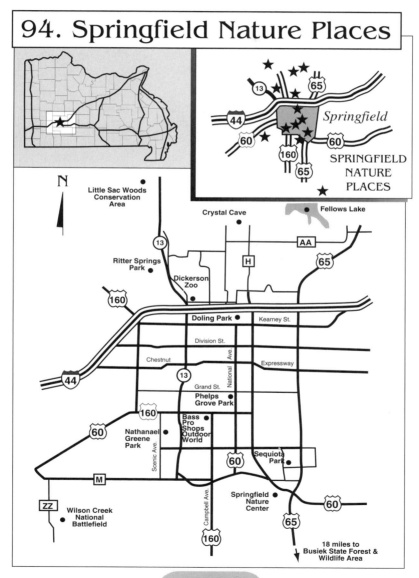

94. Springfield Nature Places

Springfield

SPRINGFIELD
NATURE
PLACES

Little Sac Woods
Conservation
Area

Crystal Cave

Fellows Lake

Ritter Springs
Park

Dickerson
Zoo

Doling Park

Kearney St.

Division St.

Chestnut

National Ave.

Expressway

Grand St.

Phelps
Grove Park

Bass
Pro
Shops
Outdoor
World

Nathanael
Greene
Park

Scenic Ave.

Sequiota
Park

Springfield
Nature
Center

Campbell Ave.

Wilson Creek
National
Battlefield

18 miles to
Busiek State Forest &
Wildlife Area

NATURE WALK
94

TRAIL 94A: *Springfield Conservation Nature Center*

*S*pringfield Conservation Nature Center is considered to be the premier nature center in the Missouri Ozarks. The Missouri Department of Conservation's suburban retreat offers 6 interconnecting miles of hiking with lots of boardwalks, foot bridges and paved all-weather paths plus fantastic displays and exhibits at the 16,000-square-foot nature center. The 80 acres includes old fields, woodlands, creeksides, glades, savanna, hillsides, restored prairie, marsh and Lake Springfield. There are educational seminars, films, special programs, guided walks, an auditorium and wildlife viewing areas.

*F*rom the intersection of U.S. Hwy. 65 and U.S. Hwy. 60 in southeast Springfield, travel 1 mile west on U.S. Hwy. 60/James River Freeway to the Glenstone exit. Exit and go left, crossing over the overpass to the frontage road and turn left (east) and continue to the visitors center parking area.

Area:
Ava-Cassville/Springfield Nature Places

Address/Phone:
4600 South Chrisman
Springfield, MO 65804
(417) 888-4237

Schedule:
Open Year Around
except Thanksgiving, Christmas and New Year's Day

Hours:
Hours: Tuesday-Sunday, 8 a.m - 6 p.m.

Fees:
Donations accepted

NATURE WALK
94A

TRAIL 94B: *Bass Pro Shops Outdoor World*

*B*illed as the "World's Greatest Sporting Goods Store," Bass Pro Shops Outdoor World may be the ultimate urban "nature walk" in the Missouri Ozarks. There are indoor waterfalls, huge aquariums and even a trout pond and the American National Fish and Wildlife Museum. Outstanding dioramas of North American wildlife in their native haunts are featured. The museum entrance is through the warehouse clearance area at the northwest end of the Outdoor World showroom. This is also a great place to look for hiking and camping gear. Four million individuals pass through the doors of "Pro Bass" yearly.

*F*rom I-44 exit 77 south on Mo. 13/Kansas Expressway and drive to the intersection of U.S. Hwy. 160/Sunshine Street and turn left (east). Proceed to the intersection of Campbell Avenue and turn south. Go about two blocks to the spacious parking lot on the right (west) side of Campbell Avenue.

Area:
Ava-Cassville/Springfield Nature Places

Address/Phone:
1935 South Campbell Avenue
Springfield, MO 65898
(417) 887-1915

Schedule:
Open Year Around

Hours:
Monday-Saturday, 7 a.m. - 10 p.m.
Sunday, 9 a.m. - 6 p.m.

Fees:
museum admission fee

NATURE WALK
94B

TRAIL 94C: *Dickerson Park Zoo*

*D*ickerson Park Zoo is nationally respected for its programs for endangered species. A couple miles of paved all-weather pathways loop about the menagerie of caged exotic animals. "Missouri Habitats," a cooperative program between MDC and the Zoo, encompasses five acres and includes native Ozark fauna such as black bear, bobcats and river otters. Additional points of interest include live animal programs, contact animal area, pony rides, gift shop and concessions. There are also wheelchair and stroller rentals.

*E*asy access from I-44 by exiting 77 north on Mo. 13 and turning right (east) immediately on Norton Street. Follow Norton Street about three blocks to the zoo entrance on North Fort Avenue. Plenty of free parking.

Area:
Ava-Cassville/Springfield Nature Places

Address/Phone:
3043 North Fort Avenue
Springfield, MO 65803
Phone: (417) 833-1570

Schedule:
Open Year Around except mid- to late-October
Halloween Event

Hours:
April 15-October 15, 9 a.m. - 6 p.m.
November 1-April 15, 10 a.m. - 4:30 p.m. weather permitting

Fees:
admission fee

NATURE WALK
94C

TRAIL 94D: *Springfield City Parks*

Park Board Office
1923 North Weller
Springfield, MO 65803
Phone: (417) 864-1049

Ritter Springs Park
Mo. 13 North of I-44
to FC 94 to FC 129/Fantastic Caverns Road
nature trails, cave, lake, picnicking, day camp

Sequiota Park
3500 South Lone Pine
caves, lake, birding, picnicking

Phelps Grove Park
800-1200 East Bennett
flower and rose garden, xeriscape garden,
picnicking

Nathanael Greene Park
2400 South Scenic
7.5 acre Japanese Garden (fee),
botanical center and city nursery,
oldest farmstead in Springfield,
picnicking

Fellows Lake
I-44 North on Hwy. H
to FR 66 to FR 197
hiking trails circle the lake, shelter picnicking

Frisco Rails-to-Trails
Future 30 mile bike and hike trail
from Springfield to Bolivar

NATURE WALK
94D

TRAIL 94E: *Crystal Cave*

*O*nce inhabited by Native Americans, this "Mom and Pop" commercial cave displays evidence backing such a claim. Cave formations include "Upside Down Well," "The Cathedral," and "Rainbow Falls." There are natural paths with hand rails and stone steps and 80 minute guided tours.

*F*rom I-44 exit 80B and go north on Hwy. H, driving 5 miles. Turn left (west) to the parking area and the signed site.

Area:
Ava-Cassville/Springfield Nature Places

Address/Phone:
Route 1, Box 590
7225 North Crystal Cave Lane
(417) 833-9599

Schedule:
Open Daily
(weather permitting)

Hours:
Seasonal Hours
9 a.m. - 2 p.m.

Fees:
admission fee

NATURE WALK
94E

TRAIL 94F: **Little Sac Woods Conservation Area**

*T*his 772 acre MDC property (urban metro forest) is located about 17 miles northwest of Springfield. Two loop hikes lead 3 miles through forest and old fields but the property barely borders on the Little Sac River. Trail follows a single track, forest roads and some powerline swath. This is a good day hike just outside the city and features primitive camping and seasonal hunting.

*F*rom I-44 exit 77, and go north on dual lane Mo. 13, 11 miles, turning west on Hwy. BB. Drive half a mile west on the crossover Mo. 13 south bound lane and continue on Hwy. BB 3.2 miles to FR 115 and turn left (south). Follow FR 115 and go 1.4 miles to the parking area and trailhead. An area map is posted.

Area:
Ava-Cassville/Springfield Nature Places

Address/Phone:
Contact: MDC District Forester
2630 North Mayfair
Springfield, MO 65803
(417) 895-6880

Schedule:
open year around

Hours:
dawn to dusk unless camping

Fees:
none

NATURE WALK
94F

TRAIL 94G: **Wilson Creek National Battlefield**

*W*ilson Creek National Battlefield is the site of the first major Civil War battle west of the Mississippi River occurring on August 10, 1861. The Confederates called the military clash the Battle of Oak Hills. The military site is named for the stream that crosses the battlefield where 2,300 men from both North and South were killed or wounded.

*T*he 5 mile auto tour (fee) accesses several miles of self-guided hiking trails that lead to historic interpretive sites such as Bloody Hill in a restored prairie savanna. The visitor center features a film, battle map and a museum. Guided tours, special events and other interpretive services are provided. A picnicking area is available. This site is administered by the National Park Service.

*T*he battlefield is located 3 miles east of Republic and 10 miles southeast of Springfield. From I-44 take exit 70 Hwy. MM south to U.S. 60. Cross U.S. 60 and continue three-quarters of a mile to Hwy. ZZ. The battlefield is located 2 miles south on Mo. ZZ.

Area:
Ava-Cassville/Springfield Nature Places

Address/Phone:
6424 West FR 182
Hwy. ZZ and FR 180
Republic, MO 65735
(417) 732-2662

Schedule:
open year around

Hours:
8 a.m. - 5 p.m.

Fees:
auto tour fee

NATURE WALK
94G

TRAIL 94H: *Busiek Conservation Area*

*T*he 2,505 acre Missouri Department of Conservation property is located 20 miles south of Springfield in Christian County and is bisected by U.S. Hwy. 65. The 15 miles of single and forest road trails lead along Camp Creek (west of U.S. 65) and Woods Fork (east of U.S. 65). This is one of the most popular all-terrain bike areas. Rocky hills, gravel creeks and 270 acres of miniature prairie glades (elev. 900-1,290 ft.). Hunting, fishing, and camping and more (U.S.G.S. Map 1:24,000 Day).

*F*rom Springfield, drive south on U.S. Hwy. 65 about 20 miles and exit left (east). There is a parking area on each side of the conservation area that the highway bisects.

Area:
Ava-Cassville/Springfield Nature Places

Address/Phone:
Contact: MDC District Forester
2630 North Mayfair
Springfield, MO 65803
(417) 895-6880

Schedule:
open year around

Hours:
dawn to dusk unless camping

Fees:
none

NATURE WALK
94H

TRAIL 95: **Henning Conservation Area**

Dewey Bald Overlook of Branson

*T*he Henning Conservation Area overlooks the glitz and glitter of encroaching Branson, a world apart from these White River Hills. The steep, forested hills (elev. 800-1,300 ft.) are punctuated with rocky open glades which comprise the 362 acre White River Bald Natural Area. A half mile segment of Roark Creek flows through the northwest perimeter of the conservation area. Several natural features of the area were immortalized in Harold Bell Wright's book, *Shepherd of the Hills*, including Dewey Bald and Boulder Bald. Hikers will follow portions of the "trail that nobody knows how old," along the four walking paths.

*S*hepherd of the Hills Farm, a National Literary Landmark, lies adjacent to the Henning Conservation Area. Here Wright's characters acted out life's drama in the early 1900s, and today at the farm, outdoor stage plays of the novel are acted out for tourists.

*T*he main trailhead and parking area is accessed from Mo. 76 at Cedar Bald, about 1 mile north of the Shepherd of the Hills Expressway intersection. The half mile Dewey Bald Trail begins and ends at the south end of the parking area. The paved loop path ascends 1,300-foot Dewey Bald where a 46-foot observation tower overlooks Branson. Author Wright refers to "climbing the Old Trail to the lookout on the bare shoulder of Dewey" (page 82) which "like a great sentinel, was the round treeless form" (page 151).

NATURE WALK
95

*T*he trailhead for the double loop, 1 mile Glade Exploration Trail and the lower loop Streamside Trail (1.6 miles) begins at the north end of the Cedar Bald parking area. The wood chipped Glade Exploration Trail follows the "Old Trail at the base of Boulder Bald" into the White River Balds Natural Area. The scenic glades are home to the smoke tree, Ashe juniper, collared lizard, Missouri tarantula, prairie warblers and wildflowers. The Streamside Trail interconnects with the Glade Exploration Trail near Dewey Cove and leads downhill, looping back along an intermittent stream to rejoin the glade loop. Naturalist walks are scheduled from May to October.

*T*o reach Henning Conservation Area at Cedar Bald from U.S. Hwy. 65, go right (west) on Mo. 76 and drive about 5 miles to the parking area on the right (east) side of the highway. The area may also be accessed from U.S. Hwy. 65 west to Mo. 248 to the Shepherd of the Hills Expressway, and Mo. 76 north.

A second separate trailhead and parking area for the 3.7 mile Henning Homesteaders Trail loop is at the northeast edge of the conservation area along Roark Creek. A trail brochure is available and corresponds to the 15 stops that interpret the cultural and natural history. The trail was constructed by Boy Scout Troop 2001.

*T*he Roark trailhead is reached by driving west from the intersection of U.S. Hwy. 65 and Mo. 248. Go west and north on Mo. 248 about 5.5 miles to Road 248-20/Sycamore Log Church Road and turn left (south). Follow Road 248-20/Sycamore Log Church Road south 3.7 miles (underneath the railroad trestle) to the gravel parking lot. Park and walk across the low water bridge on Roark Creek. The trail is blazed orange.

Area/Location/County:
Ava-Cassville/Branson/Taney and Stone counties

U.S.G.S. Map(s):
1:24,000 Garber

Trail(s) Distance:
four loop trails total nearly 6 miles

Acreage:
1,534 acres

Activities:
nature walks, nature study, seasonal naturalist, picnicking

Fee(s):
none

NATURE WALK
95

95. Henning Conservation Area

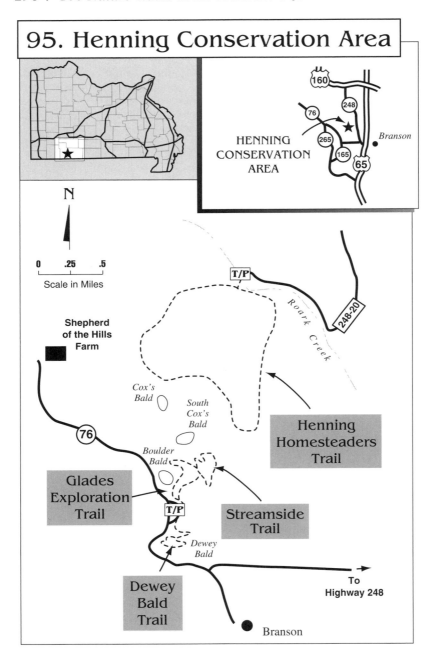

N

0   .25   .5
Scale in Miles

Shepherd
of the Hills
Farm

160
248
76
265
165
65

HENNING
CONSERVATION
AREA

Branson

T/P

Roark Creek

248-20

Cox's
Bald

South
Cox's
Bald

Henning
Homesteaders
Trail

76

Boulder
Bald

Glades
Exploration
Trail

T/P

Streamside
Trail

Dewey
Bald

Dewey
Bald
Trail

To
Highway 248

Branson

NATURE WALK
95

TRAIL 96: ***Shepherd of the Hills Fish Hatchery***

Aquarium at Visitors Center

*L*ocated at the tailwater of Table Rock Lake Dam, Lake Taneycomo or White River, Shepherd of the Hills Fish Hatchery is the largest trout rearing facility operated by the Missouri Department of Conservation. The visitor center features exhibits, a trout aquarium and auditorium media presentations. Self-guided and guided tours (Memorial Day-Labor Day) of the hatchery are available.

*T*he visitor center is open daily from 9 a.m. to 5 p.m. with extended hours from Memorial Day to Labor Day. The visitor center is closed Thanksgiving, Christmas Day and New Year's Day. For hikers, the grounds are open sunrise to sunset daily.

*F*our short trails ranging from three-tenths of a mile to 1.6 miles, lead visitors from the shoreline of Lake Taneycomo (or the banks of White River) to the high rocky bluffs overlooking the valley and dam.

Trail Summary:

*T*he White River Corridor Trail is a four-tenths of a mile linear path that begins at the east end of the shaded picnic and parking area downstream from the visitor center. A foot bridge over a cascading tributary stream marks the trailhead. The scenic path follows the riparian forested bank downstream to connect with the three-tenths of a mile Canebrake Trail and a second trailhead and parking area.

*C*ontinuing downstream along the narrow canebrake path there are boardwalks, foot bridges, waterfalls and ravines. A spur path leads to a wildlife viewing blind overlooking a waterfowl area (old fish rearing

NATURE WALK
96

96. Shepherd of the Hills Fish Hatchery

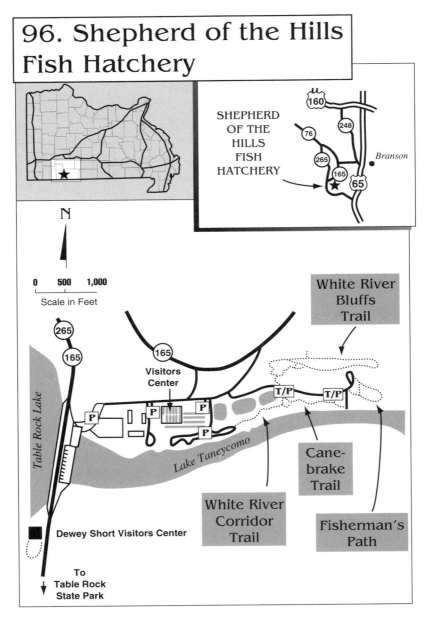

SHEPHERD OF THE HILLS FISH HATCHERY

Branson

N

0   500   1,000

Scale in Feet

White River Bluffs Trail

265

165

165

Visitors Center

T/P   T/P

Table Rock Lake

P

P   P

P

P

Lake Taneycomo

Cane-brake Trail

Dewey Short Visitors Center

White River Corridor Trail

Fisherman's Path

To Table Rock State Park

pond). The paw paw trees along the Canebrake Trail are outstanding and there are thick stands of native hardy bamboo (*Arundinaria ginantea*) or "canebrake." The trail concludes at the boat launch ramp and third trailhead and parking area. Retrace your steps. Both linear paths form a point-to-point seven-tenths of a mile trail and there are three trailheads.

NATURE WALK
96

*T*he Fisherman's Path begins and ends at the turnaround end of the hatchery road where there is roadside parking. The four-tenths of a mile trail loops about the wooded area, accessing the river lake via a wooden staircase from the bank down to the river.

*T*he longest trail is the 1.6 mile White River Bluffs Trail which begins and ends across from the parking lot adjacent and east of the lagoon. The double loop trail has a shorter loop of six-tenths of a mile. From the signed trailhead, the wood chipped path leads uphill and loops along the glade dotted bluff, curving back along the property perimeter next to a trailer park, to return downhill to the hatchery road and parking area.

*T*he Shepherd of the Hills Fish Hatchery is located 6 miles southwest of Branson, on Mo. 165 on the north side of the Table Rock Dam. Watch for the signs.

*S*outh across the dam one-quarter mile on Mo. 165/125 is the Dewey Short Visitor Center administered by the Army Corps of Engineers. Overlooking Table Rock Lake, the center features exhibits about the Ozarks history, folklore and wildlife. Films are presented in the auditorium. A 1 mile paved loop trail begins at the south entrance of the visitor center and ends at the parking lot. The Dewey Short visitor center is free and is open daily from April 1 to October 31.

*F*arther south about three-quarters of a mile on Mo. 165/125 is Table Rock State Park. In addition to lakeshore waters, the half-mile-long Chinquapin Trail is available for walking. The trail leads from the amphitheater parking lot to campground No. 2 and is blazed with blue arrows with a short green arrow loop. The DNR state park is fully developed and is a fine place to watch for winter birds such as loons, bald eagles and grebes on the 52,300 acre reservoir lake.

Area/Location/County:
Ava-Cassville/Branson/Taney County

U.S.G.S. Map(s):
1:24,000 Table Rock Dam

Trail(s) Distance:
four trails total nearly 3 miles

Acreage:
311 acres

Activities:
nature walks, nature study, naturalist, visitors center, aquarium, exhibits, fish hatchery tours, picnicking, fishing, boating, launch ramp

Fee(s):
none

NATURE WALK
96

TRAIL 97: *Piney Creek Wilderness*

Lichen-Covered Boulder

*F*ree-flowing Piney Creek is the heart of this southwest Missouri wilderness. Piney Creek, with its myriad of small springs, drains the entire 5 mile watershed, sending its waters to the James River Arm of Table Rock Reservoir Lake. The rugged wilderness is deeply dissected with narrow ridgetops, long, steep, forested slopes and deep trough hollows (elev. 900-1,400 ft.). Shortleaf pines dot the ridges, slopes and bottoms, intermixed with the prevailing oak and hickory deciduous forest. Small patches of glades appear on the southwest, sun-intensive slopes. The Piney Creek area has been a wilderness since 1980. There are two trailheads that access the Piney Creek Wilderness.

NATURE WALK
97

*P*ineview Lookout Tower is the north trailhead access point. To reach the trailhead from Cassville, travel east on Mo. 76 about 20 miles and turn right (south) on Lake Road/76-6 (2 miles southwest of Hwy. EE). Proceed on gravel Lake Road/76-6, 1 mile to the lookout tower and the trailhead parking area.

*S*iloam Springs is the south trailhead access point. To reach the trailhead from Cassville, travel east on Mo. 76 about 15 miles to Mo. 39 and turn right (south). Follow Mo. 39 approximately 2 miles to Lake Road/39-1 on the left (east) side of the highway. Continue 4 miles on Lake Road/39-1 to the trailhead.

*B*e advised, hikers, that a map and compass are necessary. The easy to rugged, unmarked trails can proved challenging. The wilderness area is popular with equestrians and the trails reflect their heavy use especially on ups and downs. The stream bottom can be overgrown and the trail confusing. Although there are 13 miles of maintained trails, a 6 mile loop connecting the two trailheads is suggested.

*F*rom Pineview Lookout Tower, walk south and follow the rough and rocky path downridge about 1.25 miles, descending gradually and sometimes steeply, to Piney Creek. At the creek bottom, the suggested route junctions with a hiking-only linear trail that follows Piney Creek upstream and eventually upridge, to conclude at the southwest wilderness boundary. Despite the fact that the trail is designated for hiking only, horse riders use the path heavily. Also, at the streamside trail junction, hikers may shorten the 6 mile loop to about a 3.5 mile loop by following the creekbed trail downstream to a second trail junction and turn left (north), going back upridge to Pineview Lookout Tower.

*T*he suggested 6 mile trail loop continues up Siloam Spring Hollow from Piney Creek and eventually arrives after 1.25 miles at the Siloam Spring south trailhead where there is a parking area and bulletin board. The loop trail continues east from the Siloam Spring trailhead and then goes north on an old, fairly level, forest ridgetop road above Buck Hollow. The old growth shortleaf pines along the ridge and the views are outstanding. After 1.5 miles, the trail descends to Piney Creek and a trail "T" junction. Going right (east) will lead to the St. James River (narrow and often muddy, and compacted). Going left, the suggested route, the trail follows Piney Creek upstream about one-quarter mile to a trail junction. Go right (north) and continue a steep climb upridge. Follow the ridgetop north to the Lake Road/76-A and follow the gravel road left (west) back to the Pineview Lookout Tower. The final road section is necessary because the final trail segment is obscure, overgrown and generally lost.

NATURE WALK
97

97. Piney Creek Wilderness

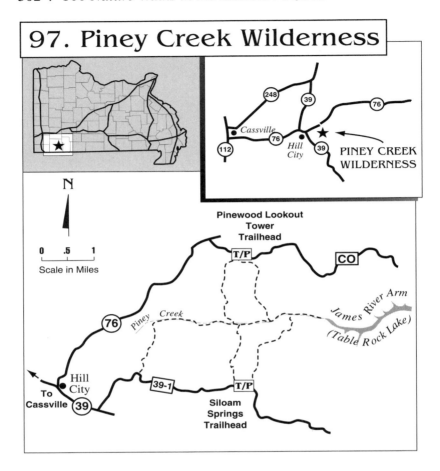

Area/Location/County:
Ava-Cassville/Cassville/Barry and Stone counties

U.S.G.S. Map(s):
1:24,000 Shell Knob, Cape Fair

Trail(s) Distance:
13 miles total
suggested 6 mile loop

Acreage:
8,142 acres

Activities:
hiking, backpacking, nature study, seasonal hunting, equestrian
use

Fee(s):
none

NATURE WALK
97

TRAIL 98: **Roaring River State Park**

*D*onated to the State of Missouri in 1928, Roaring River Spring, Missouri's twentieth largest spring, forms the headwaters of Roaring River. Twenty million gallons flow daily from a pool at the base of of a 90-foot-high bluff, considered by many the most scenic spring setting in the state. The spring-carved valley of Roaring River stretches through the state park, carrying its rushing, cool waters southeast to the White River and Table Rock Lake (7.5 miles from spring to confluence at Eagle Rock). A variety of geological rock formations are found within the park, mostly within the spring area. The greater portion of the state park, 2,075 acres, is dedicated as Roaring River Hills Natural Area. The popular park has high visitation especially by weekend trout fishermen from March 1 to October 31. Fishing resorts line Mo. 112 south from Cassville to the state park.

*T*here are six maintained hiking paths that range in distance from two-tenths of a mile to 3.5 miles. The trails are well trodden and the surfaces vary from easy, level and smooth to difficult, steep and rough. Hikers will experience the scenic spring, rocky streamsides, dry hollows, prairie-like glades and high knobs.

Trail Summary:

*R*iver Trail is a seven-tenths of a mile linear path that follows the east bank of Roaring River between the lodge and park store southeast to campground No. 3. The riparian trail also accesses the amphitheater. This is a picturesque streamside trail along the rocky base of a steep bluff.

*D*eer Leap Trail is a two-tenths mile spring and fish hatchery loop and the park's most popular trail. The trail begins along the spring pool and fish hatchery rearing pools and follows the paved edge, curving into the spectacular canyon gorge where the spring emerges. Before the spur trail enters the spring gorge, the loop trail follows the bluff uphill on stone steps, past the junction with the connecting spur of the 3.5 mile Fire Tower Trail.

*C*ontinuing uphill, Deer Leap Spring flows from a waterfall bluff down to the larger spring pool a hundred feet below. Deer Leap boardwalk overlook gives a bird's eye view of the spring and hatchery. The trail descends along a wooden staircase back to the trailhead parking area.

*D*evil's Kitchen Trail is a geology hike. The 1.5 mile loop is signed with blue and yellow arrows and circles a 1,400-foot-high ridge just west of the spring. Caves, chert outcrops and forest, and the boulder breakdown of Devil's Kitchen are the trail's highlights. An excellent trail booklet is available from the nature center and naturalist near campground No. 3. Trail access points are situated in the picnic area,

NATURE WALK
98

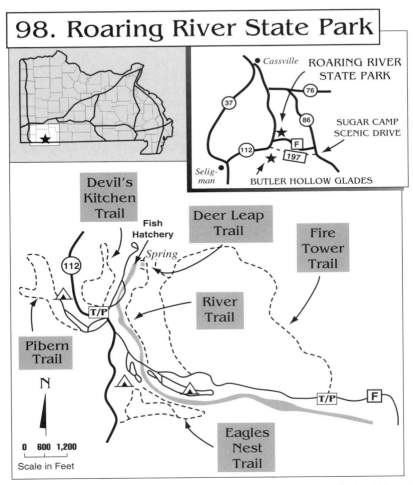

98. Roaring River State Park

Cassville ROARING RIVER STATE PARK

37

76

86

SUGAR CAMP SCENIC DRIVE

112

F

197

Seligman

BUTLER HOLLOW GLADES

Devil's Kitchen Trail

Fish Hatchery

Deer Leap Trail

Fire Tower Trail

112

Spring

T/P

River Trail

Pibern Trail

N

T/P

F

0   600 1,200

Scale in Feet

Eagles Nest Trail

across the park road from the lodge and the intersection of Mo. 112 and the hatchery road.

*T*he 1.5 mile Pibern Trail (one way) is orange blazed and follows the ridgeside slopes above campground no. 1. Taking in the campground road will form a complete loop. Trailhead access is at the north end of campground No. 1 and behind campsite No. 55. Visitor parking for non-campers is at the campground gate entrance.

*E*agles Nest Trail begins and ends at campground No. 2, campsite No. 105. The 2.3-mile rugged trail follows the south bluff slope above Roaring River to the lower and upper loop. There are excellent vistas after the leaves fall. Rocky bluff outcrops are found along the lower loop. This is a quiet corner of the park. The trail is marked with yellow and green (lower loop) arrows.

*F*ire Tower Trail is a 3.5 mile easy to difficult hike that traverses the Roaring River Hills Wild Area. It is signed with yellow and brown (Deer Leap spur) arrows. It is essentially a forested ridgetop trail to the climbable fire tower (elev. 1,400 ft.) but has vistas only after the leaves fall. Directly northwest of the fire tower in Ketchum Hollow is the 120 acre Roaring River Cove Natural Area, an old growth, dry upland chert forest.

*S*ince the trail does not form a complete loop (unless you hike busy Hwy. F), a suggested route is to hike the brown arrow Fire Tower Trail spur from Deer Leap Trail and the fish hatchery parking area, and go left at the trail "T" junction to the fire tower and retrace your steps. Recent tornado winds have opened up some ridge top vistas enroute to the tower. There are three trailheads for the Fire Tower Trail: Camp Smokey, the wild area parking lot on Hwy. F and the Deer Leap Trail.

*R*oaring River State Park is located 7 miles south of Cassville on Mo. 112.

*W*hile in south central Barry County, consider a side excursion to the U.S. Forest Service's Sugar Camp Scenic Drive. From the intersection of Mo. 112 and Hwy. F at the state park, drive south on Mo. 112 about 3.5 miles to Sugar Camp Scenic Drive/FS 197 and turn left (east). The scenic drive is 8 miles long, ending at Barry County Road 97, north a quarter mile to Mo. 86, just south of Eagle Rock. Enroute there are two picnic areas at Sugar Camp lookout and Onyx Cave. The 285 acre Butler Hollow Glades Natural Area lies half a mile south of the scenic drive and Sugar Camp lookout on FS 1004. There are no trails, however the forest service road makes a good trail substitute.

Area/Location/County:
Ava-Cassville/Cassville/Barry County

U.S.G.S. Map(s):
1:24,000 Eagle Rock

Trail(s) Distance:
six trails total approximately 10 miles

Acreage:
3,372 acres

Activities:
nature walks, nature study, naturalist, nature center, spring, fish hatchery tours, picnicking, shelters, amphitheater, fishing, swimming pool, equestrian stable, dining lodge, park store, cabins, motel, camping, group camp

Fee(s):
shelter rental, camping, rentals

NATURE WALK
98

TRAIL 99: *George Washington Carver National Historic Site*

Visitors at Carver Boyhood Statue

*T*his National Historic Site honors George Washington Carver (1864-1943), botanist, horticulturalist, agronomist, artist, educator and humanitarian. Born a slave, young George was reared by Moses and Susan Carver as if he were one of their own sons. His natural curiosity about plants and nature continued from boyhood into adulthood. Carver received an education at Iowa Agricultural College (now Iowa State University) and taught at Tuskegee Institute in Alabama. He rose to national prominence by age 55. He first received national attention

NATURE WALK
99

for his work in extracting an array of products from peanut, soybean and sweet potato plants.

*T*he three-quarter mile Carver Trail loop begins and ends at the visitors center. A trail guide is available at the visitors center for a nominal fee. The easy level trail leads to 12 interpretive stops including Carver's birthplace site, a statue of Carver as a boy, Carver Spring, the 1881 Moses Carver house, a persimmon grove, walnut tree fence row, the Carver family cemetery and 140 acres of restored native tallgrass prairie. There are four small stream crossings and a pond.

*T*o reach the historic site from I-44 exit 18 south onto U.S. Hwy. 71 Alt. and drive 6.2 miles south to Diamond and the junction with Hwy. V. Go right (west) on Hwy. V 1.9 miles to Carver Road/160 and turn left (south), or from U.S. Hwy. 71 take V Hwy. east 5 miles towards Diamond. Proceed seven-tenths of a mile on Carver Road to the parking area and visitors center. The hours are from 9 a.m. to 5 p.m. daily for the visitors center. Follow the highway signs.

*W*ithin the vicinity is Diamond Grove Prairie Conservation Area. The 571 acre area is one of the few large remnant prairie tracts remaining in Missouri. The upland tallgrass prairie is a refuge for the prairie chicken and for several unique prairie plants.

*P*ark at the roadside entry gate and walk along the linear service road that follows the high ground and bisects the property (half a mile one way). The MDC property is located 4.2 miles west and north of the George Washington Carver National Historic Site. From the Carver Road entrance to the historic site, drive west on Hwy. V about 3 miles to Lark Road and turn right (north). Continue on gravel Lark Road, 1.25 miles to the locked gate and park in the roadside pullout.

Area/Location/County:
Ava-Cassville/Diamond/Newton County

U.S.G.S. Map(s):
1:24,000 Fidelity, Joplin East

Trail(s) Distance:
three-quarter mile loop

Acreage:
240 acres

Activities:
nature walk, nature study, historic site, visitors center, bookshop, picnicking, tours, programs, films

Fee(s):
none

NATURE WALK
99

99. George Washington Carver National Historic Site

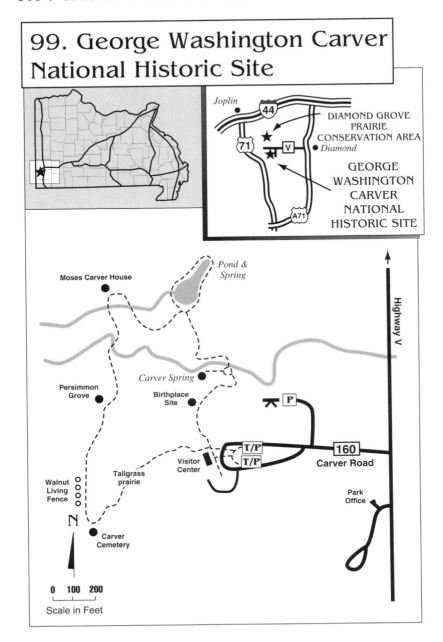

Joplin

DIAMOND GROVE PRAIRIE CONSERVATION AREA

Diamond

GEORGE WASHINGTON CARVER NATIONAL HISTORIC SITE

Moses Carver House

Pond & Spring

Highway V

Carver Spring

Persimmon Grove

Birthplace Site

P

T/P
T/P

160

Carver Road

Visitor Center

Walnut Living Fence

Tallgrass prairie

Park Office

N

Carver Cemetery

0   100   200

Scale in Feet

NATURE WALK
99

TRAIL 100: *Buffalo Hills Natural Area*

Monarch Butterfly

*A*cquired in 1984, this Missouri Department of Conservation property is situated on high hills (elev. 950-1,050 ft.) overlooking the Buffalo River, about 5 miles east of the Oklahoma-Missouri state line. Most of the acreage is covered with old growth oak and hickory forest but there are west property portions that are open fields. Nearly half of the property (206 acres) has been designated a natural area.

A foot trail leads northwest from the parking area uphill to the natural area following an unmarked but obvious path. The trail winds along the hilltops of the predominately black oak forest with a plentiful understory of dogwood. The trail emerges from the natural area to an edge of a field at a "T" junction.

NATURE WALK
100

*G*oing north at the "T" six-tenths of a mile, the trail continues its linear way on a farm lane along field and forest edge and through forest to conclude at the extreme northwest property boundary. Retrace your steps.

*G*oing south at the "T" three-tenths of a mile, the trail leads along the forest edge to an old homestead and concludes. Retrace your steps. From the "T" junction, retrace your steps back to the parking area, a total walk of 4 miles round trip.

*B*uffalo Hills Natural Area is located 2 miles south of the Newton-McDonald County line. From U.S. Hwy. 71 at Goodman, drive west on Hwy. B about 7 miles to the parking area on the right (west) side of the road. The natural area is 2.1 miles west of the junction of Hwy. B and Hwy. Y.

*A*nother MDC property to consider visiting while in McDonald County is the Huckleberry Ridge Conservation Area. The 2,106 acre property is located southeast of Pineville on Hwy. K, 4 miles east of U.S. Hwy. 71 (U.S.G.S. Map 1:24,000 Jane). There are two parking areas near mid-property along Hwy. K within yards of each other. There are 14 miles of service roads but few loop. The best area to hike is along Greer Creek.

Area/Location/County:
Ava-Cassville/Goodman/McDonald County

U.S.G.S. Map(s):
1:24,000 Tiff City

Trail(s) Distance:
2 miles one way

Acreage:
206 acre natural area
486 total acres

Activities:
nature walk, nature study

Fee(s):

100. Buffalo Hills Natural Area

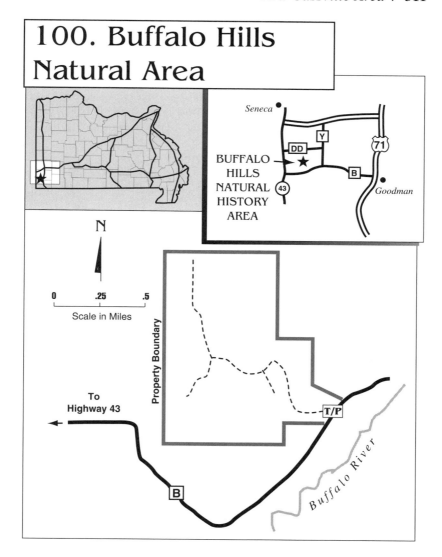

Helpful Books

Beveridge, Thomas R. *Geologic Wonders and Curiosities of Missouri.* Missouri Division of Geology and Land Survey, Educational Series No. 4. Rolla, Mo. 1978.

Beveridge, Thomas, R. *Tom Beveridge's Ozarks.* Pacific Grove, Calif.: Boxwood Press, 1979.

Bretz, Harlan J. *Caves of Missouri.* Missouri Division of Geological Survey and Water Resources, 1956.

Carra, Andrew J., ed. *The Complete Guide to Hiking and Backpacking.* New York: Winchester Press, 1977.

Chapman, Carl Haley. *The Archaeology of Missouri.* Vols. 1 and 2. Columbia, Mo.: University of Missouri Press, 1975-1980.

Clawson, Richard L. *The Status, Distribution, and Habitat Preferences of the Birds of Missouri.* Jefferson City, Mo.: Missouri Department of Conservation, 1982.

Cliburn, Jerry and Wallace, Ginny. *A Key to Missouri Trees in Winter.* Jefferson City, Mo.: Missouri Department of Conservation, 1992.

Cochran, Doris M. and Coleman J. Goin. *The New Field Book of Reptiles and Amphibians.* New York: G. P. Putnam's Sons, 1979.

Cohen, G. L., ed. *Interesting Missouri Place Names.* Rolla, Mo.: G. L. Cohen, 1982.

Denison, Edgar. *Missouri Wildflowers*, rev. and expanded 4th ed. Jefferson City, Mo.: Missouri Department of Conservation, 1989.

Federal Writer's Project. *Missouri: A Guide to the Show Me State.* Hastings House, 1941.

Flader, Susan, ed. *Exploring Missouri's Legacy: State Parks and Historic Sites.* Columbia, Mo.: University of Missouri Press, 1992.

Frey, Kelly and Baron Steve. *Trails of Missouri.* St. Louis, Mo: Show-Me Outdoors, 1995.

Gass, Ramon. *Missouri Hiking Trails.* Jefferson City, Mo.: Missouri Department of Conservation, rev. 1990.

Godsey, Helen and Godsey, Townsend. *These Were the Last: Ozark Mountain Folk.* Branson, Mo.: Mountaineer Press, 1977.

Hagen, Harry M. *The Complete Missouri Travel Guide.* St. Louis, Mo.: Missouri Publishing Company, 1984.

Hall, Leonard. *Possum Trot Farm: An Ozark Journal.* St. Louis, Mo.: Caledonia Press, 1949.

Hall, Leonard. *Stars Upstream.* Columbia, Mo.: University of Missouri Press, 1969 rev.

Hawker, Jon L. *Missouri Landscapes: A Tour Through Time.* Rolla, Mo.: Missouri Department of Natural Resources, Division of Geology and Land Survey, 1992.

Hawksley, Oscar. *Missouri Ozark Waterways.* Jefferson City, Mo.: Missouri Department of Conservation, 1989 rev. ed.

Heitzman, Richard J. and Joan E. *Butterflies and Moths of Missouri.* Jefferson City, Mo.: Missouri Department of Conservation, 1987.

Henry, Steve. *The Mountain Biker's Guide to the Ozarks.* Birmingham, Alabama: Menasha Ridge Press, 1993.

Hubbell, Sue. *A Country Year: Living the Questions.* New York: Random House, 1986.

Johnson, Tom R. *The Amphibians and Reptiles of Missouri.* Jefferson City, Mo.: Missouri Department of Conservation, 1992.

Keller, W. D. *The Common Rocks and Minerals of Missouri.* Columbia, Mo.: University of Missouri Press, 1961 rev. ed.

Key, James S. *Field Guide to Missouri Ferns.* Jefferson City, Mo.: Missouri Department of Conservation, 1982.

Kohler, Steve and Schuchard, Oliver. *Two Ozark Rivers: The Current and the Jacks Fork.* Columbia, Mo.: University of Missouri Press, 1984.

Lafser, Fred A., Jr. *A Complete Guide to Hiking and Backpacking in Missouri.* Annapolis, Mo.: Fred A. Lafser Jr., 1993, 5th ed.

LaVal, Richard K. *Ecological Studies and Management of Missouri Bats.* Jefferson City, Mo.: Missouri Department of Conservation, 1980.

Matthews, John Joseph. *The Osages, Children of the Middle Waters.* Norman, Okla.: University of Oklahoma Press, 1961.

Miller, Orson K. *Mushrooms of North America.* New York: Dutton, 1972.

Missouri Department of Conservation. *Missouri Nature Viewing Guide.* Jefferson City, Mo.: Missouri Department of Conservation, 1995.

Nelson, Paul W. *The Terrestrial Natural Communities of Missouri.* Jefferson City, Mo.: Missouri Department of Natural Resources and Missouri Department of Conservation, 1985.

Nordstrom, Gary R. *Rare and Endangered Species of Missouri.* Jefferson City, Mo.: Missouri Department of Conservation, 1977.

Oesch, Ronald D. *Missouri Naiades: A Guide to the Mussels of Missouri.* Jefferson City, Mo.: Missouri Department of Conservation, 1984.

Overby, Charlotte, ed. *Missouri Conservation Atlas: A Guide to Exploring Your Conservation Lands.* Jefferson City, Mo.: Missouri Department of Conservation, 1995.

Palmer, Kay, ed. *A Guide to the Birding Areas of Missouri.* Priv. printed by the Audubon Society of Missouri, 1993.

Parrish, William E. *Missouri: The Heart of the Nation.* Arlington Heights, IL: H. Davidson Company, 1992.

Pflieger, William L. *The Fishes of Missouri.* Jefferson City, Mo.: Missouri Department of Conservation, 1975.

Phillips, Jan. *Wild Edibles of Missouri.* Jefferson City, Mo.: Missouri Department of Conservation, 1979.

Phillips, Roger. *Mushrooms of North America.* Boston, MA: Little, Brown and Company, 1991.

Rafferty, Milton D. *Missouri: A Geography.* Boulder, Colo.: Westview Press, 1983.

Rafferty, Milton D. *Historical Atlas of Missouri.* Norman, Okla.: University of Oklahoma Press, 1982.

Rafferty, Milton D. *The Ozarks: Land and Life.* Norman, Okla.: University of Oklahoma Press, 1980.

Rhodes, Richard. *The Ozarks*. New York: Time-Life Books, American Wilderness Series, 1974.

Robbins, Mark B. and Easterla, David A. *Birds of Missouri: Their Distribution and Abundance*. Columbia, Mo.: University of Missouri Press, 1992.

Sauer, Carl O. *The Geography of the Ozark Highland of Missouri*. The Geographic Society of Chicago Bulletin No. 7. Chicago, Ill.: University of Chicago Press, 1920, reprint AMS Press, 1971.

Schwartz, Charles Walsh. *The Wild Mammals of Missouri*. Columbia, Mo.: University of Missouri Press, rev. MDC ed., 1981.

Steele, Phillip W. *Ozark Tales and Superstitions*. Gretna, LA: Pelican Publishing Company, 1983.

Steyermark, Cora. *Behind the Scenes*. St. Louis, Mo.: Missouri Botanical Gardens, 1984.

Steyermark, Julian A. *Flora of Missouri*. Ames, Iowa: Iowa State University Press, 1963.

Steyermark, Julian A. *Spring Flora of Missouri*. Columbia, Mo.: Lucas Brothers Publishers, 1964.

Summers, Bill. *Missouri Orchids*. Jefferson City, Mo.: Conservation Commission of the State of Missouri, 1981.

The Nature Conservancy, Missouri Chapter. *Discover Natural Missouri*. St. Louis, Mo.: priv. printed by the Missouri Chapter, 1991.

Thom, Richard H. and Iffrig, Greg. *Directory of Missouri's Natural Areas*. Jefferson City, Mo.: Missouri Department of Conservation and Missouri Department of Natural Resources, 1985.

United States Weather Bureau. *Climatological Data, Missouri 1897-1965*. Volumes 1-69. Asheville, N.C.: The Bureau, 1897-1965.

Unklesbay, A. G. *Missouri Geology: Three Billion Years of Volcanoes, Seas, Sediments, and Erosion*. Columbia, Mo.: University of Missouri Press, 1992.

Vickery, Margaret Ray. *Ozark Stories of the Upper Current River*. Salem, Mo.: Salem News, 1969.

Vineyard, Jerry D. and Feder, Gerald L. *Springs of Missouri*. Rolla, Mo.: Missouri Geological Survey and Water Resources, 1974.

Weaver, Dwight H. *Missouri: The Cave State*. Jefferson City, Mo.: Discovery Enterprises, 1980.

Weaver, Dwight H. *The Wilderness Underground: Caves of the Ozark Plateau*. Columbia, Mo.: University of Missouri Press, 1992.

White, Louis C. *Ozark Hideaways*. Columbia, Mo.: University of Missouri Press, 1993.

Wilson, Terry P. *The Osage*. New York: Chelsea House, 1988.

Wright, Harold Bell. *Shepherd of the Hills*. Minneapolis: Bethany House Publishers, reprint of the 1907 original edition.

Wylie, J. E. and Gass, Ramon. *Missouri Trees*. Jefferson City, Mo.: Missouri Department of Conservation, 1980.

Zuschlay, Nancy L. *Common Missouri Spiders*. Jefferson City, Mo.: privately printed, 1985.

Appendix I
Birds of Wappapello Lake

* Indicates species rare to the area
** Indicates species endangered and/or rare to the area

Acadian flycatcher
Alder flycatcher
American bittern**
American black duck
American coot
American crow
American goldfinch
American kestrel
American redstart
American robin
American tree sparrow
American white pelican
American wigeon
American woodcock
Bachman's sparrow**
Bald eagle
Bank swallow*
Barn owl*
Barn swallow
Barred owl
Bell's vireo
Belted kingfisher
Bewick's wren*
Black vulture
Black-and-white warbler
Black-bellied plover*
Black-billed cuckoo
Black-crowned night-
    heron*
Black-throated green
    warbler
Blackburnian warbler
Blackpoll warbler
Blue grosbeak
Blue jay
Blue-gray gnatcatcher
Blue-winged teal
Blue-winged warbler*
Bobolink
Brewer's blackbird*
Broad-winged hawk*
Brown creeper
Brown pelican
Brown thrasher
Brown-headed cowbird
Canada goose
Canada warbler

Carolina chickadee
Carolina wren
Caspian tern*
Canvasback
Cedar waxwing
Cerulean warbler
Chestnut-sided warbler
Chimney swift
Chipping sparrow
Chuck-Will's-widow
Cliff swallow*
Common Goldeneye*
Common grackle
Common loon*
Common merganser*
Common moorhen
Common nighthawk
Common snipe
Common tern
Common yellowthroat
Cooper's hawk
Dark-eyed junco
Dickcissel
Double-crested
    cormorant*
Downy woodpecker
Eared grebe*
Eastern bluebird
Eastern kingbird
Eastern meadowlark
Eastern Phoebe
Eastern screech-owl
Eastern wood-pewee
European starling
Evening grosbeak*
Field sparrow
Fish crow*
Forster's tern
Fox sparrow
Gadwall
Golden eagle
Golden-crowned kinglet
Golden-winged warbler*
Grasshopper sparrow
Gray catbird
Gray-cheeked thrush
Great blue heron

Great crested flycatcher
Great horned owl
Great yellowlegs
Green-backed heron
Green-winged teal
Hairy woodpecker
Hermit thrush
Herring gull
Hooded merganser
Horned grebe*
Horned lark
House finch
House sparrow
House wren
Indigo bunting
Kentucky warbler
Killdeer
Lapland longspur
Lark sparrow
Least bittern*
Least flycatcher
Least sandpiper
LeConte's sparrow*
Lesser golden-plover*
Lesser scaup
Lesser yellowlegs
Lincoln's sparrow*
Little blue heron
Loggerhead shrike
Louisiana waterthrush
Magnolia warbler
Mallard
Merlin
Mississippi kite*
Mourning warbler
Mourning dove
Nashville warbler
North rouch-winged
    swallow
Northern bobwhite
Northern cardinal
Northern flicker
Northern harrier
Northern mockingbird
Northern oriole
Northern parila
Northern pintail

Northern shovler
Northern waterthrush
Orange-crowned warbler
Orchard oriole
Osprey**
Ovenbird
Palm warbler
Pectoral sandpiper
Peregrine falcon**
Philadelphia vireo*
Pied-billed grebe
Pileated woodpecker
Pine grosbeak
Pine siskin*
Pine warbler
Prairie warbler
Prothonotary warbler
Purple finch
Purple martin
Red crossbill
Red-bellied woodpecker
Red-breasted merganser*
Red-breasted nuthatch*
Red-eyed vireo
Red-headed woodpecker
Red-shouldered hawk
Red-tailed hawk
Red-winged blackbird
Redhead*
Ring-billed gull
Ringed-neck duck

Rock dove
Rose-breasted grosbeak
Rough-legged hawk*
Ruby-crowned kinglet
Ruby-throated
    hummingbird
Ruddy duck*
Ruffed grouse*
Rufons hummingbird
Rufous-sided towhee
Rusty blackbird*
Sandhill crane
Savannah sparrow
Scarlet tanager
Semipalmated plover*
Semipalmated sandpiper
Sharp-skinned hawk*
Snowy egret**
Solitary sandpiper
Song sparrow
Sora
Spotted sandpiper
Summer tanager
Swainson's thrush
Swainson's warbler*
Swamp sparrow
Tennessee warbler
Tree swallow
Trumpeter swan*
Tufted titmouse
Tundra swan*

Turkey vulture
Veery*
Vesper sparrow
Virginia rail
Warbling vireo
Whip-poor-will
White-breasted nuthatch
White-crowned sparrow
White-eyed vireo
White-fronted goose*
White-throated sparrow
Wild turkey
Willow flycatcher
Wilson's warbler
Winter wren
Wood duck
Wood thrush
Worm-eating warbler
Yellow warbler
Yellow-bellied
    flycatcher*
Yellow-bellied sapsucker
Yellow-billed cuckoo
Yellow-breasted chat
Yellow-crowned night-
    heron*
Yellow-rumped warbler
Yellow-throated vireo
Yellow-throated warbler

Source for this information: Birds of Wappapello Lake, published by the U.S. Army Corps of Engineers, St. Louis District, in cooperation with the Scenic Rivers Audubon Society.

Appendix II

Animals of Roaring River State Park

* indicates species rare to the area
** indicates species endangered and/or rare to the area

Fish
Blackspotted topminnow*
Bluegill
Brown trout (introduced)*
Carp (introduced)
Central stoneroller
Creek chub
Duskystripe shiner
Fantail darter*
Green sunfish
Hornyhead chub

Largemouth bass
Longear sunfish
Mottled sculpin
Northern hog sucker
Northern studfish*
Orangethroat darter
Ozark madtom*
Ozark minnow
Rainbow darter*
Rainbow trout (introduced)
Smallmouth bass

Southern redbelly dace
White sucker

Amphibians
American toad
Blanchard's cricket frog
Bullfrog
Cave salamander
Central newt*
Dark-sided salamander
Eastern gray tree frog

Gray-bellied salamander
Green frog*
Grotto salamander**
Northern spring peeper
Oklahoma salamander**
Ozark red-backed
    salamander
Pickerel frog
Slimy salamander
Southern leopard frog*
Spotted salamander*
Western chorus frog
Woodhouse's toad

Reptiles
Black rat snake
Broad-headed skink*
Common snapping turtle
Easter garter snake
Eastern coachwhip*
Eastern collared lizard**
Eastern hognose
Eastern yellow-bellied
    racer
Five-lined skink
Great Plains ground
    snake*
Great Plains rat snake*
Ground skink
Map turtle*
Midland brown snake
Midland water snake
Northern fence lizard
Northern flat-headed
    snake*
Northern red-bellied snake
Northern water snake
Ornate box turtle
Prairie king snake*
Prairie ringneck snake
Red milk snake*
Red-eared turtle*
Rough earth snake
Rough green snake
Six-lined racerunner*
Southern copperhead
Speckled king snake
Three-toed box turtle
Timber rattlesnake*
Western pigmy
    rattlesnake**
Western worm snake

Birds
Acadian flycatcher
American crow

American goldfinch
American kestrel*
American redstart
American robin
American tree sparrow
American woodcock*
Bachman's sparrow**
Bald eagle**
Barn swallow
Barred owl
Bell's vireo**
Belted kingfisher
Bewick's wren*
Black vulture*
Black-and-white warbler
Black-billed cuckoo
Blackburnian warbler
Blackpoll warbler*
Blue grosbeak
Blue jay
Blue-gray gnatcatcher
Blue-winged teal
Blue-winged warbler
Broad-winged hawk**
Brown creeper
Brown thrasher*
Brown-headed cowbird
Canada goose
Carolina chickadee
Cedar waxwing
Cerulean warbler
Chimney swift
Chipping sparrow
Chuck-Will's-widow
Cliff swallow*
Common goldeneye*
Common grackle
Common nighthawk
Common yellowthroat
Dark-eyed junco
Downy woodpecker
Eastern bluebird
Eastern kingbird*
Eastern meadowlark*
Eastern Phoebe
Eastern wood pewee
European starling
Evening grosbeak*
Field sparrow
Fox sparrow
Gadwall*
Golden-crowned kinglet
Gray catbird
Gray-cheeked thrush*
Great blue heron
Great crested flycatcher

Great horned owl
Greater roadrunner**
Green-backed heron
Hairy woodpecker
Harris' sparrow
Hermit thrush*
Hooded merganser*
Hooded warbler*
House sparrow
Indigo bunting
Kentucky warbler
Killdeer
Lesser scaup*
Little blue heron**
Long-eared owl**
Louisiana waterthrush
Mallard
Mourning dove
Northern bobwhite*
Northern cardinal
Northern flicker
Northern mockingbird
Northern parula
Northern pintail*
Northern shoveler*
Orchard oriole
Osprey**
Ovenbird
Painted bunting**
Peregrine falcon**
Pied-billed grebe*
Pileated woodpecker
Pine siskin*
Pine warbler*
Prairie warbler
Prothonotary warbler
Purple finch
Purple martin
Red-bellied woodpecker
Red-breasted nuthatch*
Red-eyed vireo
Red-headed woodpecker
Red-shouldered hawk**
Red-tailed hawk
Red-winged blackbird
Rock dove (pigeon)
Rough-winged swallow
Ruby-throated
    hummingbird
Rufous-sided towhee
Scarlet tanager
Scissor-tailed flycatcher*
Screech owl
Semipalmated plover*
Sharp-skinned hawk**
Snow goose

Song sparrow
Spotted sandpiper*
Summer tanager
Swainson's thrush*
Swainson's warbler**
Tufted titmouse
Turkey vulture
Warbling vireo*
Weery*
Whip-poor-Will
White-breasted nuthatch
White-crowned sparrow
White-eyed vireo
White-throated sparrow
Wild turkey
Willow flycatcher**
Winter wren
Wood duck
Wood thrush
Worm-eating warbler*
Yellow warbler
Yellow-bellied sapsucker*
Yellow-billed cuckoo
Yellow-breasted chat
Yellow-crowned night
    heron*
Yellow-rumped warbler
Yellow-throated vireo
Yellow-throated warbler

Mammals
Armadillo
Beaver
Big brown bat
Black bear**
Bobcat*
Common cotton rat
Coyote
Eastern chipmunk
Eastern cottontail rabbit
Eastern fox squirrel
Eastern gray squirrel
Eastern mole
Eastern pipistrelle bat
Eastern wood rat
Gray fox
Hoary bat*
Least shrew*
Long-tailed weasel**
Mink
Muskrat
Opossum
Prairie meadow mouse
Prairie white-footed
    mouse
Raccoon

Red fox
Short-tailed shrew
Southeastern shrew**
Southern flying squirrel
Striped skunk
Texas mouse**
White-tailed deer
Woodchuck

Butterflies and Moths
Azalea sphinx
Baltimore
Banded hairstreak
Blind-eyed sphinx
Broken nash
Buttercup moth
Cabbage white
Catalpa sphinx
Checkered white
Chickweed geometer
Comma
Common checkered
    skipper
Common sulphur
Dogface butterfly
Dusted skipper
Eastern black swallowtail
Eastern tailed blue
Fall webworm
Gemmed satyr
Giant swallowtail
Great leopard moth
Great spangled fritillary
Green marvel
Hackberry butterfly
Hickory tussock moth
Hog sphinx
Imperial moth
IO moth
Juniper geometer
Least skipperling
Lettered sphinx
Lichen moth
Little wood satyr
Little yellow
Luna moth
Many-lined angle
Maple prominent
Meal moth
Monarch
Mourning cloak
Northern metalmark
Northern sphinx
Orange sulphur
Ozark swallowtail
Painted lady

Pawpaw sphinx
Pipevine swallowtail
Polyphemus moth
Question mark
Red admiral
Reversed tigermoth
Roadside skipper
Silvery crescentspot
Sleepy duskywing
Snout butterfly
Spicebush swallowtail
Spring azure
Striped hairstreak
Tawny-winged skipper
Tent caterpillar
The beggar
The orange wing
Tiger swallowtail
Underwing moth
Virgin
Walnut caterpillar moth
Zabulon skipper
Zebra swallowtail

Other Insects
Acorn weevil
Alderfly
Annual cicada
Ant lion
Assassin bug
Bald-faced hornet
Band-winged grasshopper
Bee fly
Black carpenter ant
Black-winged damselfly
Blister beetle
Bumble bee
Caddis fly
Carpenter bee
Carrion beetle
Cave cricket
Click beetle
Common stonefly
Cuckoo wasp
Deer fly
Dobsonfly
Field ant
Field cricket
Gall wasp
Green darner
Green June beetle
Ground beetle
Halictid bee (sweat bee)
Honey bee
House fly
Ichneumon

June beetle	Stag beetle	Mosquito
Katydid	Subterranean termite	Mud dauber
Ladybird beetle	Tree cricket	Paper wasp
Leafhoppers	Unicorn beetle	Periodic cicada
Lightning bug	Walking stick	Potter wasp
Mayfly	Water strider	Praying mantis
Midge	Wood cockroach	Rhinoceros beetle
Minute pirate bug	Wood gnat	Rove beetles
Mosquito	June beetle	Stag beetle
Mud dauber	Katydid	Subterranean termite
Paper wasp	Ladybird beetle	Tree cricket
Periodic cicada	Leafhoppers	Unicorn beetle
Potter wasp	Lightning bug	Walking stick
Praying mantis	Mayfly	Water strider
Rhinoceros beetle	Midge	Wood cockroach
Rove beetles	Minute pirate bug	Wood gnat

Source for this information: Roaring River State Park Animal Checklist, published by the Missouri Department of Natural Resources.

Appendix III

Hiking Places
in the Arkansas Ozarks

Alum Cove Recreation Area
Beaver Lake
Beaver Lake State Park
Blanchard Springs Recreation Area
Buffalo National River
Bull Shoals Lake
Bull Shoals State Park
Devil's Den State Park
Greers Ferry Lake
Horsehead Lake Recreation Area
Lake Charles State Park
Lake Fort Smith State Park
Lake Wedington Recreation Area
Mammoth Spring State Park
Norfolk Lake
North Sylamore Creek Hiking Trail
Old Davidson State Park
Ozark Highlands Trail
Pea Ridge National Military Park
Pedestral Rocks
Shores Lake/White Rock Loop Trail
Withrow Springs State Park

Index